'The stories and the models in *Sustainable Peak Performance* show that business commitment to people and the planet enhances profitability, and makes the world a better place.'

- **SIR STEPHEN TINDALL,** Founder and Director, The Warehouse Group Ltd

'*Sustainable Peak Performance* is a rich addition to the field, providing a new set of performance tools that will have an immediate benefit for CEOs.'

- **ADAM WERBACH,** Global CEO, Saatchi & Saatchi S and former President of the Sierra Club

'Mike and Helga have pulled together examples of businesses who are leading the way in sustainable business practice. Clearly, green business solutions are giving business a competitive advantage. In an age of pessimism, every business needs to read this book for fresh ideas and hope.'

- **CHRIS MORRISON,** Founder of Phoenix Organics and chair of the Sustainable Business Network

world is the theory derived from the collective insights. Together, the stories and the theory help present sustainable business practices as both realistic and achievable.'

- **DR JULIET ROPER,** Professor of Management Communication and Associate Dean Sustainability, Waikato Management School, University of Waikato, New Zealand; President Asia Pacific Academy of Business in Society

'*Sustainable Peak Performance* shows that everyone can do something to make the world a better place; consumers through the choice of what they buy and who they buy from; investors through the choices of which enterprises they fund, and businesses through a commitment to people and the planet as well as profitability.'

- **VISCOUNT ROTHERMERE,** Executive Chairman, Daily Mail and General Trust plc

Sustainable
Peak Performance

PEARSON

Business lessons from Sustainable Enterprise Pioneers

Dr. Mike Pratt and Helga Pratt are founders of Sustainable Enterprise Ltd, a company dedicated to helping enterprises to develop towards sustainable peak performance.

Mike and Helga have assisted the leaders of more than 100 companies over the last decade, including large multinational companies and small and medium sized enterprises. Mike is currently Professor of Leadership and Sustainability at the University of Waikato, in New Zealand.

For 18 years Mike was Dean of the Waikato Management School, New Zealand's #1 research-led business school.

Helga is an Occupational Therapist and academic specialising in neurology, wellbeing and enablement of meaningful occupation.

When not working with clients they live next to the sea in New Zealand's beautiful Bay of Islands.

by Mike Pratt & Helga Pratt

www.pearsoned.co.nz

Your comments on this title are welcome at feedback@pearsoned.co.nz

Pearson
A division of Pearson New Zealand Ltd
67 Apollo Drive, Rosedale, North Shore 0632, New Zealand

© Pearson 2010
First published by Pearson 2010

ISBN: 978-1-4425-3161-1

Associated companies throughout the world.

Produced by Pearson

Design by Dow Design
Printed in Australia by Ligare Pty Ltd

PEFC™

PEFC/21-31-17

This book has been printed on paper certified by the Programme for
the Endorsement of Forest Certification (PEFC). PEFC is committed to
sustainable forest management through third party forest certification
of responsibly managed forests.

The greenhouse gas emissions associated with researching and
publishing this book are being offset by a native tree planting
programme on regenerating land in Okiato, Bay of Islands, New Zealand.

PEARSON ORIGINALS
is an imprint of

A division of Pearson New Zealand Ltd

Contents

Foreword **by Kevin Roberts**   10
Preface   14

Part one   20

One   Why Sustainable Enterprise?   22
Two   Putumayo   36
Three   Stonyfield Farm   48
Four   The Body Shop   60
Five   The Eden Project   78
Six   Forum for the Future   90
Seven   Snowy Peak   101
Eight   Comvita   111
Nine   Patagonia   122
Ten   Dilmah Tea   134

Part two   150

Eleven   Sustainable Enterprise   152
Twelve   People   160
Thirteen   Potential   167
Fourteen   Philosophy   178
Fifteen   Practices   189
Sixteen   Positivity   221
Seventeen   Performance   247
Eighteen   Just do something!   258

Endnotes   270

List of figures

Fig. 1   Sustainable Enterprisers   153
Fig. 2   Sustainable Enterprise
          dynamics   154
Fig. 3   Sustainable Peak Performance
          theory   158
Fig. 4   People   160
Fig. 5   Leadership perspectives   165
Fig. 6   Potential   167
Fig. 7   Unsustainability issues   171
Fig. 8   Activism   173
Fig. 9   Philosophy   179
Fig. 10   Saatchi & Saatchi S
          sustainability philosophy   183
Fig. 11   Saatchi & Saatchi S Purpose
          statement   187
Fig. 12   Practices   189
Fig. 13   Value creation model   195
Fig. 14   Sustainable Enterprise
          practices   197
Fig. 15   Positivity   221
Fig. 16   Happiness: choice   228
Fig. 17   Happiness: activities   232
Fig. 18   Performance   247

Sustainable Peak Performance is dedicated to our children Susie Pratt and Martin Pratt.

As with so many aspects of our lives, they have been the inspiration to research and write this book.

It won't be possible to resolve the social and environmental issues that threaten our future using the same economic and business thinking that created the problems in the first place. So we hope that our transformational ideas will make some modest contribution to enabling enterprise to make the world a better place in which our children and their children can flourish.

Dedication

by Kevin Roberts / CEO Worldwide, Saatchi & Saatchi

Foreword
A personal view

Anita Roddick was one spirited woman. In her interview in this book by Mike and Helga Pratt, *Sustainable Peak Performance*, she speaks of The Body Shop as a communications company that sold some great products. She was upfront about being an activist fighting injustice, making the world a better place, and creating opportunities for everyone. The messages and communications had to be, she says, daring, exciting, sexy, and riveting – "without, like, hitting you on the head." I shared a conference stage with Anita in 1998, in San Francisco, at the State of the World Forum. I was presenting, for the first time in North America, a new theory on inspirational leadership that I had developed with colleagues from the Waikato Management School in New Zealand, Mike Pratt, Clive Gilson, and Ed Weymes. I was not long into the role as CEO of Saatchi & Saatchi, having taken on one of the highest profile turnaround roles a company could throw at you. I was searching, searching for some fast keys to unlock the intuitive "Nothing Is Impossible" spirit of

Saatchi & Saatchi while accelerating it out of perilous financial waters. And I wanted to know the secrets for staying at the peak once you arrived. I had learnt everything I knew up until then from working in some of the world's great corporations – Gillette, Procter & Gamble and PepsiCo – and while being awed by their rational capabilities, I felt vulnerable and lacking in something more emotionally sustaining.

Mike and I felt that corporate case methods were driven largely by military metaphors – target, deploy, capture, conquer; and we felt that learning about corporations by studying other similar corporations had been exhaustive and exhausted! Instead we turned to the hyper-competitive world of professional sport to see what we could learn. We felt there were enough differences and parallels between sport and business to make a productive study. And we loved sport!! We weren't so much interested in the players on the field as we were intent on discovering the underlying spirit of each organization and the metaphors and practices they had developed, both consciously and subconsciously, to stay on top year after year.

The big question we set ourselves: "How do you stay on top?" In business we wanted to apply our learnings to the core problem that besets many organizations – have two good years, then a down year, two good years, another down year. Breaking this cycle and sustaining continuous growth and improvement – without sacrificing your values, beliefs, and principles – is the Holy Grail. We were after a western version of Kaizen.

After immersion in a dozen of the world's top sports organizations, we were surprised, and delighted, at what we found and with the model we deduced. First, as always, there was language: *inspiration; inspirational dream; inspirational player.* Inspirational Leadership became our framework for defining purpose, harnessing emotion, stimulating the unreasonable power of creative culture, unleashing game-changing ideas, and developing mental toughness in corporate organizations. Command and control was displaced by unleash and inspire. Dream / Challenge / Focus became the defining action structure. And Family. Family is the most demanding unit possible – equally demanding of high performance, and dedicated to making people feel loved. Family is the tough option, not the soft one; dynamic tension, constantly evolving, adding and integrating new members, always balancing

past, present and future; both stable and chaotic.

Our book *Peak Performance: Business Lessons from the World's Top Sports Organizations* was published and we started a consultancy to teach and apply our methods in some of the world's top companies. Mike and I continued to pump away with the "what's next?" question and arrived at the same place via different routes. In 2000 I wrote a memo to the CEO of a company suggesting they embrace the coming green revolution. It would be a major connection point with consumers; it would help the environment because they used natural resources, they would save cost, and they would be positioned as thought leaders and innovators. It was a case of arriving well before time, and it took a couple of years before I had a home for this restless and not fully formed thinking.

Meanwhile Mike had turned the Waikato Management School on its head and committed it to sustainability – in their own day-to-day practice, and in theory development. This was important. I often quote Edward de Bono – "There's no point in being brilliant at the wrong thing." Mike brought together many collaborators from business, academia, the media, central and local government, utility companies – and started a deep and ongoing conversation. The starting point was that sustainability needed to operate through a wide lens: economic, social, cultural, and environmental. My personal sustainability commitment is to youth justice, I support the Turn Your Life Around Trust in Auckland. My corporate commitment is to bring sustainability into the heart of Saatchi & Saatchi, and in 2008 we acquired the Act Now consultancy in San Francisco led by Adam Werbach. Favorite saying: "Act now, apologize later." Adam has been associated with Wal-Mart's program to turn each of their million-plus people into personal sustainability advocates. At Saatchi & Saatchi we have shifted the language from Green to Blue to focus on individual nano-practices. Do One Thing. DOT. Do Another Thing. DAT. And so on.

The big question Mike and Helga asked for this book was: "Is there a better way?" A sort of rhetorical question because the overwhelming answer is "YES". You'll meet several entrepreneurs across the world (including Putumayo Music founder Dan Storper who I met on a plane years ago) who with inspirational purpose have developed fantastic companies that a) make great products and b) have social change as their purpose. None of these companies have "corporate social responsibility" programs – this is their entire business! In *Sustainable Peak Performance* we meet up (again) with the wonderful phenomena of Flow (energy+joy). We get to explore with people who have the foresight to anticipate what is becoming or what could be. There are a bunch of value creation models you can start implementing in your own company today. There is language to change your world. There is a ton of spirit, which (I remember) comes from the Latin *spirare* – to breathe.

I am a radical optimist. I want to inspire everyone to help make the world a better place. Where to start? In the words of Anita Roddick, *"Just do something!"*

by Mike Pratt and Helga Pratt

Preface

The story of sustainable enterprise is in many ways the story of our lives. Mike has instigated a variety of small enterprises for fun and profit. Helga has dedicated her life to social enhancement as a health professional in both developing and developed countries. Both of us have a deep commitment to equity, and through our love of nature, especially the sea, and our life in the natural beauty of New Zealand we care deeply about the environment.

We have been academics in management and health for the last thirty years and for the last ten of these have embraced storytelling both as a research methodology and as a mode of sharing our findings. So this book is a storytelling project. In one of our earlier projects throughout the 1990s we grew kiwifruit for the global export market. We developed the orchard from full-on chemical sprays to Bio-Gro certified organic, and it was this experience that deepened our involvement with the sustainability movement.

For 18 years Mike was Dean and Professor of Management at the Management School at the University of Waikato in New Zealand. Waikato Management School is accredited by AACSB, EQUIS and AMBA, one of only about thirty business schools in the world to achieve this distinction. In 2002 the faculty made a commitment to sustainability at the core of the school's purpose. Unusually, the school has faculty across every discipline who are active researchers and teachers of sustainability in business. Individually and collectively they have been an inspiration to create our business dedicated to the implementation of sustainable enterprise ideas in practice. Mike retired as dean in early 2008 to take up a part-time role as Professor of Sustainability and Leadership, and to focus on working with enterprises to assist them in their journeys towards sustainability.

Ten years ago, Mike with three colleagues Clive Gilson, Kevin Roberts and Ed Weymes, commenced a research journey to discover business lessons from the world's top sports organisations. The resulting book, *Peak Performance,* was published in 2000. In *Peak Performance* we told the stories of peak performance at ten iconic sports organisations, and then developed a theory of peak performance from these stories. Key findings from this research were that clarity of shared purpose and inspirational leadership in a family-like environment provide the best foundations for flow and peak performance. *Peak Performance* has sold more than 100,000 copies and resulted in the creation of an organisational development business, Inspiros Worldwide Ltd, devoted to the implementation of peak performance principles in global organisations. Inspiros has implemented these ideas in more than 50 different companies (see www.inspiros.org). Mike and Helga with Kevin Roberts and Clive Gilson regularly conduct peak performance workshops with iconic clients around the world. Through these experiences we came to realise the potential for companies to do well by doing good through building sustainability principles into their business models, but learned how few were actually doing so.

Three years ago Mike and Helga embarked on this global research journey to tell the stories of the genesis of iconic enterprises that were founded on sustainability principles and have become globally recognised brands. From these stories we have created a theory of sustainable enterprise to help other companies to embrace sustainable development within their business models and practices.

Business enterprise has always been an energiser for human progress. Yet in recent years, corporate and environmental scandals, population growth, world poverty and ecological overload have called into question the validity of current business models.

The concepts of sustainable development and the business case for sustainable development – operating profitably while nourishing the environment and strengthening society – are getting increasing airplay. Member nations of the UN have endorsed that organisations should focus on sustainable development and have committed to implementing sustainability action plans in their own countries. And business networks have sprung up world over to link like-minded companies who see both the moral imperative and competitive advantage in operating sustainably.

There is a lot of rhetoric about the need for sustainable enterprise development, but little by way of theoretical and practical guidance about what this entails. Much of the business focus has been on large corporations' environmental practices, community responsibility and their role in developing nations. Yet the vast majority of the world's businesses are small to medium-sized enterprises (SMEs)[1]. They are major employers. They are embedded in their community. They are the backbone of every nation's growth and development. Where does sustainability fit with these smaller and medium-sized firms?

We wondered how a grassroots enterprise could create economic and social wellbeing in their communities. We wondered how it was possible to conceive, establish and grow to international success a business founded on sustainability principles. How would such a business weather the uncertainties of entrepreneurship, survive mid-stride growth pangs and succeed in a global market, without diluting or deviating from its founding values?

And what lessons might there be in their experience – for aspiring entrepreneurs, for established firms seeking a roadmap to sustainable business success and for strategists charged with regional and national development? How do these organisations contribute towards making the world a better place?

As citizens we make choices daily in what we buy, use and throw away. Ultimately we are all individually and collectively the authors of enterprise through these daily choices. We can choose to buy from companies that destroy the environment, impoverish communities, and exploit workers and children through their activities. Or we can choose to buy from an increasing number of sustainable enterprises that produce products which are altogether healthier, are produced in such a way as to nourish or do no harm to the environment, build communities and enrich the quality of life. And the good news is that sustainable products need not cost more. As citizens we can make the world a better place through the daily choices we make.

In *Sustainable Peak Performance* we tell the stories of nine trail-blazing sustainable enterprises that were founded on sustainability principles and have grown from grassroots to international success. We explore the genesis of the business idea, examine their business models, purpose and spirit, and review the steps on their journey. Primarily these stories are about their founders; a remarkable group of foresighted people with deep commitment to sustainability and a better world. What does it take to be a super-successful sustainable entrepreneur? And what can citizens the world over learn from their leadership?

We extend our sincere thanks to the many people who have contributed to the development of this book. The founders of the sustainable enterprises and their colleagues gave generously of their time and hospitality to provide the stories that gave rise to Sustainable Peak Performance theory. Kevin Roberts, Worldwide CEO of Saatchi & Saatchi, wrote the inspirational foreword to the book and introduced us to Dan Storper, founder of Putumayo. The insights derived from working with Kevin Roberts and Clive Gilson on Peak Performance over more than a decade inform all aspects of our thinking about business performance. Adam Werbach, CEO of Saatchi & Saatchi S, Julie Nelson CEO of Wise Group and Pat McGillycuddy CEO of Gazeley Ltd kindly gave approval to include their sustainability philosophy and purpose statements as illustration. Charlie Panakera, Lecturer in Tourism at the University of Waikato, acted as our mentor, guide and interpreter in our visit to the Solomon Islands and shared his own stories of sustainable enterprise. Frank Dixon, sustainability advisor to Gazeley Ltd, kindly gave his approval to include an extract from our conversations about system change. Sarah Knox introduced us to Anita Roddick, Founder of the Body Shop and to Simon Dowe, friend of Anita and Director of Children on the Edge, the charity that she founded. Tracey Lowndes assisted in some of the enterprise visits and interviews and provided valuable editorial advice on early drafts of the manuscript. Jaki Heta and Wendy Talsma accurately transcribed the many hours of interviews, and Wendy checked and formatted all the references. Susie Pratt, research fellow at the University of Wollongong completed valuable literature reviews on unsustainability issues and assisted in crafting the sustainable enterprise model. She also contributed towards writing one of the stories. Angie Knox has made a huge contribution to the book through crafting initial drafts of some of the stories and through a careful editorial review of the final draft of the manuscript. Dr Juliet Roper, Professor of Management Communication and Associate Dean of Sustainability at the University of Waikato, and Dr Eva Collins, senior lecturer in strategy and human resource management at the University of Waikato provided valuable and insightful academic feedback on the final draft of the manuscript. Our long-time publisher Pearson made the publishing stage of the project easy and fun. Dow Design of Auckland did great work on the design of the book and are a joy to work with. Putumayo, AnitaRoddick.com, Patagonia, Forum for the Future, Snowy Peak, and the Eden Project kindly provided

photographs of the founders
which are included in the book.
The photograph of Yvon Chouinard
is by Meredith Ogliby, courtesy
of Patagonia. The photograph of
Anita Roddick is by Joel Anderson,
courtesy of AnitaRoddick.com. Other
photographs are by the authors.
We extend a sincere thank you to
all those involved.

1.

In **Part One** of this book we explain why we believe sustainable enterprise is the future of business and share a series of stories about our experiences of sustainable enterprises around the world. The approach is one of appreciative enquiry, or learning from success.

Reflection...

At the conclusion of each chapter we reflect on the key insights we learned.

Part 2.

In **Part Two** we build a theory and practice of sustainable success induced from these stories.

One.

Why Sustainable Enterprise?

Charlie's dad was a head-hunter. Not, you should understand, the sort that tap you on the shoulder saying "Have I got a job for you", but a real one. As a paramount chief of the island of Rannong in the Solomon Islands, he had lived in three centuries by the time he died at the age of about 110.

For countless centuries head-hunting was a way of life in the Solomons where it was seen as necessary to sustain the health of the islands' communities; – a form of population control... But Charlie's dad was the last of the head-hunters, as the British stamped out the practice in the early 20th century. His early career severing heads did not last long and gave way to the timeless island activities of fishing, subsistence agriculture and micro enterprise. This was interrupted briefly but spectacularly by World War II during which the Solomon Islands became the major theatre of war between the Allied forces and the Japanese in the Pacific; Charlie's dad became a scout, interpreter and spy for the Allies. Millions of dollars of first world equipment and infrastructure were thrown into the Solomons over the few war years, much of it now at the bottom of the sea where it makes for interesting diving attractions. The way of life quickly reverted back to what it had always been, but it's a way of life that through global socio-economic forces is becoming increasingly unsustainable.

Charlie is an entrepreneur. He was the one from the village who was chosen to get a Western education. He was a member of the national parliament for 12 years, Speaker in the provincial government and deputy managing director of the Development Bank of Solomon Islands. As the oldest son he became paramount chief on the death of his dad. He recognised the potential of the achingly beautiful western islands as a tourist destination, and from small beginnings built a chain of hotels specialising in diving and adventure tourism. He has spawned multiple micro-enterprises and funds the education of new generation leaders in his traditional tribal area, to create a better future for his people.

But it's not easy. The Solomon Islands are a Melanesian microcosm of the unsustainability ills that beset the world. In the words of Bill Clinton, "we are stuck with a global economic system that doesn't work for half the world"[2]. Ever since independence in 1978, the Solomon Islands have experienced civil unrest and conflict. Their population growth rate is one of the highest in the world; the majority of the population is aged under 16. There is increasing migration towards urban areas which is placing intense pressure on all aspects of infrastructure, education and health. Only 70% of the population has access to safe drinking water and only 70% of children attend any form of schooling. At 70% of GDP, the only way government debt can be repaid is through negotiated debt relief (in which there has been some success recently), or unsustainable logging of tropical hardwoods, most of the profits and benefits of which accrue to the developed world. GDP growth in the last two years has been enhanced to more than 6% through this latter activity, necessitated by debt repayment requirements. There is no sustainable way the debt to the first world can be repaid.

Charlie doesn't live in the Solomon Islands any more, although he continues to conduct his chiefly duties by phone, regular visits and financial support. His leadership was paramount in the local response to the 2007 devastating earthquake and resulting tsunami. Now Charlie is a university academic specialising in tourism and entrepreneurship. He and Mike have worked together as academics for 20 years. The Solomon Islands were a midway point in our sustainable enterprise odyssey, and Charlie was our mentor and tour guide. As well as global enterprises founded on principles of sustainability, we wanted to experience sustainable enterprise from the ground up in developing nations; the so-called bottom of the pyramid[3].

As we waited in what passes as the domestic airport in the capital Honiara for our little plane to Gizo in the Western Province, and while Charlie greeted a constant stream of relatives and friends, Helga spotted two out-of-place besuited Europeans, fanning themselves with their German passports. She greeted them in their own language, and a conversation quickly ensued. Through the laws of serendipity it transpired we were all heading for the same outer island and for the same purpose – to review the progress of a sustainable enterprise project cultivating seaweed for the Japanese market. We were interested in learning about how to create grassroots enterprise. Our fellow travellers were European

One.

Union aid auditors coming for their first-ever review of the embryonic seaweed farm venture. Thus began our peek into the inner world of the self-referential global aid industry.

As we flew over the idyllic azure blue lagoons and dense tropical jungle, Charlie pointed out the multiple ugly red scars on the otherwise pristine landscape where multi-national logging companies were exploiting the nation's natural wealth. He explained how it doesn't have to be this way and that Solomon Islanders can sustainably log while preserving their habitat. He had demonstrated this through a micro-enterprise project he had founded. But it's hard for small entrepreneurs to compete with the power of global logging companies and local corruption, so the destruction goes on.

As it turned out, both parties were headed to the seaweed island the same day we landed in Gizo. Our canoe was the fastest, so we got there first. The global reach of the EU was no match for the mana[4] of a paramount chief, so the village chief spent the afternoon sharing seaweed stories and tea with us, while the EU paced the beach. The story that emerged confirmed what we had heard from officials in Honiara and through the coconut radio[5]. This village had shipped a full container of valuable dried seaweed prior to the EU project through their own enterprise. Since the advent of the aid project, a complex web of connections and alleged corruption had muddled the market, such that our village had withdrawn. This was one of many stories of aid projects that funded Western aid workers, consultants and a few local officials, with little impact on the local population. The chief nodded knowingly at the beach, saying the EU project would go away and then they would see about starting again; island time works on a different vector.

We sped home across the lagoon lashed by a tropical downpour to emerge dripping at Gizo's half-finished ferry terminal building (an aid project that ran out of money), and took a quick ride to look at the coast road to nowhere that stood as another monument to 'bandaid'. The following weekend we enjoyed a day's sailing with a couple from a New Zealand-based scientific research institute. It was fun sailing in a strong trade wind and flat seas across the lagoon to an enclosed bay that made a perfect anchorage; the tropical heat made a swim tempting. We were advised against this, however, because of an upsurge in the presence of hitherto rare crocodiles. Local villagers in a sombre mood told us that a young woman had been taken from the beach by a croc just the day before while collecting shellfish. We asked why there were so many more crocs. Three years ago a bright idea for an aid project had been a crocodile farm. But as with so many aid enterprises, the economics beyond the aid had not been properly explored and when the money swam out, so did the crocodiles; the last worker opened the farm gates.

Charlie did not take part in the aid industry. Instead he saw the future through the lens of sustainable enterprise, and through a range of ventures demonstrated how it can be achieved. For every social and environmental issue, such as those demonstrated in the story of the Solomon Islands, there is an enterprise opportunity for its resolution. Later in the book we describe how Charlie created profitable business opportunities through sustainable enterprise.

Whereas sustainability and environmental issues are often seen by traditional business as cost and problem, or as matters for governments to address not business, by contrast Charlie and the enterprisers featured in the forthcoming stories regard these matters very differently. For sustainable enterprisers, profitable business, people and the planet are inextricably interlinked. Not for them, the add-on corporate social responsibility department or token environmental policies. Sustainability – economic, social and environmental – lies at the heart of the enterprises, and is the foundation for their financial success.

On our website at www.sustainableenterprise.org you will find our views and stories of unsustainability from our global travels from both the developing and the developed world. In each story we describe the context, record the main facts that are known and suggest opportunities and risks for enterprise. The main social and environmental issues which are generally included within an analysis of sustainability, and which are illustrated in our website, are listed below. You will see many of them reflected in the opening story.

Our web stories are intended as kaleidoscopic and illustrative rather than exhaustive. We encourage you to take a look and see how many of these issues will affect your company and your lives. Our guess is almost all of them. Taken in totality they present a picture of the potential for global societal collapse[6] through business as usual; and conversely the potential and

One.

priority for sustainable enterprise. It is axiomatic rather than dramatic to state that the future of the human race depends upon it.

It's not our intention to detain you here with stories of unsustainability. You will know about many if not most of them, and have your own stories to tell. We are continuously confronted with these issues in the media and in our daily lives. Rather, our question is what can we all individually and collectively do? And if not us, then who?

We believe that solutions lie with enterprise. Value can be created through a sustainable enterprise frame of reference and destroyed by ignoring sustainability issues. For example, enterprise directed towards low cost and low or no carbon-emitting sources of energy, fresh water treatment and purification, and enhanced food production are

Social & environmental issues		
	Agriculture	Energy
	Aid	Fair trade
	Animal ethics	GMOs
	Biodiversity	Health and safety
	Child labour	Human rights
	Climate change	Industrial pollution & waste
	Conflict	Malnutrition
	Corruption	Obesity
	Debt – Third World	Overfishing
	Deforestation	Poverty
	Demography	Transportation
	Desertification	Urbanisation
	Eco-footprint	Water
	Education	Women's rights

all obvious enterprise opportunities as the world population escalates from about 6.7 billion people in 2009 to about 9.5 billion people in 2050.

Sustainable Enterprise is a 21st century paradigm for peak performance and business success.

Sustainable Enterprise

The classic definition of sustainable development (or development towards sustainability) as formulated by the Brundtland Commission[7] is forms of progress which meet the needs of current generations without compromising the ability of future generations to meet their needs. Sustainable development as defined by Forum for the Future is "a dynamic process which enables all people to realise their potential and to improve their quality of life in ways which simultaneously protect and enhance the Earth's life support systems"[8].

The word enterprise derives from the French 'entreprendre', to take in hand or undertake. The word often relates to a bold, risky, difficult or challenging undertaking. We use the term sustainable enterprise to refer to new, innovative or pioneering ventures that create sustainable value for entrepreneurs, their people, society and the environment through addressing the multiplicity of unsustainability challenges with

which human society is beset.

The elements of sustainability are often presented as a three-legged stool of the economic, social and environmental consequences of human activity; or more colloquially – profit, people and the planet. We see sustainability as an ethical choice. Enterprises can choose to pursue profit without regard to the social or environmental consequences, or they can choose to take a more proactive approach to people and the planet. As a consequence we add to the traditional elements of sustainability a fourth dimension of ethics. The addition of this fourth leg provides theoretical and metaphorical stability.

We describe these dynamics as follows:

Sustainability

Conventional	Sustainable Enterprise	
-	Ethics	Principles
Economic	Economics	Profit
Social	Equity	People
Environment	Environment	Planet

Sustainability ethics is about moral choice; about perceptions of right and wrong. Sustainable enterprises have clear views about what they stand for and where they stand on the various issues set out in

One.

the issues table above and in the subsequent stories.

Is there a sustainable way? When we started this research odyssey we were not sure. We were sure that transformational change in science or society seldom comes from within a paradigm; it comes from the edge. Our home base is New Zealand, and we are inspired by the vantage view that this tiny, beautiful nation on the edge of the world gives us. It was this edge that we looked from to explore how peak performance in sport could be applied to business, and we have subsequently taken these edgy ideas to some of the biggest and most successful companies in the world.

For a decade now we have worked with the chief executives and senior leaders of global corporations to assist them towards the achievement of peak performance. Our work is based on research for *Peak Performance: Business lessons from the world's best sports organisations*[9], which was formulated as Peak Performing Organisations, theory and practice. Companies we have been privileged to work with have included Procter & Gamble, Toyota, Carrefour and Saatchi & Saatchi, each of which in their chosen industries seek to be leaders in sustainable and ethical business, and profitability. Together with our clients

we learned how to implement the principles of peak performance in a variety of different industries.

In this new research we resolved to seek out a set of companies that had been based from the beginning on sustainability principles, and have gone on to become global success stories. We knew of some (like The Body Shop and Patagonia, for example) that personified sustainability and ethical values long before it became fashionable to do so. So it was that we resolved to explore sustainable enterprise through the stories of the founders of such enterprises, assuming we could find enough of them. At this stage we had no idea whether they would have anything in common, or whether each would have stories as independent and iconoclastic as their enterprising founders.

The focus in this sustainable enterprise project was to learn from the founders what prompted the instigation of the company and how it grew to global success. One of the criteria for this study was that the founders needed to still be associated with the company so that we could learn about the journey from early beginnings to the current time.

This book is about positivity and potential, opportunity and optimism, not problems. We determined to seek out and talk with companies from around the world that had been founded on principles of sustainability and had grown to global success as a consequence. We set no special number in mind, but decided that we would apply the principles of theoretical saturation which had worked well in *Peak Performance*. The research approach that we adopted was based upon the same approach of learning from success as used for *Peak Performance*.

We adopted a grounded theory[10] perspective, using an appreciative enquiry methodology[11], rather than working from a normative[12] perspective in which it is then usual to attempt to prove or disprove hypotheses based on a priori theory. Appreciative Inquiry utilises a four-stage process focusing on:

We spent time talking with members of each organisation, especially the founders, because the study is focused on the genesis and development of the business idea and the purpose and values of the organisation. We read everything we could about the organisation before the interviews. In many cases the founders had themselves written about their enterprises which made our job easier. If we started to hear similar ideas across different

1.

Discover

The identification of organisational processes that work well.

2.

Dream

The envisioning of processes that would work well in the future.

3.

Design

Planning and prioritising processes that would work well.

4.

Deliver

The implementation of the proposed design.

One.

companies, cultures and countries, then there could be the potential forthe development of generalisable theory. If we found nothing in common after the first few companies then we would abandon the project.

We chose the companies for inclusion in the project based upon the following criteria:

- Explicit commitment to sustainability

- The founder still engaged with the company and available to respond to questions

- An internationally recognised brand [known outside the country of origin] and/ or operating in multiple countries

- Each enterprise from a different industry

- Recognised sustainability leadership in their industry.

Sadly we were not faced with a long list of companies to choose from!

All the companies met all the criteria at the time of the research. Anita Roddick, founder of the Body Shop, tragically died shortly after our interview with her. The Body Shop story was reviewed by her friend Simon Dowe. This story differs from the others In the book, in that it is completely in Anita's own words as we recorded them in the interview.

Some of these companies are well known and their stories have been

Enterprise	Founders	Country	Industry
Patagonia	Yvon Chouinard	USA	Sports & outdoor clothing
The Body Shop	Anita Roddick	UK	Body care
Stonyfield Farm	Gary Hirshberg Samuel Kaymen	USA	Yoghurt
Comvita	Claude Stratford Alan Bougen	New Zealand	Natural health
Snowy Peak	Peri Drysdale	New Zealand	Fashion
Forum for the Future	Jonathon Porritt Sara Parkin	UK	Education and strategic advice
The Eden Project	Tim Smit	UK	Tourism
Putumayo World Music	Dan Storper Michael Kraus	USA	Music
Dilmah Tea	Merrill J Fernando	Sri Lanka	Beverage

told in books, case studies and journal articles. Others are less well known and their stories are told for the first time here. In comparison with our peak performance clients, all are small or medium sized enterprises. We did not set out with this intention, but this outcome was largely a consequence of the choice criteria, especially that of the founder being still involved with the company and available for interview. Together they represent the first set of enterprise stories assembled with a view to inducing a theory and practice for sustainable enterprise development.

Students of sustainable enterprise will note a number of well-known sustainability ambassadors that did not make it onto our list. For example:

Ray Anderson of Interface has done much to promulgate the cause of sustainable business, and his book *Mid Course Correction*[13] is a classic. Interface was excluded from our study on the grounds that it was not founded on sustainability principles, but rather instigated a 'mid course correction'.

Ben Cohen and Jerry Greenfield of Ben & Jerry's icecream are also well known in sustainability circles, but at the time of our research they were no longer associated with the company[14] after the sale to Unilever.

John Mackay of Whole Foods Markets has instigated a hugely successful retail chain based on sustainability principles. However, we concluded that Whole Foods Markets was not a good fit with the purpose of our book because of the company's alleged anti-union stance and the controversy that surrounded Mr Mackay in regard to anonymous anti-competitor blogging at the time we were completing our research.

Tom and Kate Chappell of Tom's of Maine was the company that got away! We would have loved to have included them in the book, but at the time of our research they were embroiled in the Colgate take-over and declined to meet with us. Fortunately Tom's book *Managing Upside Down: The Seven Intentions of Values-Centered Leadership*[15], paints a comprehensive picture of the company and we have used some of these insights in our research.

Our global odyssey commenced in New Orleans just before the floods, where we interviewed Dan Storper the founder of Putumayo World Music, and concluded some two years later in the tea gardens of Sri

One.

Lanka with Merrill J Fernando of Dilmah Tea. Along the way we met some amazing people. We asked the same question of everyone. "What does sustainable success mean to you, and how do you achieve it?"

From these stories we hoped to develop a new theory of sustainable enterprise success with a view to inspiring others to accelerate their own sustainable success in business and in daily life. A theory is simply an explanation of the relationship between concepts. There is nothing so practical as great theory, because by understanding relationships it is possible to implement the concepts in different contexts.

Patterns

A pattern is a succession of repeating events. The existence of patterns in research evidence can be a starting point for theory development. At the completion of the set of interviews with each of the sustainable enterprises, we identified the key insights and ideas that emerged. We note these ideas at the end of each of the forthcoming story chapters 2-10. As the stories unfolded, a pattern began to emerge, with similar ways of working becoming apparent across the very different businesses. The following is a summary of these key findings.

1. Enterprise is a way of life for the iconic founders. Sustainability is intrinsic to who they are. Their personal beliefs and philosophy become intrinsic to the business. Often a dyad of founders with complementary technical and entrepreneurial skills provided the catalyst for the enterprise idea.

2. The enterprises derive from deep insights about world social, cultural or environmental movements, and from the creation of clear business ideas and value propositions that open up whole new markets or market segments.

3. The enterprises developed through close emotional relationships with suppliers, customers and users. These are based on deep listening, humility and respect. Enduring relationships with users are achieved through imaginative public relations and unconventional, inventive marketing.

4. The enterprises are infused with an independent spirit and activist orientation to make the world a better place.

5. The enterprises have a clear set of beliefs and philosophy

about what they stand for. There is consistency of action with these beliefs, come what may. The beliefs focus on one or two dimensions of sustainability while embracing sustainability thinking as a whole.

6. The entrepreneurs seek and embrace significant challenges, create opportunities and seize on serendipitous events. They pursue these with overwhelming persistence and optimism. This enables them to prevail through major setbacks.

7. The enterprises are based on a focused enterprise model to which there is sustained passionate commitment. The core business is clear and there is a relentless focus on its development.

8. The entrepreneurs developed strong brands based on exceptional quality and sustainability. Customer and consumer education is central to market and brand development. The approach to customer and consumer education is based on authentic engagement with significant social or environmental issues within which the benefits of enterprise products or services are contextualised.

9. All aspects of the enterprises are carefully and systematically constructed taking a long-term perspective. It took at least a decade to build the businesses to global success.

10. The enterprises operate in a family-like environment based on sustainability with high levels of loyalty, investment in people and fun. This family-like environment is extended to embrace the communities within which the enterprises operate.

11. Wellbeing is achieved through mutual respect, togetherness, and willingness from everyone to take personal responsibility. This leads to high levels of personal commitment and focus.

12. The entrepreneurs have an absolute passion, deep knowledge and love for their products and services. This is embraced by people throughout the enterprise.

13. The enterprises enjoy an upbeat, positive, optimistic spirit and there is a confidence of success.

14. Continuous streams of transformational ideas that come from everyone grow the enterprises.

15. There is a passionate

One.

commitment to quality of experience for the customer and consumer. The entrepreneurs are their own toughest critics. Everything is carefully considered and deliberately executed.

16. The challenge of succession beyond the entrepreneurial founders is consciously addressed in a variety of different ways. The sustainable enterprise community is closely connected and learns from one another. There is a developing understanding of how to go for growth whilst remaining true to sustainability beliefs.

17. The founders develop their enterprises to be role models to show how business can do well by doing good. They share their stories of a better way of doing business through books, presentations, influence on other businesses with whom they trade and openness to those who seek to learn from them.

18. The founders embrace philanthropy as a natural expression of their enterprise philosophy.

At the completion of the research, we shared this pattern with the sustainable enterprise companies, a few adjustments were made, and they confirmed that it was indeed consistent with their philosophy. So we had the basis for a theory.

A list is not a theory, although lists are common in business books, eg *In Search of Excellence*[16], *Good to Great*[17]. The problem with lists is that they do not explain the relationships between the components, and therefore it is hard to know where to start or the likely effects of specific actions.

Conclusion

In the next nine chapters which constitute together with this chapter Part 1 of the book, we share the stories as we experienced them. In Part 2 we induce a theory from these experiences to explain as best we can the factors that appear to lead towards sustainable enterprise success. We also share some of our experiences of implementing these ideas in a range of companies, large and small, across different countries and industries, with a view to assisting you to practise sustainable enterprise in your own business and daily life.

We conclude this introductory chapter with two key insights that emerged for us from the project:

1. Sustainability is not just about the environment; just as

importantly it is about economic outcomes for the enterprise and its participants, and about the social outcomes of the enterprise activities.

2. Sustainability does not need to cost enterprises more; exactly the opposite, in fact. Authentic sustainable enterprise activities create value, inspire opportunities and minimise risk.

Two.

Putumayo

"I'd always believed that business could be a force for positive social change. Even in the 1960s when I was trying to run businesses out of my dorm room and most kids on campus were opposed to the Vietnam War, and the world kind of got divided between people who were anti-establishment and those who were 'establishment' and into things like business, I was always in the middle. I said you can't rule out business – business I don't think has to be by definition bad for the community, bad for society, and at the same time I'm not saying that business is a purely social endeavour: it has to find a way to balance both issues."

— Dan Storper, founder Putumayo World Music

"I think there is a kind of spirit that people feel working for Putumayo that they're doing a good thing. That in their small way maybe it's going to help change the world, as trite as that might sound. You know it can change people's lives and in so doing it can change their world in its own little way, in their communities wherever they might be. That's why I feel good about what I'm still doing."

— Michael Kraus, co-founder Putumayo World Music

Think music executives, and many people conjure up images of shadowy powerbrokers cocooned in their prestige offices picking 'the next big thing' from a pile of demo tracks. Not Dan Storper and Michael Kraus, founder and co-founder respectively of Putumayo World Music, an unorthodox business producing world music compilations 'guaranteed to make you feel good'.

This entrepreneurial duo parlayed Dan's interest in global culture and retail experience and Michael's salesmanship and music background into a business idea aimed at supplying world music, not just through traditional music stores but through retailers such as bookshops, gift shops, health food stores, cafes and other specialty shops. The idea was to make people – customers, store staff – feel good, and at the same time introduce them to other cultures in an inspirational way.

Our foray into the fascinating world of world music marked the beginning of our sustainable enterprise journey of discovery. It was to be a prescient beginning. We got to New Orleans with a couple of days to spare before our meeting with Dan Storper, CEO and founder of Putumayo World Music. So we took the opportunity to explore some of the unique and vibrant city, its street life, night life, enduring jazz, culture, context and history. We found ourselves wandering through the French Quarter and chanced on a museum complex in Royal Street that housed the Historic New Orleans Collection of books, manuscripts and cultural artefacts. Putumayo Louisiana CDs were on sale in their museum store. We were treated to a tour of the museum and learned about the levy and flood protection system that preserves this city which is built on average six feet below sea level. Our knowledgeable tour guide was eerily certain that the city would imminently be flooded. It was only a few months later that Hurricane Katrina broke the city's sea defences, thereby creating the USA's worst ever natural disaster and simultaneously a symbol of awakening awareness of global warming.

We found Dan Storper in his quintessential New Orleans villa in the Faubourg Marigny community in the French Quarter. Dan chooses to live in New Orleans and New York, both vibrant centres of the global music scene. Dan and family survived the devastation with no ill effects, and the villa survived with damage to the roof. The joy of jazz is once again filling the streets and bars of this slowly recovering city. The passion for music is unabated, and it's this same passion that drives Dan and Putumayo.

"Music seemed so clearly something that was ideal to introduce people to other cultures. It has been called the universal language. I would venture to guess that if you put a great world music track alongside some pop hit around at the moment, and you grabbed a random 100 people in almost any city and said which of these do you like better, you would get a pretty sizeable number saying they prefer the world music track."

Dan's own story of how world music grabbed his attention is a great example of the power of authenticity. After taking a degree in Latin American studies, Dan set off in 1974 to see the region for himself firsthand. 'I started going to

Two.

places like La Paz, Bolivia to collect handicrafts and I would sit in the clubs like the Peña Naira in La Paz and I'd listen to some of these incredibly skilled musicians playing traditional indigenous Andean music and I just loved it. It was such an incredible environment.'

Back in the US, in 1975, Dan opened a tiny handicraft and clothing shop in New York which he named Putumayo after the Putumayo River, a 1,000 mile long navigable tributary of the Amazon River which runs through southern Colombia where he spent time collecting crafts. The business caught a wave of interest in ethnic craft and clothing and one store grew to a chain of seven, each filled with carefully collected items from Dan's travels. Through his travels and the crafts that he bought and sold, he developed a deep understanding of the differences between global cultures, but more importantly their shared humanity.

Dan's musical epiphany happened during a walk through Golden Gate Park in San Francisco. "There was an African band called Kotoja performing and there were probably 300 or so people dancing – it was a gorgeous day – and it was one of the most multicultural crowds I'd ever seen. There was a Chinese woman dancing with an African guy, and they weren't dancing to the juju-based music of Nigeria, they were doing a kind of salsa. There they were, kids, grandparents, Chinese, African, Latin, all having a great time, and I was really struck both by that scene and by the music – how powerful it was."

A few days later, back in New York City and visiting one of his stores, he was horrified to hear heavy metal music playing that was profoundly alien to the cultures that the store represented. To create a sense of escape from the city streets of New York and to ensure consistency with his stores' theme of world clothing and craft, he started seeking out international music in local record stores. This was in the early 1990s, and he was surprised how little was available and known, but he bought what seemed interesting.

With the help of a company specialising in in-store play music, he put together a four- hour tape mixing music he'd brought back from his travels in South America with the music of artists from Brazil, South Africa and beyond, along with tracks from his favourite artists such as Van Morrison and Bonnie Raitt. It was an eclectic mix, he told us, "but always driven by good melodies, beautiful voices, interesting songs".

The effect was electric, Dan recalled. "About two hours after one of those first tapes went into one of the stores, I got a call from the assistant manager who said, 'Dan, you have no idea what's going on here' -- I remember the call distinctly – she said, 'I've never seen the staff so happy, they are bopping around the store and the customers are coming up to the counter every couple of minutes asking what's this song and what's that song.' So that was the first sign that there was something really going on there."

"Dan has been the real missionary behind this whole thing," Putumayo co-founder Michael Kraus told us on a flying sales visit to New Zealand. A former professional musician and serial entrepreneur, Michael was a long-standing friend, and was an obvious choice as business partner when Dan came up with the idea of starting their own record label in 1992. "Michael was somebody who always had these enthusiastic ideas about starting a new business," Dan recalled. "He had been doing everything from selling t-shirts, renting roller skates in Central Park, to managing a comedy club, and I just think, man, if he had something really good like fun, world music CDs to sell, he would be great."

Michael takes up the story. "Over the years, he'd mentioned different ideas to me, and I didn't like any of them

until it was music, because that's my background. So when he came to me and said, 'Do you want to help me start a record label, do you want to join me?', I said , 'Make me an offer!' He made me a great offer and the rest is history!"

Today Putumayo employs more than 100 staff in New York, New Orleans, Amsterdam and 12 other offices around the world, and distributes its music in 100 countries. Sales reached $24 million in 2007, but Putumayo has never been just about profit. An invited member of the Social Venture Network of businesses for social responsibility, since the early 1990s, Dan Storper drew inspiration from people like Anita Roddick of The Bodyshop and Ben Cohen of Ben & Jerry.

It was through the Social Venture Network, that Dan met the founder of Rhino Records, Richard Foos, who was deeply committed to social responsibility. That connection was to prove a turning point, as Dan explained: "I went to Richard and I said, 'There's an incredible response to this music I'm playing. How about if we collaborate on putting together a series or even just a single world music collection?' He said, 'It's funny you mention that because we've talked about it for the last couple of years, but weren't sure what to do. Collaborating with you might be fun and profitable.'"

Two.

Under the deal, Dan was to pick the music and take care of the liner notes and the design, while Rhino Records handled the licensing and manufacturing. Distribution was to be split, with Putumayo focussing on the non-traditional market and Rhino selling to record stores.

Within eighteen months, four Putumayo collections had been released – with their distinctive folkloric artwork by Nicola Heindl and packaged not in the usual plastic 'jewelcase' but in a cardboard digipak sleeve. The packaging caused a month-long argument with Rhino Records' production manager, recalled Dan, but typically he was not to be swayed from his vision for Putumayo. "We were in the production office of Rhino, and I kept telling them I hate plastic jewelcases, they break, they are ugly, you can't see the artwork and they are not environmentally friendly.

"Then I looked over and there on the end of his desk was a digipak CD package that was made out of cardboard, and I said, 'That's what we want' and he said, 'No, you don't' and I said, 'What do you mean we don't?'. He said first of all retailers hate it because they were very hard to use in anti-theft devices. I finally got the president of Rhino, Richard, to overrule his production person, because I said we are going to a market that isn't about plastic jewelcases; we want to create a package that combines music, culture and travel and that can also be purchased as a gift."

Dan and Richard had also decided that a portion of the proceeds from each of the albums would go to a different non-profit organisation that worked towards social or environmental causes in the region where the music came from. Rhino Records and Putumayo subsequently parted ways, but the social activism element of Putumayo's business model has remained strong. For example, the Music from the Coffee Lands album has raised $50,000 for Coffee Kids to support children and their families from coffee-producing countries in Latin America. Organisations dealing with homelessness, global poverty and the effects of war also receive support; and closer to home Putumayo has been involved in bringing dance and music programmes into inner city schools in Harlem and New Orleans. The company has donated more than $1 million to non-profits since it began.

Dan explained the thinking behind Putumayo's not-for-profit alliances. "We pick an organisation based on research tied in usually with a theme:

Are they working in the communities where the music comes from? So would this money come back to these communities? That's critical. And also, are they worthwhile?"

He says the underlying purpose and real strength of Putumayo to reach people took a step forward when the company launched its children's CDs and multicultural activity kits and teacher training programmes for underprivileged schools. The initiative came from a teacher who was using Putumayo CDs in her classroom and came to the company with a proposal to create teaching materials which tied in with the music. "We ultimately invited her to help start the children's and education division which we created after we saw how positively people were responding to the World Playground Activity Kit," Dan told us.

Putumayo Kids has now released 15 albums – aimed at "young children who can learn about the positive sides of other cultures that are often depicted in the media mostly through their problems like poverty, disease and war," said Dan. The albums are designed to encourage kids to learn and to counter prejudice.

The synergy between Dan and Michael is evident when they talk about their business. Here's Michael on what success means to him:

"It's not just about the money. It's also about turning people on to an artist and different cultures that they otherwise would not have been exposed to. We've made it accessible, and I think that's really where the success emanates from. Putumayo really does bring people closer together. There is a certain sort of community feeling and outreach."

That sense of social engagement runs right the way through Putumayo. And it begins with the customer. The company's sales have grown about 20% a year since 2001, but Dan and Michael still spend much of their time on the road doing what they call 'store busting' – a sort of face-to-face cold-calling. They and their team drop in on retailers across the world, ranging from coffee shops to museums, to introduce the product or check on how sales are going.

Store busting is Putumayo's point of difference, the key to building a bond with existing customers and finding new ones. Dan told us he'd developed the idea of store busting from his clothing company days when he'd take trips around the country, partly for design inspiration but also to visit retailers. "I realised it's one thing when you talk to somebody on the phone, it's another thing when you see it. And I started to see all these stores where

Two.

Putumayo wasn't really appropriate or the staff didn't like playing the music. And I started seeing stores we were not in, that we really should have been in. And so we began the process of doing these store busting trips to visit retailers. It's a really big part of what Putumayo does."

"Dan and I have been doing this so long we can drive down a street and we know what store would be a good match for Putumayo, so a lot of those types of stores we'll just give CDs to," Michael explained. "At first, people said no, we're a gift shop or clothing boutique, we don't want to sell music, or it's not our thing. Lots of times we wouldn't pressure those people, but we'd say here are a couple of CDs, this is our little prospect package. Then we'd call them back a couple of weeks later, and you know what, people were saying they were getting a great response to the music they were playing. And before you knew it we had a new customer."

As well as stores, Putumayo gives CDs to restaurants, cafes, clubs and DJs – what Dan calls 'taste makers'. In the US alone, Putumayo's taste makers number 8,000, with perhaps another 2,000 in Europe. "We produce more sample CDs than probably anyone in the world, including major labels, because we believe it's critical

that people hear the music." CDs and store displays, he told us, are the biggest investment Putumayo makes in marketing. The relationship marketing strategy has paid off: now more than 50% of Putumayo's sales are made through non-traditional music outlets, and it remains the driver of the company's growth.

The relationship goes both ways: store busting and the taste makers network allows Putumayo to gather feedback on what works and what doesn't. "It's a constant interaction," the company's marketing manager Mary Alice told us. "We're constantly listening to our consumers, we get bounce back cards – they are inserted in most of the CDs – and people not only give us information about themselves, but they are constantly providing interesting things that they'd like to see, suggestions for the label, and we really do try to pay close attention to that."

"One of the great things about working with Putumayo sales is that every time we visit a retailer we're received with such a huge smile, so it's great," the international sales and marketing manager Candice Vargas told us. "It's not like selling something, it's almost like you're creating a partnership with the person. You say, I'm from Putumayo and we're going to introduce one of these CDs and that puts a smile on their face. So that's really great. We just love going store busting because we make many friends and we have really good experience from visiting them."

For Dan Storper, this kind of staff engagement is what makes Putumayo special. He told us the company does a lot of brainstorming with the staff "to make sure they get both the purpose on the one hand and also understand and are a party to the marketing and promotion decisions that are made".

This philosophy has brought in people from all walks of life who clearly value the Putumayo way. There's Mary Alice, the former record store sales assistant who became Putumayo's marketing manager after first experiencing Putumayo through store busting. There's Mona Kayhan, Putumayo Kids division manager, who studied music in Mali and then considered a career in music therapy. She told us Putumayo represented her ideal of spreading multiculturalism through music throughout the world.

Former actor Chad Kraus, who incidentally is son of Putumayo co-founder Michael Kraus, started out as the company's part-time receptionist; he's now national sales manager. Chad has a real feel for what kind of retailer is likely

to become a Putumayo fan. "I'm looking for gift shops that have a different feel, whether it be that they have some items that I've never seen before, or just have a nice layout to the store that is more non-traditional. I'm looking for a hip coffee house, one that is playing music or has comfortable chairs, that is a place to relax and enjoy."

When we visited Putumayo's Amsterdam office, we found another group of dedicated people who obviously find fun in their work. The big thing they really valued was the authenticity of the company. Igor Rooselaar is responsible for Putumayo's sales and marketing in Europe, and regularly sets off on store busting trips on a bike with a backpack full of CDs. "The joke is of course that we say, yeah, we came all the way from Holland on bicycles. Which is so much Putumayo's style to do that. Besides, we wouldn't be able to do half of the shops if we didn't have these mountain bikes. We can go anywhere and just leave the bicycle, jump in, jump out. Forget trying to do that on public transport or if you had to rent a car." Igor told us the reason he liked working for Putumayo was that the company operated on the street level and kept in touch with customers. "We almost feel naked if we don't have any CDs on us," he joked, "even on weekends or vacations."

Two.

For European marketing director Gwena Jaouen, a veteran of the music industry, what makes Putumayo different is Dan Storper's philosophy. "It's so clear and so straight, and it's really personal and people can feel it very well. This is a company with a strong philosophy." Gwena told us that in her previous job, dwindling budgets had made selling into traditional markets increasingly difficult. "That's the big difference with Putumayo: when you come into the shops and propose a product and explain what the philosophy is, people love it and that's why they buy it."

It was inspiring to spend time with people passionately discussing the core Putumayo beliefs. The same words came up time and again: passion, creativity, quality, the balance between business and social responsibility, sharing cultural traditions, staying close to the customer. Music researcher Jacob Edgar summed it up: "I feel great at the end of the day because I feel like we are making a difference."

Two or three times per year the company puts on a party with an artist and food, and brings in a music and culture expert for that particular region to talk to staff. It's a way to combine learning with making staff feel part of the family. Initiatives

like these have been important as Putumayo has sought to negotiate the shift to a more corporate structure. Dan explained that it was about "finding a way to negotiate being a much bigger company which requires structure while maintaining informality, without losing identity, and sense of personality, and without bringing people into an environment where it's just a nine to five suit job and nobody knows anybody."

The fun extends to marketing too, from kids colouring contests to concerts. Putumayo organised belly-dancing lessons in a New York club to launch its North African Groove album, and when it put on a release party in Mexico there were 25,000 people following a truck playing world music from places like Africa and Indonesia.

So how did Putumayo make the shift from bringing world music to US consumers to taking world music out to the rest of the world? Very, very slowly, Dan told us. He made the decision to focus initially on the English-speaking world, and in 1995 – a year after the split from Rhino Records – the company started working with distributors in Canada, Australia and New Zealand. A year later, Putumayo started in the UK, but it was at the MIDEM music business conference in Cannes,

France, that the global market really took off.

"We had appealing CD covers; people had started hearing about Putumayo, and we just had lines of people who were interested in distributing Putumayo," Dan recalled. "I was able to find some good distributors in seven countries that year." Putumayo still holds an annual meeting for all distributors at MIDEM to talk about upcoming releases and some of the company's approaches on both the traditional and non-traditional markets.

Going global has brought its own challenges – not least ferreting out the right people with the right passion to tackle the non-traditional retail market. One of those people is Beverly Meyer who distributes Putumayo CDs in New Zealand and more recently in Australia. Less than six months after starting out, she'd opened up 200 accounts in New Zealand. "She's a shining example for the rest of the world in terms of what she's been able to do on this island of four million people. It has been a phenomenal success," enthused co-founder Michael Kraus.

A South African who has settled in New Zealand, Beverly knew and loved Putumayo music, and knew that it just had to be in New Zealand. "I contacted Michael and it just went from there," she told us. "We've had

an incredible ride with Putumayo in a short time. I've seen so many restaurants, for instance, like this Indian restaurant, I walked in there -- and they were playing the radio. Beautiful table settings, the way they dressed, exquisite food, but they were playing the radio. The thing is, putting Putumayo's Asian Lounge [album] in there has even changed the way the staff come across; the way they serve you, the way they walk, everything changes. It's incredible. We absolutely love it and the reps love it too. That's what this music does to you."

Internally too Putumayo has had to become more flexible. Dan Storper told us his greatest frustration along the way has been getting staff to take an international perspective. "I think the main challenge is to make the inside company start to understand how to go global, to understand that we have a beautiful concept and it is great, but what applies to the West may not apply to other countries. So it's really to be able to understand what the basic concept is, understand what and where you want to go, understand our purpose very well and be able to adapt it in each country."

Putumayo is tackling this internationalisation of the company by making sure it's international inside as well as outside. In Putumayo's international office in New York alone,

Two.

there are people from the US, Canada, France, Japan, Colombia, Jordan and Argentina. The results speak for themselves: Dan told us that sales in the Latin America market had tripled in eighteen months.

Outside of the US, Putumayo now maintains offices in Amsterdam, Paris, London, Barcelona, Stockholm, Rome, Quebec, Vancouver, Brazil, Cape Town, Tel Aviv, Mumbai and Tokyo. As well as using on-the-ground reps with local knowledge, Putumayo also issues its album liner notes in English, Spanish and French.

Putumayo's next big challenge is to manage growth without losing sight of its purpose. The company has had its own globally syndicated radio show since 1998, and it is looking to move into TV. Putumayo also markets complementary products, such as books and DVDs, and is developing marketing alliances with other like-minded companies that share their dream.

Dan Storper is committed to maintaining control of the company. "I've never valued success by saying I've achieved a billion dollar business and a ten million dollar or hundred million dollar profit. There's no question that this could be a much bigger company in terms of volume and probably profitability if I cared more purely about sales

and profitability," he told us. "I've passed along a lot of opportunities along the way including investment opportunities where I felt I'd rather be able to control the direction of the company than sell out to investors."

Quality is paramount for Putumayo. It was a theme that came up again and again with everyone in the company that we talked to. Dan told us he was definitely concerned about quality. "Don't put anything out until it's ready, and everything does take longer to develop and get to the point where you feel it's ready than you can imagine," he said when we asked him what lessons he had for aspiring sustainable entrepreneurs.

"I look at a couple of benchmarks. I can't feel successful if the company isn't profitable. I can't feel successful if there is not a really strong positive response to the majority of our albums we'll release in a year. To some extent, success comes from a sense that you really do get great positive feedback, both from the public and your peers."

He gave us a great example of the impact Putumayo has had on the music world. "I remember giving Jackson Browne's girlfriend a copy of the CD by Habib Koite who is a Malian artist that had been signed by Putumayo; a very talented guy. And she called me up three days later saying that she, Jackson and all her friends were gaga over his music, and within about a year he [Jackson] was flying to Mali to spend time hanging out writing with him."

Music researcher Jacob Edgar summed up Putumayo's purpose eloquently: "It's basically a business. We are trying to sustain ourselves and have to be concerned about making a profit, but at the same time there is a social purpose underlying what we are doing, underlying Dan's passion. It's music that we sell but really the product is culture. We are a company whose product is basically introducing or supporting the notion of cultural diversity and supporting the learning and understanding and appreciation of other cultures. Music is the vehicle, music is the tool; but we have plans to develop other products and use other tools to do that as well."

Reflections

At the end of each of our enterprise visits we took time to discuss the key insights that emerged. Much earlier in our lives we spent a winter in Falmouth, England, after a year's sailing cruise in the Atlantic. By chance we were anchored alongside Robert Pirsig, author of Zen and the Art of Motorcycle Maintenance. At the time Robert was writing Lila, his sequel to Zen. He showed us and

explained his technique of using squares of paper for recording ideas as they emerged from his research. The squares can then be sorted and categorised to enable ideas to emerge intuitively for theory development. We used Post-it notes for this purpose which we gradually assembled across a large wall in our New Zealand office. We found the visceral and visual experience of the notes worked well for theory development in conjunction with our computerised qualitative analysis systems.

Key ideas that found their way onto our notes after our experiences with Putumayo were:

- *Enterprise philosophy is the foundation for the enduring success of the company*

- *Learnings from prior enterprise experience were leveraged to energise the establishment of this enterprise*

- *Passion and enthusiasm characterise the enterprise's spirit and are deliberately nurtured*

- *Direct and unconventional marketing lies at the heart of the business model*

- *A commitment to outstanding quality goes hand in hand with sustainability.*

Three.

Stonyfield Farm

"I think one could say we are excellent yoghurt makers who know that making money cannot be the exclusive point, because otherwise there will be no planet left."

"I've never felt that what we've done here is terribly ingenious – I think it's in fact brutally pragmatic. We wanted our farmers to get a reliable source of support; we wanted to break in to a market that is daunting at the very least. There was no way we could outspend with a marketing budget that is essentially a rounding error next to my competitors! When you identify with concerns that the average person has, you cut through all of that."

— *Gary Hirshberg , founder Stonyfield Farm*

Stonyfield Farm is an hour's drive north of Boston in Londonderry, New Hampshire. We found the dairy factory underneath a giant yoghurt cup that proclaims the company's presence and purpose. Carmelle Druchniak, Stonyfield's chief of 'moos releases' and storyteller par excellence, had already warned us not to expect to see too many cows. That's OK, we said, we've seen lots in our home country, New Zealand. And so it was; the only cow we experienced was a life-sized plastic one in the front reception. But the spirit of cows was omnipresent!

At Stonyfield Farm's Yoghurt Works Visitors Centre we chuckled as we encountered moos releases; moos letters – which go out to 600,000 consumers; an adopt a cow scheme; personalised cow stories featuring Tuttle, Priscilla, Luv, Libby, Spiffy and many more, and celebrities in the moos (celebrity endorsements). The Stonyfield communication team enjoy a theme that enables a never-ending supply of puns and fun to flow. There's a purpose to all of this, however, beyond creative fun. The good 'moos' story that flows around Stonyfield is all about creating enduring emotional connection to the company and its products; and it's about educating people about where their food comes from and how it is produced.

Education of consumers is central to the Stonyfield Farm commitment to 'healthy food, healthy people and a healthy planet'. And this commitment in turn is core to the wellness value proposition that has helped Stonyfield become the world's leading organic yoghurt maker and a model to show the whole business world that environmentally friendly and socially responsible business can be profitable too.

The man behind Stonyfield Farm's success is Gary Hirschberg – dubbed the philosopher king of the organics industry by *Business Week* magazine. His own team describe him as the company's essence or DNA. Our meeting with Stonyfield Farm's president and CE-YO began (how else?) with ritual yoghurt sharing. Celebratory yoghurt eating is a usual feature of Stonyfield meetings, and Gary ensures he tries every one of the product flavours and varieties at least once a month as part of his personal commitment to sustained product quality.

"Stonyfield Farm has not just talked the talk, but walked it as well," he told us. "I think we've built a lot of loyalty. Actually our percentage of spending on marketing has decreased as we've spent more and more on farmers and on fulfilling our mission. It's much more of a word of mouth product, but word of mouth is a result of an emotional connection and that emotion is loyalty. And that loyalty comes from people being comforted not just by what's in the cup, but by our whole business approach."

Stonyfield Farm started out with just seven cows in 1983 as the fundraising arm of an organic farming school, founded by engineer-turned-hippy Samuel Kaymen. Samuel had approached Gary for some business advice, and in the course of their discussion on windmills, power generation and other ideas to financially support the Rural Education Centre, Samuel revealed his delicious recipe for yoghurt. The astute entrepreneur in Gary recognised an opportunity and suggested that yoghurt production could be a viable way to create value for the Centre. Samuel's other two recipes were beer and pickles, so yoghurt turned out to be a fortunate choice! The engineer and entrepreneur went into business, and now the yoghurt enterprise Stonyfield Farm is a $320 million business that shows environmental education is good for the bottom line.

Like most of the enterprises featured in this book, Stonyfield Farm emerged through a dyad of founders with complementary technical and

Three.

entrepreneurial skills. It's rarely the case that a single person snatches an enterprise plan out of the ether and takes on all roles of entrepreneur, engineer, technician, marketer and manager. Michael E. Gerber refers to this heroic image as the E-Myth[18].

Even with this solid partnership, Stonyfield Farm was by no means an easy ride to success. Gary and Samuel refer to the first ten years as "the bad old days". Everything went wrong, as Carmelle explained, "The local dairy they enlisted to help them in terms of milk supply ended up going bankrupt and all Stonyfield's equipment was seized". Money had to be scraped together from family and friends; even the support of the local order of nuns was enlisted for a loan.

To focus the enterprise model in the middle of a crisis, Stonyfield created an operating board to share the load. Gary explains the benefits.

> In 1988 we did $2.5 million in sales and we lost $1.4 million and that meant that we were losing about $30,000 per week and I had to raise that money. We crafted something that we called an operating team in the midst of that crisis where we got all of our key decision makers together and started meeting once a week. And that group became the

group that was sharing the load instead of it just being Samuel and Gary. The value that the board always played was that the board meetings forced me to really get my head together. I'd have to get my agendas and my arguments all lined up so it was a little bit like writing a business plan. The product was not the point, it was the process. We got through some real crises with this board, they would poke me and kick me, but mostly the work was done before the meeting even opened.

Through the board, Stonyfield Farm was able to relentlessly focus on and develop the core business. A central part of the business is working with family farms to produce organic milk. Stonyfield Farm started life as a family farm – Meg Hirshberg and her husband Gary, Louise Kaymen and her husband Samuel, plus all their children. To this day 100% of the milk used by Stonyfield Farm comes from family farms. Stonyfield Farm has formed close relationships with their family farm suppliers to achieve the highest quality product they can and simultaneously benefit the community within which they operate.

By securing their source of sustainably produced organic milk, both Gary and Samuel knew they had a high quality product with potential – the best yoghurt they'd ever tasted. They persevered, inspired by the need to share a sustainable success story that no other food business was telling; in the United States only Ben & Jerry's came close:

> As an environmentalist, as a climate change advocate, as an advocate for renewable energy and organics back when I was an academic, I just came to the conclusion that business is the only way to advance these ideas and that we must prove to the world that its highly profitable to do so because otherwise we were just going to be a really cool lonely company on a dead planet. We have to change the way other businesses do business. This model would never work if our yoghurt wasn't superior. Period. My view is that you use the vehicle of an excellent product or service, to then become a more adept communicator of the principles you stand for.

Gary and Samuel's personal conviction that farmers should be environmental stewards, caring for the land by avoiding pesticides and hormones, is intrinsic to Stonyfield. Their activist beliefs derive from an insight into the environmental degradation caused by popular farming practices that endorse abrasive synthetics over natural nourishing cycles. Agricultural models that rely on synthetics deplete soil nutrients with chemicals, requiring ever-increasing amounts of fertilisers and hormones to bump up the soil and livestock fertility. Stonyfield was at the forefront of pushing for organic farm management and family farmers to improve the environment and sustain a healthy population. Gary and Samuel's insight in the 1980s positioned Stonyfield Farm at the crest of the wave in the new burgeoning organic market in the mid-1990s.

Starting with seven cows to prove that zero toxins create a healthier and tastier product, the challenge was to show others how to save the world through a different model for business. Their business, or model for living, would educate consumers on social, cultural and environmental issues and create economic solutions, while fostering close consumer engagement. This innovative strategy of inviting the consumer into the brand recognised the benefits of a relationship that listened to and respected consumers, as Gary explains:

> I always say that the Coke & Pepsi model is really obsolete, their model is make the product as

Three.

cheap as you possibly can, then with the huge margin that is left, spend that on seduction, on manipulation and hopefully you'll get awareness which will hopefully lead to trial which will eventually at the end of a long string of maybes, possibly lead to loyalty. And well, we can't afford all of that, so what we do is we go straight for loyalty! We just skip that whole curve.

The marketing strategies Gary created for 'skipping the curve' are closer to activism than conventional advertising. His background was as an educator and a windmill builder, and he sometimes refers to himself and others in the Stonyfield family as "environmental educators masquerading as yoghurt makers". He told us: "I knew about environmental education and I always took the attitude that marketing is just another form of education and that education is the best kind of marketing. That by informing people you not only help them to learn, but you demonstrate a certain kind of competency and consciousness."

The environmental and educational consciousness or spirit that infuses Stonyfield Farm inspired its early activist campaigns, such as using the tops of yoghurt lids as a space for raising awareness of climate change, advocating for gun control and inviting people to consider a multiplicity of social and environmental issues facing society. This is one of Stonyfield's most successful ideas that continues to this day. Amongst the thousands of brands in supermarkets and stores Stonyfield Farm is one of the few that lift their product out of the supermarket trolley and contextualise it in significant environmental and social issues. Gary describes how the products signal to the consumer that Stonyfield Is actively involved in creating solutions to individual issues such as low immune systems or global issues like climate change:

> The average consumer who rushes in to the store with a kid on her hip and one in the car doesn't have the time to get a lecture on why glaciers are receding, but she wants to see some signals that this is a company who is trying to be part of that solution. So if you see our organic guarantee or you see my signature or you see that 10% of our profits go to the planet or you see other discussions, people get the feeling that we are informed and we are certainly trying to inform them. We really have a lot to say and I take the reciprocal attitude that if you don't like what we're saying, you can

vote by buying somewhere else. But obviously it has been working.

Gary attributes the company's success to this open invitation to the consumer.

We were never just a brand – we always, from the very first package, invited people to be part of Stonyfield. The first thing I wrote on the package was "let us hear from you". We put our signatures on the package. Nowadays everybody does it, but we were one of the first, because we wanted to say, hey, we are not just a company that's anonymously out here producing tonnes of product, we are people who you might like to know, but who certainly would like to know you and please write to us.

Like any true activist, Stonyfield Farm is most comfortable on the streets, rather than on glossy retouched billboards. The protest banner may have been exchanged for clever packaging and the information clipboard turned into a corporate website, but the community-based handshake remains the same. Stonyfield Farm's Vice-President of Communications, Carmelle, Druchniak, describes how it's done:

There was no venue too small for Stonyfield product to be given out to the masses. And as Gary says, once they taste the yoghurt they would come back again and again, and it's that handshake with the consumer that Stonyfield is built on. We continue to market the yoghurt by way of community events – we give out tens of thousands of samples every year. We sample on subway platforms; we salute commuters for using public transportation by giving them yoghurt.

All this well-meaning consumer engagement would be for nothing without a great quality product. Stonyfield Farm led the shift of organic food away from mealy apples and lumpy yoghurt at the hippy co-op, to become a premium quality, healthy product aimed at a wider market. Simply having a sustainable purpose and product is not enough to swing consumers over. If the product is as good as or better than its competitors, then sustainability can spark enduring emotional engagement.

Having the mindset that you can make something better coupled with the determination to succeed is the formula Gary attributes to successful sustainable enterprise:

I've learned that determination is probably one of the most undervalued but most essential

Three.

qualities needed to succeed. It's human nature I think to try and simplify things and to take for granted the kind of backbone, the vertebrae, that is needed to create something. When I see people with great ideas, the one who is more determined is the one I'm going to bet on!

Stonyfield Farm is an inspiring example of what determination can do. Optimism and drive helped Gary and Samuel to embrace challenges through initial setbacks of failing electricity and near bankruptcy. And, as Carmelle illustrated in a great story, Gary has the ability to turn challenges into opportunities:

> One day someone called and said there is a radio disc jockey in Boston and he's saying that yoghurt tastes as bad as camel manure. So Gary of course -- Mr Optimism -- he went to a local petting zoo that had a camel and he had them package up camel manure, and he drove to Boston and went to the radio station and went to the receptionist and said, "Hello, I make yoghurt and I'm here to challenge your DJ to an on air taste test between my yoghurt and camel manure." And he ends up on the air for an hour! I mean you can't pay for advertising like that.

Stonyfield Farm people have a clear philosophy about what the company stands for – a healthy planet. They embrace sustainability thinking as a whole, with a focus on educating consumers and producers on the value of environmental and organic methods of food production and support of family farmers. As enterpriser, Gary was instrumental in establishing the enterprise's purpose and continues to embody the company's spirit. His passion continues to fuel the purpose and Inspire others. Carmelle explains:

> I really think that he's assembled a like-minded team. The purpose is engrained in everything we do so we can't digress. Gary's DNA is imprinted in the purpose and so we joke sometimes about channelling Gary which I'm doing right now actually! The brand is truly ingrained in the psyche of the consumer as well.

"Channelling Gary" happens to everyone in the Stonyfield family. Take Carol Chapman, manager of the Yoghurt Works Visitors Centre. She's been with the company from the early days, and she told us how she got caught up in the passion. "Here they were, a little tiny, tiny company, like with these wonderful goals and wonderful product, so it was very easy for me to just get so caught up in it. When I was soliciting people to taste this yoghurt they would say 'Is this your company?', but that was the passion that I felt so it was very, very easy for me."

Just as a river is cleaner downstream if chemicals are not poured into it upstream, a product is of higher quality if the upstream suppliers are nourished. Stonyfield listens to its farmers' needs; for example, the company protested alongside farmers against the introduction of the synthetic growth hormone rBST[19] and even pays farmers not to use it. To be part of the Stonyfield family, farmers have to be organic. Stonyfield Farm recognises that the three year process to become certified organic is a difficult time, so the company offers financial and in-kind support, such as loans and educational workshops during the transition period.

Gary believes Stonyfield Farm's practices and commitment to family to create future supply and share the dream of environmental stewardship strengthens the supplier relationship and minimises risk for both parties:

> We are associated with a co-op of about 800 farmers, but then there is also fruit and sugar and cocoa, and we've really got a tremendous track record that I'm very proud of as far as helping to sustain our upstream partners. There are hundreds of farmers now of course profiting where they might not have even survived, and they'll be the first to tell you that. And that's my proudest achievement, the long list of farmers who are not only having their most profitable years ever now, but they are having the only profitable years that they've ever had.

The careful consideration with which Stonyfield treats upstream suppliers is also extended to their relationship with customers and consumers. One of the letters we were shown by Gary came from a young consumer asking about a cow she had adopted.

> I am 8 years old. I adopted my cow when I was 4 and I wanted to check on her – is she alive? Does she have a calf, if she did, did the owner give it away? I want to know if the owner gave her calf. Bye, love Natasha. P.S. Don't eat Fiona (that is the cow's name). I love her.

Adopting a cow, as this eight-year-old demonstrates, is an emotional process which requires a careful and thoughtful response. In keeping with the transparency of the rest of the company's processes, Stonyfield Farm decided to openly educate children and adults on natural cycles, and has developed a whole bibliography on loss. Gary explains:

Three.

We gave the parents references so they could sit and talk to kids about loss, because we thought it was better to face up to the circle of life. We believed this would build relationships. Parents really appreciated that we were so sincere about this instead of us just fluffing it over. I think the fundamental way that we grew our business was by being people who talked to other people. We didn't act bureaucratic, we didn't act like executives, we didn't assume that there was a wall either between us and the outside world, our consumers, or even for that matter our employees.

Although Gary describes his approach to business as "brutally pragmatic", his decisions and insights about world social, cultural and environmental movements have carefully positioned Stonyfield into a new market with strong value propositions. "We've been out in front about what goes in the cup; we've also been very vocal about our whole process and my background is in climate change, so I've been talking about this stuff for 25 years, even though for 23 of those years no one has really been listening!" he told us.

Events such as Monsanto's push for legal approval of the synthetic growth hormone rBST in the mid-1990s, the movies *Fast Food Nation* and *Super Size Me*, and McDonalds' statement that it would endeavour to reduce hormones in its food have all served to increase awareness, Gary believes:

How many consumers are going to put up their hand and say, no I'll take the one with more hormones! Once you choose to be aware, you have to choose organic products, particularly as parents, because it's really the only surefire way of ensuring you are going to minimise toxins to your family.

Gary also sees political events such as the Iraq war as a tipping factor for Stonyfield Farm. "Educated people saw this as another Vietnam and saw a need to be more secure and I think organics is a form of security." Consumers are no longer using their purchasing power to invest in enterprises whose sole function is creating more money to push more products. Rather people want security and emotional connections, they are what Rolf Jensen refers to as "in the market for convictions[20]". Gary believes sustainable business can meet that need. "What has happened, is that as our political leaders have really failed us I think a lot of people have turned to conscious businesses or businesses with a cause to give them a little bit of personal comfort," he told us. "And because Stonyfield has not just talked the talk, but walked it as well, I think we've built a lot of loyalty."

It came therefore as a deep surprise and source of dismay to many that Gary chose to sell to Groupe Danone in 2001. Many observers felt that this multinational takeover would result in a watering down of Stonyfield's purpose and beliefs. But Gary created an unconventional deal with Groupe Danone that would allow both enterprises to flourish and share the Stonyfield dream of a healthy planet with a larger audience.

> The deal I struck with Groupe Danone was really a marriage of strengths but with a lot of respect. It was not a classic acquisition by any stretch, in fact it was a most unconventional partnership and is to this day, but I think that has inspired others that they can do the same thing -- and there have been others. Tom [Tom's of Maine] did it, Cadbury's acquisition of Green & Black's in the UK was very definitely influenced by this, and I've been associated with a half a dozen deals where the entrepreneur has really been nourished by the parent without being squashed.

The challenge of succession is faced by all successful enterprises. The Groupe Danone partnership Gary created demonstrates the potential for merger and growth possibilities whilst remaining true to sustainability beliefs. Stonyfield now has access to new technology, capital and expanded marketing channels and collateral, while retaining its organic and sustainable identity, with Gary remaining firmly in charge:

> At the Groupe we are having an enormous impact on everything from climate change policy, philanthropy, marketing approach, to concrete things like the waste water plant which is a net energy producer. It's a methane digesting facility which heretofore has never been used in any yoghurt plant in all of Danone globally – you know 75 plants around the world. It has been a smash success – Danone initially didn't want us to do it, because they were fearful of it, but I told them we were going to do it because we had to do it, because it is part of our mandate to turn waste into food and plug leaks. And they reluctantly agreed, and now they're thrilled because Stonyfield has been a guinea pig. Next we're doing a new heat recovery system that's also never been approved.

Three.

Greater growth and profits for Stonyfield Farm mean greater profits for the environment, as since 2000 the company has had a policy of giving 10% of its profits annually to initiatives and programmes that help create a healthier planet. This policy remains under the Groupe Danone ownership.

Stonyfield Farm constantly pursues opportunities consistent with its purpose of making excellent yoghurt and contributing to a healthy planet. They are often the first to trial new concepts and technologies. For example, they were the first manufacturer in America to make their plant a zero emissions facility through mitigation and offsets, well before the concept of offsets was known to the business world.

Stonyfield was initially set up as an educational enterprise, and perhaps one of the most important educational lessons it imparts is setting an example for other enterprises. As well as acting as a role model that shows how business can do well by doing good, Gary runs an annual workshop for entrepreneurs.

We are proving here that you can make more money doing these things, whether it's installing solar cells on our roof, or putting in this waste treatment plant, or supporting family farmers

whose yields over time come up and whose costs go down. The Stonyfield Entrepreneur Institute is a real boot camp for entrepreneurs and I try to impart some of the learnings from all of my many mistakes and it's pretty powerful; I get 70 or 80 entrepreneurs there and it takes place every March. Many, many of these folks would say that they've really avoided some of the problems or been helped because of us.

The natural products industry as a whole has benefited from Stonyfield and a number of peer companies including Patagonia by just getting proof and confirmation that this idea of building a company based on relationships, advocacy and activism can work, in the same way that I got my inspiration from Ben & Jerry's who were out in front of me by about seven years.

As for the future, Gary remains characteristically upbeat. He recognises that he needs to find a successor so that Stonyfield Farm can "outgrow its founder", as he puts it. But the big challenge ahead is securing supply as demand for organic products grows, which in turn will bring down costs for the consumer. "My optimism is rooted in the fact that ecology really is long-term economics," says Gary. "The other reason I am optimistic is that I started doing this stuff 25 years ago, and I was dismissed at best and ridiculed at worst. But now I get presidential candidates visiting me all the time."

Reflections

POSITIVITY writ large was the standout insight that found its way onto our Post-it notes at the end of our Stonyfield conversations. Gary personified it and his positivity was contagious to the organisation. Quality also featured large, to the extent that we started to see sustainability as an extension of quality into the 21st century. We wished we had had this idea back in 1979 when we met Pirsig during his exploration of quality through telling the story of Lila! The nexus between the technical skills of Samuel Kaymen and Garys Hirshfield's enterpriser skills and passion for sustainability struck us as an ideal cauldron of potential sustainable enterprise ideas. As this dyad story was similar to that of Dan Storper and Michael Kraus at Putumayo, we wondered whether this would prove to be a common feature of sustainable enterprise creation. The discussions about succession and the sustainability of the enterprise itself in the light of Gary's decision to expand the business by selling to Danone gave us food for thought that we determined to explore in the subsequent case study interviews.

Four.

The Body Shop

This chapter records an interview with Dame Anita Roddick shortly before her death in September 2007. Here Anita, the inveterate storyteller, tells the story of how she instigated The Body Shop, grew the company as an ethical sustainable enterprise to become a global brand, and of her hopes for the future. We have chosen to present the story entirely in Anita's own words, partly because she tragically died before being able to give us feedback and partly as tribute to her incomparable gifts as a storyteller. We have edited only for readability. Simon Dowe, Anita's good friend and director of the charity she founded Children on the Edge, listened to the tapes to check the authenticity of the transcript and verify facts.

The start of the Body Shop was all about survival. I was a trained teacher so communication was one of my absolute planks in a platform of ability to be a leader. If you don't have that, you are just not there. Secondly, I came from a family that was very visual, so those two things are what I brought to the table when I opened up The Body Shop. And I had travelled, and travel was my university without walls. So I knew about community – this is really important when you look at ethical companies. I knew about communities that are connected to the land because as a student I won a scholarship to study in Israel to do my paper on education – the children in Kibbutz. There was nothing more exciting in the 1960s than living in a community where the community is grounded to the land, where the community protects each other. So travel, my experience with the community, storytelling (which is major) and a sense of aesthetics are all things I brought to the table without me knowing it. I opened up a little café restaurant. Gordon went and wanted to travel for two years across South America; it was survival because I was only going to do The Body Shop for two years until he came back and we were immigrating to Australia.

So women are really good at taking what they are good at and what they are interested in and fashioning a livelihood. It wasn't a business, it wasn't going to be big, it was 'treading water'. It just so happened that while he was away, I opened up another little shop. I think that was to do with the fact that there is a sense of pathological optimism in entrepreneurs like me, an enormous sense of work ethic coming from an immigrant family and I was loving it, so it was becoming an extension of myself – the storytelling, the anecdotes of the products. Then really when he came back we decided to stay put and not go to Australia. It was survival; if I had to determine success then, it was getting paid or earning enough to survive. Then that success in a way metamorphosed into "God how many people are we employing now – we are employing 10, now we are employing 20". So that was a measurement of success.

The tipping point was our relationships with the NGOs. We were activists; we were both active in the anti-war movement, in the civil rights movement, in the student union – we were activists. We helped shape a charity called Shelter for homeless people, so we were turning our little hotel into places for the homeless. I think what shaped us was we had an antenna for things that were out there because we were both travellers. We brought in who we thought and believed were the thought leaders, moral thought leaders for us, who were giving us information; our relationship with Greenpeace on the Save the Whale, our relationship with Friends of the Earth, our relationship with Amnesty. That absolutely shaped our moral agenda far more than any economic magazine – forget the bloody Forbes; forget the Fortunes, they were never really magazines for entrepreneurs anyway. So we really had no signpost for what we wanted. We brought the heart into the workplace; we wanted to only work with friends and activists. And I think truth be known, it was a communications company. We sold great products, but it was a communications company all the way.

It wasn't ever meant to be a product led company. It was about taking the skills that we had and marketing, without even having a marketing department for 20 years, and taking issues that we passionately cared about and vesting them in the shops. We wanted the shops to be like wells – in a traditional society where people gathered around the well and they chatted and they gossiped; that's what we wanted the shops to be. Yes, just gather around it. Sign a letter, save a life, whatever.

Go back to any entrepreneur and look at what fashions their identity.

Four.

Because what they are taking into the work place or whatever they are doing in the business is an alter ego, it's an extension of themselves. It is no more complicated than that. They are to a person totally unable to manage themselves out of a paper bag. More often than not the most interesting are the social entrepreneurs, people like ourselves, like Ben & Jerry, who were shaped more by the Quakers and Scandinavian business practices. None of us ever went to business school so we were mercifully saved from this economic theory that business is financial science.

We networked and we networked and we networked. So we had this feeling that ideas have wings, and there were other people around the world doing the same as we were, thinking the same, which they were. And I think what helped shape us was the earlier days when we got together and found in America there was an organisation called Social Venture Network which was a crazy group of inherited wealth kids, NGOs, progressive businesses – all getting together into a sort of conference on really how to make business kinder. And this was in the early 1980s and it was amazing, we felt God was on our side, we were putting two fingers up to the international chamber of commerce, we thought we were

what we learnt from each other. What we failed to recognise is that we were patting ourselves on the back; we just didn't get what was really going on, we didn't change the laws and we weren't political enough. But it was networking, it was running around seeing who's got the best idea and replicating it and keeping that sense of a work place having to be a development of the human spirit as well as production.

There were some major milestones. At first we were too hokey pokey; we were called hippy capitalists! The beauty industry didn't give a damn about us. Then when we started getting bigger we became a moral threat, a threat of good example on some of the issues that we were taking. I could identify this timeline – our first correspondence and relationship with Greenpeace was major because we realised then that the shops could be an avenue, a distribution point for Greenpeace to gain more members. Brilliant. The second major one was language. We used poetry, we used metaphysics, and we used philosophy as our language. We took more language out of the poetry of Walt Whitman than anybody else and so our language was an economic language. Our language was a sort of language of joy, it was a language of wonderment and awe, and we found our language to be absolutely embedded in the poetry of Walt Whitman. That was major. Everybody had that sense of something happening. The third was when we went public. A major milestone was when we had people looking at our shops. Mostly women saying, "Christ, if you can do this, I can do this." You know, we only had 20 products so we put them in five sizes and made it look like we had 100 with all that stuff. And women who either we didn't know or we did know were coming in saying, this could be an enterprise. Nobody called it a business. We called it a business, it was a livelihood, and it became an enterprise. There was such a sense of co-operation, so by bringing in the franchise people (people that we didn't know were called franchisees then, they were friends) we set up with a network of shops. Our vision when we knew we were going to get a tad bigger was to have this moral network of shops.

From day one the enterprise was ethically based. From day one we said we are going to make skin and haircare products, we are going to have the language of a puritan, we are going in the opposite direction. We had made a very, very strong strategic move which was saying if the beauty industry is going that way, we are going to go this other way.

We were quite iconoclastic. Quite childish. If the financial industry is going to go that way, we'd go the opposite way. We liked going to bed with the NGOs. We liked going to bed with the more progressives. We weren't interested in anything that was coming out of formal business. And that is very childish, but it worked for us.

We had an absolute commitment to telling the truth. I'll tell you something really stupid, we didn't know you were allowed to tell lies and that is quite ironic when you think of the beauty business I'm in! So we thought you could go to prison if you told lies. Hey, we made a honey and almond oil and I found this out from a Roman historian Pliny. He was talking about what Roman women did for beauty. So we made our honey from a hive, and we had put rosewater in and beeswax and when my mum who filled some of the pots realised there was some black bits in she said "My God, what's this?" And I said, "Oh, that's the bloody dirty footprint of the bees when they go off the garden path," and so we had these little cards that had written on them 'Don't worry about the black bits, they are the dirty footprints of the bees, just scoop them out'. People gave us permission that said oh Christ, they've screwed up again, but they'll get there. There was an

Four.

absolute permission to do this type of thing as long as we were telling them things and the reason why.

And we didn't know, and I think that was what saved us. We didn't think business was financial science. We hadn't read a book by Milton Friedman or whatever his name was, we didn't know anything like that. We just didn't think that life was any more complicated than love and work and the stories around the products. I think what we did too, which was fascinating, which shaped the identity, was we had a real reverence for women. Women's wisdom. So we kept on looking at the past and going and spending time with grandmothers or collecting anecdotes about the body, the rituals of the body, my travels, and coming back and saying, well you know the women in Pakistan cover their body with yoghurt. So out of all this information and anecdotes, we'd throw them in to the pot and say okay, maybe we'll make those. So that travel was very important. One of the big things before we went on the stock market was opening up shops in London because the world came to London, not like a little town like Chichester. And we started to get excited by opening up in a major retailing area called Covent Garden when hundreds and then hundreds of people were knocking on our door.

Now, this is where we lost the plot! We didn't realise we could have been a small giant. We didn't have the language of saying forget it, I don't want to go on the stock market. Let's just roll it on and let's just do it at our own pace. Going on to the stock market gave us an enormous amount of money to set up vertical integration, which we were very excited about. Building a factory, controlling the animal testing – no animal tested ingredients, making sure that everything was recycled. Making sure there was a sense of education on the campus, having our own child development centre. But if you look back on it we would say it was the worst mistake we ever made, but that shaped us.

Success for us was a movable feast, there is no doubt about it. I think number one it was survival. Gordon when he left on his trip for two years said "You need to take £300 a week". Second was how many people we employed, third was getting a moral framework, what is right what is wrong, what is good, what is bad message out in a way that was exciting and sexy and riveting without being like hitting you on the head. And fourth being able to do good for all the franchisees and everybody in the business.

So then we went on to the stock

market and there was a fourth success about numbers and finances and profit. We stopped once and said what is our mission? Business mission statements are usually produced by PR companies, so we said no, let's do like the letters of delegates to Congress in the development of the American constitution[21]. So we had a whole group of franchisees and staff around the world writing about what our mission should be. The first thing we did was we dedicated our company legally (it was a legal entity) in the Articles of Association and Memoranda to human rights advocacy and social and environmental change. That then became 'the purpose of the business' and nobody, not investors or anybody, could screw around with that. Then the rest followed.

I think our biggest success was our ability to communicate. We were just phenomenal at that and it wasn't just what we were saying, it was how we were saying it; the delivery systems, the videos we made, the music we produced; all about issues, all about anti-war or about freedom or whatever. Take the logo, we had no idea. I just paid 25 quid for it! I mean it made sense because we could only afford a round label and so 'hands encircling the globe' was just magic! The Body Shop name came about because I saw it in America in car repair shops! We had such a small shop fascia that we couldn't put like 'Brighton's Garlanded Emporium' so that seemed to work quite well! I mean it had to be a short name because we only had a small shop!

Then there was serendipity. We couldn't afford to put perfumes in the product so we had a perfume bar. We didn't know this, but it completely changed the perfume industry! Previously you had to buy perfume as eau de toilette or eau de parfum, not just neat. And we were telling everybody yes, just throw it in the Hoover, you know, smell it, put it anywhere you want.

There was a common purpose. I've found that people get incredibly motivated and excited when enthusiasm comes straight from the heart, when it's not the enthusiasm of a corporate CEO saying we will be the biggest and talking about business as if it's war and sport! It's about being the bravest, being the most eccentric, being the wildest and being the most up your bum; you know, that was more important to us. Our motivation was huge, and everybody felt that they were part of a social experiment. They were changing the way things were. They wanted a Monday to Friday living. This is where they spent most of their

Four.

time, meeting up in the campus, meeting up with their mums, grandmothers, kids, protecting the family with a day-care centre. We gave them love programmes which meant they could have money they could do anything they want with twice a year, but it wasn't anything to do with business or anything to do with their skill, the only thing they can't do is learn golf! You know everybody, every shop, every person had the right to go to the community and volunteer, which we paid for, and that's what made them feel great. It was all about connecting. We had lectures, we had people, we had spirit, we had liberation theologists come in, we had heads of community trade projects. So we brought the global into a very small working class community.

There was a sense of joy; there was a sense of purpose. People thought that there was more to life than putting a moisture cream on their face. It was definitely the bigger purpose. I'm very nervous about bringing the word spirituality in because its so like feminism, so reshaped, but if I take the Mahatma Gandhi statement of being in service to the weak and the frail, we've got it. That is what it is. So we made a product so you can wash the skin, clean with it; but all the while making sure our ingredients were purchased

from co-operatives or family-based organisations.

We started as a family until we got too big and then we became a community. It got too big to be a family. I mean it was The Body Shop family, The Body Shop community when we were all over the world. Our people were never employees. I would refer to them as 'sweethearts', there was a lot of lèse-majesté because that was the structure of the management style – making fun of the owners, making fun of the hierarchy. 'Beloved' is what we used a lot; 'pals' and friends'. We used 'community' because community is a place that is safe, people protect each other, they know more about each other than the nation state does, so I think community was the right choice. When you had little groups of family run Body Shops around the world it was like a multi-local organisation, where the centre had to be the moral head, not directed at just the products, who is going to do a campaign and on what.

We first of all had to get the franchisees and we had to know that if we were going to go to bed with these guys they are not going to give us any shit. Nobody speaking out against, it when, for example, we are going to do a whole campaign against the war in Kuwait; (which we did). So we found this fabulous methodology of looking for them called the Marcel Proust questionnaire[22]. Marcel Proust had this very simple questionnaire. We fantasised that you would really get to know potential franchisees when you gave them this questionnaire. We adapted it a little bit to the franchisees and we added a couple of questions. One was – what is the car you are driving and what is the car you want? And if it jumped from a little Beetle to a Rolls Royce, we went oh, Christ, we are never going to get them on our side. And we asked them questions like -what have you done in the community? What would you do if you were community volunteering? And so it was a wonderful idiosyncratic way of getting the people. And we never looked for business people who were predicted to be silly. We looked for activists, teachers; we looked for people who were in civil society who were in the care business.

And we didn't want bullies so we put in a methodology to stop bullying which was that every employee, – and at our campus down the road there was some 2,000, – had a copy of this employment manual which was as eccentric as you could get. Inside were six or seven red envelopes, and any time they were pissed off with anything that we – Gordon, I, the Board or their managers or their line managers – were doing, they could write to me and I'd see them within 24 hours. That immediately stopped hierarchy and bullying. That was very interesting.

Well, going global was a plus for us. We were global from day one – we had somebody arriving from Belgium on the back of her truck who wanted products and she opened up a little store there – so going global was never a problem. It was a problem when it was 'really' serious when you had to check everything with laws in terms of ingredients, etc, but you buy specialists for that. When we went on the stock market it gave us the ability to do vertical integration, to control everything because we trusted nobody; we didn't trust the suppliers, the ingredients; we wanted this no animal testing stuff embedded down with us. And so we put a lot of our environmental standards into practice, and again learning from Ben & Jerry's, for example, waste water – turning it in to a place where we grew our herbs; so it was a control standard.

We had 20 years of making sure that our standards were as high as anybody's could be if not better. So global wasn't a problem in those first early years. It started to get a

Four.

problem with the media. It was a disaster. Our relationships with the media went from absolute adoration to cynicism, to the extent where we had to fight for our reputation in the high courts of London, to the fact that we had a corporate stalker, to the fact that the financial press hated what we were doing (when we opened up our soap factory in Glasgow and gave 25% of the profits back in to the community they said we were stealing from the shareholders' pockets). So I think our biggest challenges were the financial press, no doubt about it. And we didn't help; I called them 'pinstriped dinosaurs', then I referred to them as 'financial fascists', so I should have kept my mouth shut more. So those were the pressures. Not on the values and the belief structure, that was never ever a problem until when I cut my umbilical cord with The Body Shop and stepped back as the driving force and became a consultant, when a lot of the values sort of were there, but they took a lower profile. That was a huge change for the company.

That was about seven years ago. And then we had another huge thing that we would never ever have foreseen which happened about the same time. We were the second biggest employer in the town and we had to make about 300 people redundant. Our business plan previously was making our money through manufacturing and wholesaling and we wanted to shift away from that to retailing. We did it brilliantly well. Christ, we should have got a pat on the back. We brought in the police, we brought in the social services, we brought in counsellors, we brought in education, we brought everybody in, and Gordon and I personally dialogued with everybody – which is not what most businesses did. We realised that when we were exhausted saying the same thing, is just the time they'll get it. We had a fund of a million pounds that anybody could access to set up as an entrepreneur. They could take money from that fund, and we did something I think marvellous, we said to them if you don't want to be retrained for another skill, we'll train any member of your family. So I think we were pretty good at that, even though still making 300 people redundant was pretty terrible for us. It's horrible. Absolutely horrible. And that is why when companies just tell their people by email, I just don't get it.

There were no financial pressures as we were growing, not at all. In fact the opposite was true because we never advertised. So being a big, growing consumer beauty company and not advertising is like giving a speech in church and not saying it from the pulpit! I found really creative guerrilla tactics which means low cost. All our billboards were on our trucks. We painted our trucks going up and down the highways with messages on. These were also not messages to sell our product. We didn't like the Minister of Education so we found a great quote which was "If you see education as expensive try ignorance" and then at the back of the truck we just had his home phone number and his office phone number. So we went to the highway with our messages. We trained every staff member in every shop. They were brilliantly trained to be public relations officers and their job was to go out to the community and give talks to the schools, work with the disabled, tell the story of The Body Shop in their way, in that community, to be high profile. So we had a very different way of looking at would this be expensive. It was not expensive. Think of that money we saved. Millions we would have had to pay for a stupid ad telling somebody to put bloody shampoo on their head! We used it in a different way with our values. We were absolutely true to purpose. We sent our staff to community trade, we sent over 1,000 of our staff to volunteer in Romanian orphanages.

And you know this is the irony about criticism for our motives. The media said it was all about selling a product. I said to the media and business critics, "Great, if the good things we're doing is all about selling a product, then why don't all businesses do it? If it's all about sales and profit, why don't they do the fair trade stuff? Why don't they do community trade? Why don't they do the campaign if it's so good? Follow it! Come on, be a friend, be a partner, play with me on this stuff". Of course they wouldn't because always the sales went slightly down. Only slightly, but motivation was sky high. And when you get motivated staff who never stop talking, they are proud, they are rabbitting on to their family. So we immediately already had a network of people, real people, not sultans of sleaze PR companies, that were really saying this is a good company.

I learnt from Ben Cohen from Ben & Jerry's – he said to me why don't you open up a tour. He said I've got the biggest tour in Vermont and so he said you could do that. So I opened up a tour, we had the shop, we had these Indonesian buses. We had over 200,000 people come on to our campus, and staff would be waving to them, kids would be waving to them, so that's what brought a sense of carnival in to the workplace.

The major big thing that we were changing was animal testing in the

Four.

beauty business. Major, major, major. We absolutely brought that issue to public consciousness. We showed that there are alternative ways. We didn't need to test any finished product or any ingredient when there are so many thousands of ingredients that you could have. So bringing up that issue and changing the law in England on that and subsequently in Europe I think was major for us. Oh yes, I think that if we go to heaven and He says well you are here because you changed the law and you raised the consciousness of animal testing, you've saved people's lives with campaigns with human rights like Amnesty, those have to be the big ones. And even though what the hell is a cosmetic company doing in Nigeria shouting and fighting all over Shell Oil and trying to get 20 people out of prison, which we did; why are they doing it? Because if not us, who else! Nobody else was doing it except the NGOs and they were that far removed from the public. We were like meals on wheels, we were putting these campaigns in and thousands of people were passing; hundreds were coming in to our shops, so it was an easy way of leveraging.

Our shops had a greater voice than maybe some of these NGOs because we made things sexy. We had great posters and we had intelligent staff who were always well educated. So again another subliminal plus was our consistent education of the human spirit so it was not about educating on how to sell the product; rather, it was this is the story of Amnesty, this is the story of Native American farmers. And I remember saying to staff years ago: "I looked at what the Celts used to say because they are pre-eminent storytellers; if it doesn't go through the heart, it's dangerous and that's the way they should live. Poets should be there".

Connecting to activists was our moral authority. In any campaign that we did which was either a human rights campaign or an environmental campaign, we didn't breathe without them checking everything, in fact writing the copy, making sure everything was right. Then we took that information and with our sense of style we were able to make it sexy, the right images, the right designs, the right language. So we took their information and put it into amazingly evocative, interesting material for the public. Sometimes we got it really wrong, other times we just hit the right note.

I don't think there is enough spoken about the role of behaviour in an organisation. Many of us are blessed with the type of the work that we do; it becomes a blessing to work in an organisation that admires, protects the family, has a sense of joy, a sense of decency, a sense of real creativity, not a controlled creativity – fantastic!

We had a board. The non-executive directors really protect the interests of the financial investors. We chose them so well. All of them loved the company. Really they are there to fill the holes that you are not good at. We wanted to go into direct selling, which we did. We should have had – and didn't at that time have – a non-exec director that knew how to avoid the pitfalls of direct selling. There was never ever a time that any of non-execs said to us you are going too far. In fact in the last few years it's more not going far enough, except once when I wanted every shop to challenge the Kuwaiti war and I'd organised faxes in every shop so that the customers could say anything, anything but don't let us go to war. This is 12 years ago and the Managing Director then of our company (who was a bit wimpy) said this is dangerous and I shouldn't be challenging the government, we are a company that shouldn't be challenging the government. I just said I will leave this company on this principle, because we are an activist, an advocacy company. We are a company that stands up and all our shops are supportive. Just because it's a political issue

does not mean we should back down. So what I did was (I'd never recommend anybody do this – never ever offer an ultimatum because it could have not gone so well; never in life, in relationships) but anyway I threw in an ultimatum, which is if we pull down this campaign I'm out the door! Christ, it was the worst time of my life. So we called a town hall meeting, we closed down the entire headquarters, I closed down the entire offices in London, and through electronic information I said I'll pull out of The Body Shop. I said the Managing Director says this is dangerous; I don't think so. But I knew that if I talked on and on and on about it, they'd probably say, or might say, up your bum. So just by luck I had spent a week up in my house in Scotland with about 20 staff. One was a truck driver, all grassroots people, and a lot of those guys had been in the Falklands war. They knew the horrors so they wore the cloak of authority about war and told the entire campus, about 2,000 people, about the horrors. It was their voice that changed, made them say no, we are going to campaign for whatever is wanted. Whew – that could have gone so wrong.

We trained storytellers in the company. They went to a specific college and so every two years they gathered all the storytelling, all the

Four.

anecdotes, into a booklet *Our Stories*. If you don't capture them they go, and when that goes your soul goes. And people come in, and it takes 20 years to build a brilliant brand and one year for some guy to come in and just kill it. So you've got to keep those going.

I wanted more teachers in the company. My kids went to this very progressive school and there was this wonderful teacher, very inspiring. I thought I'd spent so much time reading about the Quakers and about social enterprise – give back to the community, because the community gives you your wealth – and I'd listened and seen what Cadbury's had done. It was jaw-dropping and I wanted to do it, anyway, at least to replicate, make a bold attempt at replicating what they did. So I found a teacher and employed her. You have to have a champion, you have to have a department of volunteering, and her job was to be the champion for making every shop decide themselves what they wanted to do, and it was our thanks to the community for giving us our wealth. And it was wonderful for the staff around the world, certainly in the shops that the company owned. America, UK, Australia were huge as was New Zealand. And they chose whatever they wanted to do. But that was major and it wasn't

about selling, it wasn't about oh my God, we've got to cover our staff overhead, it was about your staff never wanted to leave you. They were so proud. You know, they don't go home dreaming of moisture creams. They wanted to be part of this experiment. I said to the Board their dreams are in music, I mean you bring some music into their lives and great lyrics and you talk about relationships, they are there, they understand it. That is why we did a whole lot of music videos around some of these issues. And so for their motivation that worked unbelievably well. And we gave out awards – for the best community trade programme, the best volunteer programme, who rose up in spite of all the crap that happens to them.

Celebration was major, and it wasn't just thank you very much for the conversation; it was sending the staff to see one of our community trade projects in India or Guyana. They had a wonderful time, and they came back local activists. They wanted to work within the community – fantastic. And most of them then wanted to leave us and go work for an NGO which, I mean, we are doing something wrong! I remember going in to this one store in New York and this woman said to me I don't like this, we have to sell, sell, sell. She said I want to talk about voters rights (because we'd just done a campaign on that) and I thought, oh, give me a break! Try and sell our products so that we can survive! There was some tension. I had to deal with it with humour. I always had to laugh at it and I always had to say, you know, get a life if we don't do this, we can't do this. It couldn't be a written thing; it had to be me going in to talk to them. You know, I was shunted around the bloody world all the time!

I've learnt that the most essential tool is communication. And that communication has to be daring and it has to be different and it has to be sexy, and when I say sexy, exciting, because no matter how passionately you care about something, if you can't communicate it with a passion you won't persuade. The difference doesn't persuade and theoretical information doesn't persuade – if you don't communicate with passion, then you are not there, no matter how much you care about it. So passionate communication would be a major.

The next thing I've learnt is to look at things that sneak up on you. And when you get bigger, hierarchy sneaks up without a doubt. And with that, things like rules and regulations come into play, and that's when creativity really dips – really dips. So you've got to have a really safe place

in a growing organisation for that sense of creativity and that sense of ethics. One of the things that we did was that we had a Centre of Values and Vision, where we had three, four or five people working on the environmental guide, social audit guide, human rights guide, etc.

Then we thought no, what we are going to try and do is integrate that through the whole company, purchasing people etc. I don't think that worked. I think when you lose the geography of place in a company, you'll find it falls down under, it starts wavering under economic rationales for doing things. The geography of place is really important. And that geography of place has to be on decision boards, whether it's the executive committee, otherwise they just can be seen as greenwashing. They've got to be a voice, to be able to persuade and cajole, to change the thinking. And their ability can only be measured by their contact with networks and the NGOs. They can't work in a silo.

I've also learnt that the NGOs aren't always the most helpful because they are all protecting their own little territory and trying to get them to dialogue is challenging. In the 30 years I've been doing this I still haven't found what their sense of camaraderie is. They need survival; it's money.

Four.

The bigger you get the more intimate you've got to be, and therefore your communications have got to be intimate and belly to belly, so the increased electronics stuff like voicemail and the internet doesn't help. And it's got to be at the shop front if you are in an organisation like retailing. The people you've got to inspire, number one, are shop staff and the part-time staff who spend 90% – 99% of their time with the customers. You go higher up the hierarchy and managers or heads of department never go into the bloody shops. I've done getting up at five in the morning and going and delivering products in the trucks just to see what it's like for the staff at seven in the morning to receive them and how they have to live their lives. You know, CEOs don't usually do that. I brought them to my home and there was no sense of hierarchy so you sit them around and have a discussion, have a conversation café about what is the future, what are the worries, tell me. It's a sort of searching for feedback on your thinking and the truest feedback is going to be the employees. I think a champion consistently championing the underdog is major. Leaders shouldn't be seen to have followers behind them, they've got to create other leaders and give them a voice and a freedom to be a leader and a safe place to be a leader.

Another thing I have learnt is that your enemies can end up being your greatest support. Hence the L'Oreal thing. Who would have ever thought in a million years they would have come down and sat and said, you know, we like your company? You can teach us; you were a thorn in our flesh for 25 years, but you were right on the animal testing, you were right on the community trade, you were right on the ethical stuff, can we buy you, with your approval? With your approval? I like that, you know. Support us and teach us.

You can take two strategies – one to be purist and complain and complain. I think it's to do with age; as you get older you are so thankful for any approximate solution! But also to be a Trojan horse; to go inside and persuade by experience. Because experiences change your values. I think we can do a phenomenal job.

This is what is so exciting for me. At this moment, The Body Shop does a hugely successful job, and could get bigger at community trade. This means that we have a purchasing programme with woman's co-operatives, family farmers, epicentres of despair (mostly agriculture around the world). Well, there are probably 15,000 families benefiting from our direct purchasing ingredients which we shove in to our products. The Body Shop is middle in size, nothing big. But if you take something like L'Oreal, which is 'the biggest', and they are willing to develop and are open to learning about and wanting to purchase from these scattered brazil nut farmers or Nicaraguan sesame oil farmers then you have got a wonderful example of village economics which is an antidote to poverty. Then you get a knock on the door from Boots, which is our biggest retailer who also wants to learn how to do the same things. So I'm sitting there thinking, shit, instead of being a little company helping 15,000 we could, by embracing, collectively embracing Boots and hopefully later on it would be Procter & Gamble, but now L'Oreal. And so, it's not about this is our unique selling point, this is our marketing edge – bullshit, this is the right thing to do. And so in exiting my relationship with The Body Shop, I'm still pursuing the right thing to do. This isn't about making something exclusive to The Body Shop; every cosmetic company should be doing this and for years I've been writing to Avon and getting no response, now through this relationship with L'Oreal and Boots I think some of those family farmers could be happy bunnies.

It's timing – it's bloody timing. I mean we were the first to come up with this fair trade or community trade. Marks & Spencer's have a new CEO who has had an epiphany, he's changed that company around. He's only selling fair traded coffees, going to be selling fair trade cotton, organic. He gets it, and when a big noise on the high street gets it – you know five years, two, three years ago they wouldn't have done this – the time was right.

It's probably my pathological optimism – I think we should be optimistically guarded for a bit. I think the ground swell hasn't happened yet. It might well happen with Marks & Spencer's coming on board, L'Oreal coming on board, but it's a big business out there and the biggest business is Wal-Mart. I think the new moral movement is workers' justice. It's like the civil rights movement in the 1950s or 60s. This is a new moral movement and if the biggest purchaser in the world (which is Wal-Mart) gets behind these and pays fair wages and all of those things and in other countries, then you've got a stab. But government should be penalising companies if they use slave labour or sweat shop labour, and they are not, and businesses are lousy at self-regulation. They just love having corporate social responsibility, which is just another talking shop. I really believe that the public are the ones pushing it, because the vigilant

Four.

consumers are now saying look, government is useless, I'm pointing my finger at this company, I really feel sympathy with the product, I do not feel sympathy with this company and as a result, I am joining up with the fair trade movement and with radical professors in colleges, I'm joining up with progressive companies, I'm joining up with the human rights movement, and they are funding and supporting these movements which Government has never done. So these vigilante consumers, ethical consumers, are pushing the envelope. I sound optimistic and I think the next phase is to really shake the tree and let the branches fall off – the greenwashing. It's got to be done. On the other hand, with the web and the blogs, regardless of whatever they say in the media, if you are smart you can get the truth on the blogs. The media won't deal with the subject, because it shaves away the advertising budget if they want to do a big expose. So I'm excited with the changes.

My next biggest challenge is giving my money away! And that's a big thing. It's a lot of money. I think this is the last 10 or 20 years of my life and the last thing I want to do is argue with my husband about how we do it, and yet we are both so political. So trying to find a methodology of giving about two or three million a year is

huge. I don't want to die rich, I think it's obscene. I'm from an old socialist background, so how I do that is going to be a real challenge but it's going to be exciting. And the company is spending a lot of time with L'Oreal in helping them to set up their values in place, and going to other brands and talking to them. That's a given – I've got about 30 or 40 days a year with them to do that.

All my activism is here. I've got the documentaries I'm funding these issues, the books I'm doing. I'm very impressed by some of the grassroots groups I spend time with. Dorothy Sayers said "A woman in advancing old age is unstoppable by any earthly force" – yeah, you got that right – it's true. Because women want to be heard and they are not worrying about what they look like any more, thank God. It's being heard in politics and community and education, and I think it's all going to be shaped, I keep on saying to people it's going to be shaped by humour. Women together, laughing cuts through fantasy.

Reflections

Helga conducted this interview with Anita in Chichester, shortly before her untimely death. Anita has given countless interviews, yet she told her story with a freshness, energy and enthusiasm as though it were for the first time. Her frankness about things that went wrong and the search for improvement was refreshing and we felt characterised a key basis for her business success. In talking about the need to lay off staff in a business downturn it was clear just how painful this had been and how it prompted a search for better ways of doing business to ensure that such actions would never again be needed.

Anita leaps out from her story as an activist making a difference to people, society and the planet. The power of storytelling is revealed both through her own story and in the way she explained the role of storytelling in The Body Shop development. Anita developed a strong philosophy, purpose and set of beliefs for The Body Shop, and used every means possible to tell the stories of the causes they represented intertwined with their products.

The development of the human spirit as the energy for enterprise and the essence of wellbeing was an exciting re-interpretation of the centrality of spirit that we had identified in the earlier Peak Performance project. Anita felt that change was needed both at the level of individual wellbeing and at the systemic level. One of her proudest achievements was in the progress towards eliminating animal testing in the cosmetics industry. As Anita's story unfolded and her business became more successful it became clear that she found her voice whilst at the same time experiencing a greater urgency for action towards sustainability. Her activism consequently took on a greater sense of urgency. She always had a new challenge ahead.

Five.

The Eden Project

"We often joke about being the equivalent to the Davos World Economic Forum both in environmental and social change. And that's what success would be, actually effecting change. And I think one of the things that has to be said about why Eden is potentially so potent is because we know from a lot of friends in the environment movement, they all say this, bloody nice for once to have a project which is glamorous and sexy and rock'n'roll that is actually coming out of the environment movement. Because no-one has ever put marketing, rock'n'roll, those sorts of things in the context of saving the world."

— Tim Smit, CEO, Eden Project

"There's a plaque in the Eden Project education centre and what the plaque says is just 'Our future depends on the choices we make today', and I think for me the crucial element that underpins everything at Eden is that it is about people persuading people to take control of their own choices and happen to the world rather than live in a world that happens to them."

— Peter Boyden, former creative director, Eden Project

A muddy manmade crater in the midst of a bleak landscape of industrial despoliation in a backwater of the UK is hardly the stuff dreams are made of. But from this unpromising site – a disused clay pit in Cornwall in south-west England – has risen an extraordinary vision made real: huge greenhouse globes or biomes showcasing productive plants from all the world's major regions, woven together with compelling stories showing how plants are "the common backcloth against which all human life is led" (p162).[23]

The quote comes from CEO Tim Smit's book, *Eden*, about bringing the Eden Project to fruition. Tim's vision was to build the world's leading example of a social enterprise, designed to inspire people with an understanding of the essential balance of conservation and stewardship with sustainable use. The process of transforming that vision to reality took eight years of hard work, determination, and unwavering belief that the project would succeed.

Vision, Tim told us when we met him in Eden, is in us all: "'Mr Smit was so visionary,' they say, and I say hang on, is there anybody in this room who when they were 12 years old did not have dreams of building castles on top of mountain tops? We all did! That wasn't visionary at all, we took something that is almost archetypally in all of us and just did it. I think a lot of people do themselves down on how unvisionary they are."

The Eden Project is a tourist attraction in Cornwall in the United Kingdom. The project aims to educate people about the relationships between people, plants and the planet through stories and experiences. The attraction features artificial biomes which house plants from around the world, landscaped gardens, an education core, food and gifts, sustainable architecture, exhibitions, events and surprises.

Eden opened in March 2001 and by July 2008 over ten million people had visited the Eden Project, and despite being tucked away in a remote corner of the British Isles, it has gained a worldwide reputation. "We always knew that we had to be the biggest and most beautiful, so we were very conscious that it was going to be global. We set it up to be a 'global must-see'. That's why we said it's the eighth wonder of the world, and before long everybody else was calling it the eighth wonder of the world!" Tim fields requests from all over the world to create similar Edens elsewhere, but he says would-be imitators are missing the point – the distinctive thing about Eden is not so much its architecturally stunning biomes, but its attitude.

Tim Smit certainly has attitude in dome-loads, as we found when we talked to him about the thinking behind the project. "I was asked in the early days by a banker, he said, 'You will not have a successful project unless you can sum it up in one sentence.' I said that is really sad, because I didn't want to work on a project that I could sum up in one sentence. However, I think you'd have to say the Eden Project is using the stage that we have created as a canvas on which to paint stories about how we might have a different future."

Peter Boyden was previously Eden's creative director. With a background

Five.

in the music industry and as a change management consultant for corporations, activist groups and government, he told us the Eden Project was a huge opportunity "to try out the things that you spend a lifetime thinking about". Peter has since moved to Dartington Hall, developing similar themes in collaboration with The Eden Project.

Peter explained to us how the Eden Project combines aspirational public service values and entrepreneurial energy.

What interests me about Eden is how we can sustain the benefits of that energetic entrepreneurial starting point, whilst understanding how in the most sensitive and flexible way we can be able to respond to the values and needs of our whole culture and the world's culture. We are very ambitious about trying to actually embrace issues of citizenship; issues which go way beyond the nations of plants and become a metaphor for the relationship between human activity and the natural environment. And that kind of breadth of interest and passion I think is the petrol in the tank of the organisation. Call it the 'un-green metaphor'.

Visionary and self-styled snake oil salesman Tim Smit has been

the driving force behind the Eden project from the start. A former archaeologist turned record producer and composer, Tim threw in his globetrotting lifestyle in 1987 to move to rural Cornwall with his family. There he discovered a series of neglected Victorian-era gardens belonging to an old estate. Enlisting the help of an impressive array of experts and enthusiasts, he went on to restore the 'Sleeping Beauty'-style gardens to their original productive condition, adding storyboards to tell the stories associated with the plants and the people who discovered them and tended them.

The Lost Gardens of Heligan have become one of the most popular botanical gardens in Britain – and, Tim told us, the gardens provided the seed of the idea that was to become the Eden Project. "We experimented at using a kind of anecdotal style to make horticulture interesting to a wider range of people who don't normally go to gardens. We realised how interesting the stories about the plants that are changing the world were to such a wide audience, and then we decided we wanted to build something at Heligan that could accommodate the stories."

Stories like how Captain Bligh and the mutiny on the Bounty figured in the journey of breadfruit from

Tahiti to the Caribbean to provide cheap food for slaves working on the sugar plantations there. Or like the story of the Duchess of Cinchon, saved from death from malaria by the powdered bark of a tree, which was subsequently named after her. Quinine was crucial in enabling Europeans to open up the heartlands of the malarial tropics to trade and empire.

These stories and others had Heligan's visitors enthralled – particularly the school parties which came in ever-increasing numbers. Tim is passionate about storytelling as a means of education. "If you go to the British Museum – a lot of stuff in there is stuff I used to study – it's ridiculously complicated and it's actually about advancing the academics. We probably have the intellect of an eight-year-old in a subject that we don't yet know about; therefore you've to engage with the eight-year-old to get excited about it."

Finding and communicating with the eight-year-old inside every visitor is the Eden Project's focus. Peter Boyden explains:

> I don't think the fact that we have a million people a year coming is because of the plants and the buildings. It's because of the story. The desire to communicate is very

much different in the sense that it's not just about the transfer of knowledge; there are many ways in which we can engage in knowledge transfer in the world and many kinds of institutions that are set up to do it. But actually being able to produce an emotional impact on people that makes them change the way they seek out knowledge and what they do with it when they've found it seems to us to be a much more interesting thing than simply to giving them lots of detailed scientific knowledge about the particular taxonomic kind of Victorian approach to the way in which we can order our world.

Creating change in people is a big ask, but it's a key aspiration for the Eden Project. Peter described it to us as "empowering people to feel connected".

> I think we live in a world where the individual feels so dislocated in terms of the processes that affect their lives that they deny any sense of accountability or responsibility for the world around them. Our great grandparents would have had much more direct relationships with the land, with the people and with the processes that made the community, and we have to find ways to actually replace them or provide ways back

Five.

to the emotional needs that they fulfilled. So the changes I would be most interested in making would be ones that actually gave individuals back the ability to feel connected, through the choices they make, to the world they live in.

As the concept of the Eden Project took shape, it became clear to Tim Smit that it would take more than a greenhouse at Heligan to do his idea justice, so the hunt began for a suitable site. Tim says when he first saw the Bodelva clay pit -- set in a landscape used for filming episodes of the cult British sci-fi TV series Dr Who -- he knew he'd found his Eden. "The basic idea was to have beautiful conservatories in clay, a hole in the ground, to create that kind of atmosphere of discovery – something hidden below the surface. We felt that the territory that was described at the edge of a pit gave a sense of loss of civilisation which we liked very much."

But he faced an immense task in turning this idea into a reality. Everyone can dream, but the ability to make things real, Tim says, is a rare alchemist's art. In his book he talks about the two ideas central to his understanding of this process: Tinkerbell Theory and Last Man Standing.

In *Peter Pan*, Tinkerbell is a fairy who exists only if people believe in her. I know that if enough people can be made to believe in something it will happen. Last Man Standing, on the other hand, is a polite way of saying that you intend to turn being an awkward bugger into an art form. In other words, you won't take no for an answer. The footnote to this is that bankers, lawyers, civil servants, investors or volunteers will have mastered the art of saying 'no' in many different ways long before you have even begun to make your pitch. Assuming that they are professionally competent, what makes people say yes when it's easier to say no is often the difference between an ordinary day at the office and a life-affirming experience that inspires the imagination. We are all human[24].

Tim put both theories to work in harnessing the support and funding required to get the Eden Project off the ground. "And suddenly there were enough people interested in the idea that it became credible. It was just a bizarre bunch of people who were excited by the idea and that seemed to excite other people, and it was amazing because all these people came from all over England for free to meet in parks and motorways and service stations, motels and various houses. So we were sure it was a critical mass of an idea that no-one else had done."

It was as if the time was ripe for something very special to happen. Tim told us that he had the sense that everything he had done in the past was preparing him for the Eden project. The project also attracted some key influencers, who Tim told us were to prove invaluable as Eden took off. "You can always tell the quality of a stereo when you turn the volume up, and what I mean by that is if you're not prepared, if you haven't got the people in place to be able to deal with success, sooner or later the wheels come off, because people don't know how to deal with something that big. So we were incredibly lucky that the people who had their mid-life crisis and joined us were people actually for whom the project grew into them rather than the other way around."

Perhaps Eden's most audacious application of the Tinkerbell theory came in response to being turned down for funding by the UK's national lottery-funded Millennium Commission. In early 1995 the Eden Project had applied for the maximum contribution of £50 million in matchfunding as one of 12 Landmark Projects intended to mark the millennium. Tim told us what happened:

> The Commission sent us a fax saying that they judged all these projects for their worthiness for funding. Grade A was 'you're in', Grade B was 'a bit more work and you're probably in' and Grade C was 'don't darken our door'. And we got this fax which said that we were Grade C. And I couldn't face telling all these people that had worked so hard that we got that response. So we held a press conference saying the Millennium Commission was encouraging us to take our work forward. And the most remarkable thing was that three months later the Millennium Commission started to believe that this is what they said. Literally it really was like a snowball starting off at the top of the mountain and picking up people along the way.

As well as surmounting what seemed to be impossible financing hurdles, creating the Eden Project required a whole range of people to do what they thought couldn't be done – from the architects and construction crew who had to design and build innovative structures to sit in a clay pit that literally changed shape from day to day, to the plantsmen who had to orchestrate the sourcing, transportation, replanting and

Five.

continuing care of tens of thousands of plant specimens, ranging from seeds to fully-grown trees, sourced from deserts through to the tropics.

This ability to get people to suspend their disbelief has been fundamental to the Eden Project's success, and Tim says it has a lot to do with personal chemistry.

> The truth is that when you start with an idea like this, my attitude to it was, this is completely preposterous, ridiculous, let's see if we can do this. Therefore, let's take it as far as we can and if we hit a wall and we can't get over it, that wall just keeps falling down. Seriously, that's how you've got to do these things. You find a way of working through, and finding your way through is initially to do with, I think, personal chemistry. No-one wants to be in a gang with people who aren't much fun, and generally we've been very good at drawing people into the fold who (a) have got intellect, (b) can deal with surprises and (c) have fun. And then what happens is people start to suspend their disbelief. And it's actually the suspension of disbelief that is the crucial thing.

To win that suspension of disbelief you also have to be prepared to put everything on the line. Tim gave us a great example from when he put the Heligan gardens up as collateral to buy a nursery to ensure that the Eden Project could open on time. The banks would only put up the money for the nursery once they were sure the project would go ahead, but as Tim explained, bidding to state institutions doesn't take account of growing seasons. "The 'killer moment' came after Heligan took huge gambles. I think some of the more serious businessy players felt if these guys are prepared to risk the current healthy business to support a risk that if it doesn't go ahead would bankrupt them, then that was convincing."

Part of Tim's skill lies in his ability to make people believe in possibility. Tony Kendle, Eden's foundation director describes his approach.

> Most people can build grand dreams in the small hours, conspiring around a bottle of wine. Unlike most of us, though, Tim still believes them in the cold light of day and wants to know when we can start. Part of the art lies in understanding the power of scale. When it comes to projects that aim to inspire people and to help them to believe that great transformation is possible, and especially when you are building things you want people to come and see, you have to fight

constantly against the tendency to be cautious, to scale down, to 'value engineer'. Tim's instincts go against the typical grain – his first principle of how to de-risk a project is to make it bigger and more ambitious! And this is also how he sees the future of social enterprise – working at a huge scale. Social enterprise should not be limited to small local initiatives; it may be the best way to manage national strategically important utilities and facilities such as railways or water supply.

Tim and Tony both believe social enterprises like the Eden Project are surfing ahead of the wave, and struggle with business institutions that were designed 50 years ago. As Tim puts it "the corporate world has outlived its sell-by date, and the new structures – social enterprises – are actually the way of the future".

Peter used a sporting analogy to explain the difference.

There's been lots of discussion in this country over the last few years about the management of the soccer clubs. Traditionally they get taken over by very successful businessmen who leave their brains in the briefcase outside the boardroom. There's no obvious reason why they would actually start tearing up £50 notes as a way of spending Saturday afternoon! Actually there's a strong sense that the emotional ownership of those clubs lies back in the 1860s and 1870s in the working-class communities that actually produced the players and the original constitution entity, such as the Manchester United Football Club. There's a kind of sense that the notion of supporters' clubs and community trust ownership are around the middle ground of social enterprise that I think in another 20-25 years will look completely different from the commercial and governance landscapes that we are walking around in now.

I think there are identifiable changes to the characteristics of organisations that fit the purpose for creating the future which would not have been characteristics of organisations that existed when the market alone determined the success or failure of a project. And [enterprise leaders] could do with replacing the instinct to control with the instinct to collaborate, the instinct to add value to other people's activities rather than simply to corral it for a small group of people within an owned environment.

For Peter, the shift towards social enterprise is currently underway,

Five.

and will be as pivotal, he says, as the impact of settled agriculture or the printing press or the Enlightenment or the Reformation. The Eden Project, he told us, was launched at a time when opportunities were exponentially growing, driven by issues around globalisation and reducing our individual, collective and corporate carbon footprints. Eden's achievement, he says, has been "in producing the stage on which we can demonstrate and play out what can happen in the world".

After 20 years spent working in corporate finance in the City of London, Eden's chief financial officer Peter Cox might be expected to provide a cautious counterweight to the project's creative visionaries. But he too is convinced that social enterprise offers a better alternative. "We made a very pragmatic decision to choose this model of being a sustainable enterprise, a social enterprise, not just because it's a nice idea, but because it actually is the most effective way of achieving what we want to achieve," he told us."I come from a world where whatever the deal was, the cake never got bigger. You know, somebody only makes money if they screw a deal out of somebody else. What I'm struck by, time and time again here, is that what seems to drive us is that it is actually possible not just to find a

win-win situation, but to find a win-win-win-win situation for everybody who is involved, all the stakeholders. We actually don't like the phrase 'social enterprise', we use it as a shorthand because other people now understand what it means, but actually we believe this is just the way all businesses should be owned. There isn't this social enterprise sector that behaves in this way and the rest of business. We want to show that it is possible to have that win-win-win-win situation and to demonstrate to all businesses that you can behave differently and still be a success."

These positive comments tend to understate just how difficult it has been to deliver the project. Managing director Gaynor Coley steered Eden through critical stages of establishing structures and winning the capital investment.

Delivering the project took huge amounts of organisation and the development of business processes that were as creative in their own way as the design and content. We often liken ourselves to a swan gliding on the river – it may look effortless on the surface but underneath we are paddling furiously to stay afloat. When we started, social enterprise was not a recognised term, and we had to pioneer legal and institutional frameworks that were never seen before. Handling grants and public investments, especially those that have some clawback provision, makes the accounts fantastically complex. Handling debt and equity is complex within a charity framework and our biggest constraint is still the difficulty of raising working capital for investments. On top of that, on a daily basis we have to work to marry the cultures of business and charity so that we can pass appraisal from every direction.

We asked Tim if he saw the Eden Project as a kind of ripple machine, role modelling changes for society. He pointed out to us that it was the way the Eden Project engaged that made the difference. "One of the reasons people like having meetings with us is because we change the rules of engagement in the way we talk. It's not just a set of values, it's actually to do with the way we engage with people and get them connected and thinking. I know I sound arrogant, but we know that people love to work with us because we bring out the best in them."

Chief financial officer Peter Cox echoed this thought. "What I think is very different about Eden, what I think underpins its potential effectiveness and its success so far, is that when we talk about values we mean there is a collection of values that we all personally were drawn to – respect and honesty, integrity and fairness, and so on. And we also believe that it is only through the application of those values down the supply chain, with the relationships we have as a business, that we can achieve sustainable success. So we want to treat our employees that way, and we also want to treat our suppliers that way. And we believe that it is only through the application of those values that we'll solve some of these global problems around the environment and the future of the planet."

It is an easy aspiration to understand, but throws up practical challenges, Gaynor says "Allowing the 'market' to set payment rates is a way of avoiding having to think too much about the consequences of what you do. But if you have an interest in growing the financial health of the whole system – looking for win-win-win – you are in territory that is much more difficult to navigate. A lot of people focus on the question of how to track and take account of the externalised costs of doing business; we are also trying to track and take account of externalised benefits as well."

Five.

Looking to the future, the Eden Project's next big challenge is, as Peter puts it, "to get out of the pit"! It's about seeing the project as a launch pad or stage; "Eden is symbolic of new beginnings," Tim reminded us. For Tim, the Eden Project has been a journey from snake oil salesman to medicine man. "I'm a busker by nature," he admitted. "So really the change for me is really profound; to be a snake oil salesman and then you suddenly realise that the snake oil is curing people! It's the most extraordinary experience. I think the pressure I feel and we all feel if we weren't joking about it is that when you've been given this good gig and people have shown so much faith in you, you start to feel a real obligation to be as good as you can. But I think that the calibre of the people who have been attracted to Eden are exactly the people who want to be under that sort of pressure to stretch every fibre."

Reflections

Eden encourages you to visit by train as more sustainable transport. We enjoy trains, so we did. The train ride from London Paddington to Cornwall has special memories for us as we took that trip many times when our sailboat was based in Falmouth between offshore cruises. Truro, not far from Eden, was also where we got married many years ago. Cornwall remains one of our favourite parts of the world, with its rich stories and legends, and magnificent, mysterious and sometimes melancholic countryside, estuaries and seascapes. Mike's ancestors originate from the West Country, and our shared voyages started there.

Eden is the story of plants from around the world, the voyages that discovered them and how they have shaped human destiny. Stories are at the heart of the project. As we wandered around the outer reaches of Eden after the interviews exploring the full context of what had been achieved, we chanced upon a Cornish faery, a professional storyteller. Her unexpected appearance from a plant-grotto seemed to summarise the enchanting experience of Eden. She entertained us with stories of Cornish life and explained (by means of a story of course[25]) how stories are like baskets of facts and experiences that enable us to connect with the past, present and future, and with each other through a shared sense of meaning and humanity.

Eden confirmed for us the primacy of storytelling already revealed at Putumayo, Stonyfield Farm and of course The Body Shop, in the creation of cause-related brands and business models. The significance of the creation of enterprise stories prior to the enterpriser's life-defining venture became clear to us at Eden. The potential for something big comes from the inspiration and insight from prior experience energised by the spirit of enterprise which Tim Smit exemplifies; a maverick spirit that turns defeat into victory, sees 'no' as merely a step on the way to 'yes', and engenders a positivity that can turn the wildest dreams into reality simply through the belief that it will be so.

Six.

Forum for the future

"We want to win the argument that a sustainable future is workable and desirable. I think there will be various ways to win that argument. Some of it will be persuading individual businesses that they can be competitive and find new customers and more authentic brands and so on by doing the sustainability stuff. Some of it will be talking to government and saying 'you can deliver public services, public value and quality of life better by taking a sustainable development approach'. Or persuading individuals that actually life could be happier and more fulfilled by buying these products and acting and living in these ways. So to start to show people, make the case that it can work, and it can and will be better is ultimately what we want to be doing."

— *Peter Madden, CEO of Forum for the Future*

Bring together a big ideas person with lots of public profile, a passionate yet strategic political activist, and a deep thinker with a thorough grounding in economics. Add to this mix a strategist at ease with the NGO and government sectors, a biologist-turned-business consultant, plus 70 other passionate sustainable enterprisers, and you have a unique mix of skills for coming up with practical ways to deliver a sustainable future.

That's the thinking behind London-based Forum for the Future, a not-for-profit organisation that works with partners in the public and private sectors to flesh out the thinking behind sustainable development in order to – as CEO Peter Madden puts it – "produce and deliver things that people can smell, touch, eat, taste, live in, walk in, drive in, that says actually this stuff is doable – not only doable, but it's better and it's a better choice".

Forum develops visions and scenarios for different areas of business and society to transform towards sustainability, identifies the changes that need to be made to get there, and works in partnership with leading businesses and organisations to make the changes happen. The organisation focuses on the following key areas: finance, built environment, retail, climate change, transport, procurement, and travel and tourism.

Peter is the strategist in the Forum mix. His sustainability credentials are impeccable: a former head of policy with one of the UK's development charities, Christian Aid, he has also run a pressure group and advised the UK government on environmental policy, including a stint as head of policy at the Environment Agency, the main environment protection body in the UK.

He took on the CEO role at the Forum in 2005, attracted by what he saw as its positive approach to dealing with the world's problems, and the organisation's unique mix of practice and theory in working with key businesses and decision-makers.

The Forum's list of partners is certainly impressive – there are 120 of them, including big corporate players such as BP, EDF Energy, Sainsbury plc, Unilever, Virgin Atlantic and Vodafone.

The Forum's rules of engagement with business are not your normal consultancy rules, says Forum co-founder Jonathon Porritt (a former co-chair of the Green Party and director of Friends of the Earth, he's the big ideas person with lots of public profile). For a start, he told us, Forum was set up as a charity. "And that was brilliant because in a way it made us do right from day one what has been the hallmark of the Forum's success with the private sector, which is to say yes, we are here to help you but in equal measure we're here to give you a hard time. The only difference is, we're going to give you a hard time and you're going to pay for it! But we're not going to give you a hard time through the media or through seeking to embarrass you and expose you to shame; we are going to give you a hard time round this table, in trust-based dialogue in ways that will always be focused on what to do about the underperformance."

Jonathon told us the Forum had a policy of not just picking sector leaders. "We work with a real mixture of companies some of which are absolutely in the vanguard, some of which are just beginning! It's more to do with the leadership commitment: we don't care where they are on the journey as long as the leadership commitment is absolutely solid and consistent. And without that we can't really do what we need to do, because we have to challenge a lot of middle management."

All business partners also have to agree to allow the Forum to take the learning from the relationship and spread it more widely through

Six.

the Forum website or through partnerships with other companies.

These aspects – challenge and shared learning – are what keep the job real for Dr Sally Uren (the biologist-turned-business advisor) who heads up the Forum's Business Programme. We asked her what it was about Forum for the Future that captured her imagination: "Working so audaciously in partnership with all these big players, particularly business," she shot back. "We really do believe that we can make a difference. So it was that potential to make a difference, and a lot of it was Jonathon, I was inspired by Jonathon. And a chance to really 'up my game' professionally, and I have, I've grown enormously. It gave me the chance to access senior level thinkers in a way that I was not able to do as a consultant."

The results have been impressive. In just the last couple of years, Forum for the Future has helped top supermarkets think through and launch their programmes on sustainability, including Tesco's climate change strategy and Marks & Spencer's much-lauded 'Plan A'[26]. It has helped companies innovate new products and services in everything from financial services to new food products, from customer reward schemes to sustainable paints[27].

"We can point to change that we've delivered, change that we've made happen," Sally told us. "They [business] are not paying lipservice to this, they are changing and they are delivering tangible outcomes, tangible change for everybody. This isn't a risk, this is a massive, massive opportunity and there is a prize for the business that has this double win of enhanced profitability, competitiveness, but also doing the right thing by society and by the planet."

Sally's passion, knowledge, enthusiasm and drive to make the connections between sustainable development and successful business leaped right out at us. Comfortable on stage, in boardrooms and at the laboratory bench, she's typical of the kind of multifaceted person the Forum attracts. The founder and director of the Sustainability Group at private consultancy Casella Stanger (now owned by Bureau Veritas), Sally has accomplished a range of scientific research including a post-doctoral project examining optimal nutrient regimes for encouraging the regeneration of logged rainforest in Borneo.

She told us there's a set of 'Forum competencies' around external networking, management and leadership, being a team player, and strong communication skills, "being able to talk to all sorts of different audiences on this issue and make it compelling," Sally explained. Shared values – respect, openness, honesty, cooperation and learning – are fundamental; the Forum holds a values survey each year to see how well the organisation is doing against its values. Relationships within Forum for the Future and with its partners are characterised by trust. "Fun is very important, we really do have fun here and we laugh a lot, which is really important." Above all, she says, Forum people have passion. "It's not just a job, it's a passion, it's this burning desire to see something change," she told us.

Forum for the Future's emergence owes much to that shared passion. A veteran of the green movement, Forum co-founder Jonathon Porritt described to us how his experience at the 1992 Rio Earth Summit shifted his thinking.

> It was a complete and utter experience. I was already beginning to think that you just can't go on building a social movement exclusively on confrontation, and I came back from Rio absolutely convinced that there was a different way of doing it, and that I was ready for it because I'd spent by that stage 20 years of my life doing Green Party and Friends of the Earth. Both of which were quite raw, often confrontational and aggressive in their orientation towards other people, and I felt that was locking a lot of my own energy. For me, there was a diminishing amount of space to continue working with the emotional responses of guilt, fear and anger, and basically that's what the environmental movement is built on. And I'd just run out of getting anything back from the flames of people's guilt, fear and anger – simple as that.

Working with two founder trustees – the late Richard Sandbrook and Janet Barlow – Jonathon began to develop some ideas for what a different kind of organisation might look like. "We thought, don't put green in the title of the organisation because that puts you in a certain box, and actually this is one organisation that is not going to go in anybody's bloody box!"

He then joined forces with a prominent 'green' academic, Paul Ekins, to explore what Jonathon called "this huge sense of a new energy". They focused initially on a sustainable economy programme. Paul's view was that many environmental problems were really economic problems in disguise and getting the economics right was

Six.

crucial to any solutions agenda.

But economics wasn't the only focus for the fledgling organisation, Jonathon told us. "The idea was that we would simply create an umbrella under which a number of different initiatives could be convened, all sharing the same common values and approach, all sharing commitment to partnerships, solutions, trust-based relationships and sustainable development. And those were the four founding precepts."

Shortly afterwards Green Party activist Sara Parkin joined them, and in 1994 they founded Forum for the Future. What united them (apart from all three of them having been leaders in the UK Green Party at different times) was that there was no other organisation out there doing what they thought needed to be done. Sara had also been active in the feminist movement and she takes up the story from a political perspective: "We moved into proposition which meant engaging with people as they went into proposition that was going to contribute to sustainable development. We didn't know everything, we'd never done it before, so by definition it was new practice; we had to work in partnership with people because

they had the expertise in how to run a university, a business or a bit of government." The essence of that proposition, she told us, was and is to accelerate change to a sustainable way of life.

With Jonathon's ability to inspire and cajole big business into giving the Forum some money, Sara's clear thinking and strong political connections, and Paul's focus on the nitty-gritty of what it takes to deliver a sustainable economy, Forum for the Future grew rapidly.

Sara explained:

> We started where we could lay the ground rules, we got a reputation of having something to say, a right to say something about higher education in universities and so we got some money from the Higher Education Funding Councils to run a whole project for the higher education sector. We also built up the business programme so there were founding corporate partners and we were working on a range of different projects and initiatives with some of them, and then we also started our local and regional government programme.

What we do is advocate solutions, and of course that is more powerful if you are doing it in partnership with one of the sectors, it's not just another gang of NGOs saying 'do this'. But we actually tried to come up not with exhortations to change, but with concrete examples of things that can help them solve the problems.

These concrete examples currently include the Overland Heaven project to encourage a shift away from air travel; the Connected initiative in partnership with Sun Microsystems, which looks at ways to 'green' ICT through its application in unleashing creativity, bringing people together and solving 'big' problems – for example, intelligent traffic management and intelligent R&D. Other Forum initiatives include a sustainable procurement toolkit for the public sector, a project looking at sustainable urban extensions, and a Masters programme in leadership for sustainable development, which already has more than 100 graduates.

The Forum's focus on partnership has meant abandoning what Jonathon calls the 'Star Wars mentality' of good guys and bad guys. He told us a great story to illustrate the point: "At one of my last Green Party conferences in Harrogate we were having a debate about the economy or something like that and a guy stood up, put his hand up and said I'm not really sure I should be here. I'm a new member, and I work for a large company. And he was booed. And I was chairing the session and I was completely mortified. I just thought, what is this? By definition working for a large company makes you a sinner?"

By contrast, the Forum operates in a more textured universe. "It's very muddy, you know what happens when you break down black and white as the polarities, you get a lot of grey, and that's the place where Forum inhabits. We are absolutely in that grey zone and very comfortable there. Don't get me wrong, I mean grey isn't boring either – grey is wonderfully contested and rich and nuanced."

In the 15 years since its foundation, Forum for the Future has experienced many of the growth pangs common to all enterprises, and at one point the organisation faced near financial collapse. It was at this point that Sally Uren joined the Forum, a time everyone calls 'the ditch'.

Basically, the programme that works with businesses was losing money. Corporates pay to become part of our network and we were losing money! So there was no financial discipline in this programme or across the Forum, there was no accountant. And what had happened was the organisation had gone from being

Six.

six or seven really interested, enthused people, it had grown really quickly so when I joined [in 2002] there were maybe 55 or 60 people. And it was just a classic of an organisation that had just grown out of enthusiasm with no discipline at all. So then we spent the next two years trying to back-fill that discipline which was painful because you basically then challenged people's assumptions about why they were here.

Forum for the Future conducted a strategic review, improved its funding base by charging more, and diversifying the sources, appointed people to handle finance, resources and HR, instituted proper career progression – which more than halved staff turnover, and put in place processes to monitor performance and provide opportunity for feedback, while reinforcing commonality of values and purpose.

Forum also took a good hard look at its charitable status, and discussed whether to become a full-profit organisation or set up a commercial arm. But ultimately the decision was to stay not-for-profit, as Jonathon Porritt explained: "The thing about a charity, everybody knows that you've got a cause, we've got a passion, that's what makes us work, and our only reason for doing it is to deliver our mission."

Reflecting on the experience of 'the ditch', co-founder Sara Parkin felt it came down to the Forum not being prepared for growth. "If you look at small business failure, one of the big failures is not knowing your market, having not very good service, but one of the key things is not being prepared to grow, not being able to survive growth because you aren't prepared for it. It's exactly the same phenomenon that we had. I'm a real thinking-ahead person, but I couldn't galvanise interest into systematising what we did as we grew."

Key lessons for any organisation seeking to be sustainable, Sara said, were "Number one, have an ultra-clear idea of what you want to do and be able to say what success would look like in the future. And then the second thing is to make sure you have in place the structures that will cope with growth, not just of the organisation, but also the people in it. And the third thing is that it is about people. I think hire the right people who have a very clear idea about what you want to do, and the rest follows."

In tackling the growth issue, Sara and Jonathon realised they had to prepare their own succession and move on. "That's been quite a mature process," she told us. "Very grown up process of deciding to do it, consulting with the staff, recruiting and putting in place the governance that meant it wasn't going to be a real poisoned chalice for the [new] Chief Executive."

That person is Peter Madden. In inheriting an organisation so heavily dependent on the relationships and profile of its founders, he admitted to us that initially the Forum's profile had suffered in the transition. "But in management terms, such a personality-led organisation probably isn't sustainable really." He sees his job as to turn the Forum into a brand "that is much stronger and bigger than any of the individuals concerned, because it's the organisational brand and ethos that is the important thing to promote".

Talking to us about his plans for the Forum, Peter said his focus would be on more visible outcomes.

> We are going to be doing a lot more scoping about positive futures. Then I want us to go and put coalitions together to actually go out and deliver real exemplars on sustainable development. What we in the Forum think is that power is in lots of places – it's in the City of London, it's in the media, it's in our big companies, it's in our communities and so

on – so we want to go out and do the non-parliamentary politics, we want to work with some of those people to make stuff happen that doesn't rely on government passing a law or regulating. We go and help build the thing, help catalyse it, and everyone says hey, that's good, let's do more of that. So it's about finding some exemplars that are going to break through the way people think about sustainable development.

Peter gave us an example of his thinking. "Getting people out of their cars – I think it is going to be very difficult. The main problem I think in the UK is that people think that you are a social failure, there is a stigma if you get on a bus. So some kind of project to change people's attitudes to what it means to get on a bus and what a bus is and so on. That kind of thing. So I'd like to help build a cutting-edge sustainable neighbourhood, and we have started to do that with our sustainable Bristol project – which involves all the major stakeholders from business, government and the third sector – in transforming the city."

On the business side, Sally Uren fleshed out for us what she saw as the next big challenge for Forum for the Future. "It's making this agenda real for the consumer. Because if

Six.

we got people more aware of these issues and help them integrate that understanding into what they bought, how they bought would just revolutionise business services." Rather than educating the general public, she told us the Forum had decided to focus on getting business to make it easier for the consumer and on encouraging financial organisations to reward more sustainable behaviour by business. "So our big focus as far as going forward is retail and finance. Align them and you jump over into more sustainable business. That's the plan."

Forum for the Future calls itself a UK-based organisation with international reach, and is still wrestling with how to become more globally relevant without losing sight of its founding values.

Jonathon told us about a Forum project with Vodafone aimed at bringing social and economic benefits to communities in Africa. "It really opened our eyes to what big companies can do to open up relationships differently." At the end of the project, he said, Forum considered moving into working in developing countries, but "actually in our hearts we knew that we really don't have enough operating experience in developing countries – we just don't. Our work is entirely

dependent on what we can achieve with someone else. Everything we do, we do for someone else. Everything. So if we over-claim in terms of what we can deliver, that puts us at risk."

Forum continues to look at individual international projects through existing or new partners, such as its largest-ever partnership to create an exemplar of sustainable tourism in Crete. It's a model espoused by CEO Peter Madden. "If we are going to offer the best of cutting edge knowledge, the solutions, if we are going to work with major transnationals in the UK, we have to understand what is happening in China and the USA and so on. So how we intend to tackle this is to try and pick probably between half a dozen and a dozen organisations in key countries and ask them to become partner organisations, asking them to join a loose network whereby we would swap ideas, staff, perhaps do joint funded projects etc. Accept more overseas contracts so that people actually go out and work in places – and make much better use of electronic communications too."

As well as the challenge of becoming more internationally relevant, Forum for the Future is also looking at becoming more of what Peter calls "a blurry edged organisation" that can quickly scale up for big projects. He described what he had in mind as "a donut, perhaps two donuts with a core Forum in the middle, a bunch of associates and people who work regularly with us and then perhaps a bunch of consultants outside, and when a big piece of work comes we run it like that". This way, Peter told us, Forum doesn't have to become a 100 person organisation and then go back down to a 70 person organisation.

Forum for the Future's role is thought leadership right at the frontiers of knowledge as opposed to delivering known ideas in large quantities. Jonathon explained the thinking to us that:

> A lot of our work has just been empowering our partners to do what they could have worked out to do themselves but often felt constrained or not properly competent. A lot of our success with our partners is doing that capacity building with them and then watching them bring in the right level of professional support, right level of in-house staffing, resource allocation and so on. For example, we do a lot of work with a medium-sized company called First Choice Holidays which is one of the biggest low cost airlines and cheap tourist operators in the UK.

> We spent seven years working with them and they've now got a team of five or six people, all the management board are bought in, most of the key staff have been trained by themselves on sustainability thinking and business planning, so you know they are still a partner of ours, but to be honest they don't really need us anymore! Although we have done one really big piece of pioneering work with them in the last year which has been brilliant. So even with partners who get better and better at it, you can always find the next challenge.

Six.

Reflections

We met Jonathon Porritt in an organic cafe close to the University of London where he was giving a lecture after our interview. It was a typical grey London winter's day drizzly and cold, of the type that we well remembered from our time working in Britain's capital, earning funds for forthcoming adventures. We were looking forward to this meeting with one of the world's leading sustainability thinkers as a highlight of the project. His book *Capitalism as if the World Matters*[28] provides an erudite exposition of how capitalism has forgotten its central premise of enhancing wellbeing and how this can be reinstated.

For Jonathon, activism is a matter of record and achievement through politics, scholarship and academia. Presciently, Jonathon and colleagues saw the potential for activism in a political sense to transform towards making a difference in the practical sense of co-creating with clients, ways in which they could develop practices which would enable them to progress towards sustainable development. Forum for the Future recognises that for sustainability to be achieved, progress is needed at the political and systems level, in education and within business, each domain having dependence on the other. We learned from Forum for the Future the pragmatic need to assist enterprises from where they are, rather than where they ought to be. We recognised that small sustainability steps and practices implemented by large businesses and/or by many smaller businesses will cumulatively make a profound difference.

Seven.

Snowy Peak

"Every now and then I cook breakfast for the whole staff. We did a presentation about the Untouched World Charitable Trust's special needs children's programme which was put together by the second group of students that participated in the programme. After that morning we were all damp eyed because the effects were so profound. In that very first special needs programme was a girl from Salisbury College in Nelson for special needs students. At first it was difficult to access her thinking and get her involved – she was cautious when she arrived on the Sunday. By Thursday she led her team, on Friday she was on camera with a big smile saying I don't want to leave, and a year later she was one of our student leaders! And that's not just a one-off. You know we are getting phenomenal stuff like that happening all the time.

— Peri Drysdale, founder and CEO of Snowy Peak Ltd

The daughter of a sheep farmer in the remote and hauntingly beautiful High Country of New Zealand's South Island seems an unlikely candidate to head up a global clothing brand that encapsulates environmental, social and cultural best practice. Yet Peri Drysdale's Untouched World lifestyle fashion garments have in the words of Cameron Silver – named by Time Magazine in 2002 as one of the 25 most influential people in fashion in the world – created an entirely new space in the international fashion arena. Untouched World, said Silver, is the future.

We asked Peri how she would describe the spirit that drives her. "Its a love of this business, it is total enthusiasm and passion for what we are doing." This, coupled with business acumen and a total commitment to sustainability, won Peri the 2008 World Class New Zealand supreme award for providing inspiration to the next generation of leaders.

Peri says Untouched World aims to create designs that inspire the spirit, and make them in fabrics that are simply the best there are – fabrics derived from nature married with modern technology. They're worn by celebrities ranging from Hollywood stars to former US president Bill Clinton. Says Peri: "The first principle

Seven.

has to be quality and performance for the customer. We then deliver that as sustainably as we can. Our goal is to get out there to make the business really successful and to have the opportunity to answer the question: well, how did you do it actually? And then you get to tell the story."

And the story is that taking care of the earth and its people is good business. Business can do well by doing good. The Untouched World story begins with a set of hand-knitted baby bootees, mittens and a little jacket. Peri was about to move to the US for a twelve month sabbatical in 1981 with her university lecturer husband and two young children, and was looking for something she could occupy herself with. "What I did know about myself at that stage was that my biggest fear was boredom, I just don't like not having something constructive to do. Even at that age, in my 20s, I was conscious that we were shipping all our wool off to the other side of the world unprocessed and we were shipping our meat off unprocessed, and that was basically the [New Zealand] economy. And so I decided to add some value to that wool and asked a neighbour to teach me how to knit."

She put her five knitted items into a cardboard box, and went down to the Trade and Industry office in central Christchurch, the South Island's main city, to find out how to export her goods. "They said it's a good idea to have a local market before you export, so I walked out of the office, crossed the square to a store that's still there and said to the manager do you want to buy these and he said yes, I'll have 40 of these, and three dozen each of those; you'd better put a label on, and I said what should I put on the label and he said, oh, put 'handcrafted in New Zealand'."

Peri says she went home and put an ad in the paper for ten outworkers. Four years later, she had 500 and then the company purchased a state-of-the-art computerised knitting machine and set up the beginnings of a commercial knitting operation. Interestingly, her first customer still buys from her "several lifetimes later", as she puts it. And she never did move to the US – the oil shock of the early 1980s meant her husband had to stay back in New Zealand and convert sugar back to ethanol – history keeps going round and round, she says!

The early focus of her company Snowy Peak – named after the sheep farm she grew up on – was creating a story around the dream of New Zealand, that dream included clean, green and safe values as well as openness and friendliness.

From the beginning the business was run on an ethos of sustainability but sustainability wasn't a word I was using at that time, it wasn't a word being used yet in the context of the planet and certainly wasn't being used yet in the business world. We just did what felt right, sharing profits across the board with all our staff, giving them time to walk every day in company time, working with natural fibres, going for high quality, timeless design.

But cracking the knitwear export market from a small unknown country at the bottom end of the world was no easy task in the 1980s. "It took a lot of energy and being prepared to challenge the status quo," recalls Peri. Despite a market survey showing there was no market for her garments in Japan, she read a book about doing business there, persuaded a Kiwi who'd once lived in Japan to come with her, and headed for Tokyo with some samples in a suitcase.

The next day we went to the knitwear floor of Takashimaya [a high end department store group] and we started taking photos, because we knew we weren't allowed to. The staff came over and indicated no photos. And I said, we're a knitwear company from a little country at the bottom of the world called New Zealand. The staff couldn't understand what we were saying so we opened the suitcase to show them, and ten minutes later it was surrounded by excited staff pulling the garments out. One went off and got the buyer, the buyer then gave us an introduction to the best wholesaler there was, and that wholesaler – after three years of courtship – eventually started selling our product. The quality of the introduction is all important. That was an introduction from a major department store – they don't come any better than that.

Peri and her colleague then went back to their tiny hotel rooms and began phoning round the wholesalers whose names they'd taken down from the backs of labels in the department store. "And the first one we rang had a son skiing at Mt Hutt right here [in New Zealand]. So they came around to our little space and we showed them the garments, and they put them straight into Isetan and Takashimaya stores. And so we had started business in Japan and have been selling in Isetan ever since."

Through sheer persistence and determination, Peri pulled off similar sales coups in North America and right across Europe, but it was hard

Seven.

work. "I used to have to go into a country, and sell New Zealand, then sell the company, then me, and then the product."

Peri told us much of her thinking on sustainability results from what she saw as she travelled the world in the late 1980s and 1990s, selling her Snowy Peak knitwear. As a child, Peri had been steeped in the natural world; she remembers drinking from crystal clear streams and always knowing about native flora – "totally connected at a really deep level" is how she put it to us. Her grandmother wrote the first book on New Zealand native trees and plants.

> I grew up in one of the most beautiful places on the planet. And I was selling Snowy Peak into resorts in some of the most beautiful places in the world as well as into busy, grey cities. But I could see from visit to visit that the environment was becoming degraded. I could see the pollution levels growing and spreading, and it was really significant as to what was happening. I was hearing about whole tracts of sea that wouldn't support any fish anymore, and whole tracts of land rendered barren through growing cotton with pesticides.

The second pivotal moment was in 2000 when she heard Ray Anderson from Interface and Paul Hawken of SustainAbility speak at a conference on Redesigning Resources. "They were pretty profound speakers and I went through something in that process. And I thought somebody has got to take a lead here, somebody has got to do something. If we all sit around waiting for the other person to do it it will be too late. So I walked back to the office here and said right guys, everything is changing as of now. And I gathered everyone together and I talked to them about what I'd heard, what I thought, what I felt. They got it straight away."

Peri signed up Snowy Peak as one of eight pilot companies in the Redesigning Resources Group, which aimed to pioneer a pathway to sustainable development "so others can come along behind us".

Peri passionately believes that New Zealand should be a global byword for environmental, social and cultural best practice, and she's put her money where her mouth is in creating Untouched World as a global brand about New Zealand, rather than a New Zealand brand.

With Snowy Peak knitwear costs rising because of the high New Zealand dollar and urged by European buyers to shift production out of New Zealand or lose sales, Peri took a long hard look at the market and saw that it was flooded with lookalike American casualwear "spreading like triffids through all the malls".

So I made up my mind I would build a well executed New Zealand lifestyle brand. This is where the first step into really consciously thinking about how to articulate the sustainability thing came through, and what I wanted to do was build the concept so strongly that it didn't matter what our dollar was doing, I could manufacture it wherever. And also if people suddenly decided they didn't want to wear sweaters anymore, the brand would umbrella whatever was relevant at the time, so long as there was a values and aesthetic/design fit.

To turn her dream into a reality, she put together a team of advisors from Italy, Japan and the USA – including Shozo Hondo who had been instrumental in transforming Prada from a 'me too' brand into a global frontrunner – and spent two years fine tuning the concept before rolling out the Untouched World brand in 1998. "We were going to take the Snowy Peak brand into that New Zealand lifestyle concept," Peri told us. "But the Italian advisor said Snowy Peak won't work as a name for what you are trying to do

in Europe; he said for us it means crampons and ice axes, whereas the American and Japanese said to them it meant virgin, fresh, clean, those sorts of sustainable values we were building the brand on." Further brainstorming threw up the name Peri's.

Vittorio, the Italian designer, was sent off to work on the Peri's concepts, and at the same time to come up with a small summer concept for the Untouched World by Snowy Peak label already in stores in Japan, this was a Biogro certified organic New Zealand wool collection. The Japanese stores were asking for something for summer for this label.

A couple of months later Peri, Honda, and Nori Nakagawa, Snowy Peak's representative in Japan, went to Italy to see how things were going. "What he'd done for Untouched World was amazing, it was different, very different to the Untouched World today, but I could see where it would go. And he had come up with the idea of the Maori kite as the inspiration for a logo, he'd researched it, and he'd even come up with the embryonic idea of the Charitable Trust. It was perfect for the major New Zealand lifestyle brand concept. To this day we never even looked at what he'd done for the other, Peri's, concept, we were

Seven.

so excited about what we could do with Untouched World."

Peri explained that Untouched World's Maori kite logo is the perfect outcome of art and natural materials, human skill and nature, the symbol of freedom. "The really interesting thing about Untouched World is that is relates to people worldwide in the most primal, fundamental way – it's just astonishing." The inspiration that ultimately led to the kite actually came from three contemporary Maori artworks that happened to be hanging in the New Zealand ambassador's office in Tokyo when Peri was visiting.

Product quality and innovation have always been of prime importance. Snowy Peak knitted the first possum and wool garment and subsequently led the way in developing the first-ever blend of possum fibre with merino wool and cashmere, using Japanese technology to create a luxury worsted yarn out of blends of brushtail possum fur, a byproduct of New Zealand's greatest wildlife and ecology threat. An estimated 70 million possums chew their way through 20,000 tonnes of native herbage every night, and millions of dollars have been spent in attempting to control this environmentally-destructive creature. Says Peri, "By using possum

fibre, we have saved hundreds of millions of tonnes of native herbage, protecting our biodiversity at the same time."

The company also sources organic cotton and organic merino wool for its signature fabric Untouched World garments, and uses a patented bamboo fabric, recycled cotton buttons, tagua nut buttons and recycled fusing. The aim, says Peri, is "to make garments in natural materials that can deliver maximum wears per dollar, minimum environmental impact per wear."

Untouched World's profits fund a charitable trust aimed at developing leadership skills in the context of social, cultural and environmental sustainability – what Peri calls deepest long term investment at grassroots level of the issues facing the planet. The Trust is based on her long-standing commitment to social activism. As she travelled around the world selling she became aware of escalating environmental issues. She explained to us that as she worked closely with partners in key markets that a short generation before had been mired in fear and conflict, she realised she had developed perceptions about these nations that she had learned from others, in the same way the children of those nations had built their own partial perceptions. She realised how much conflict in the world could be broken down if there was an opportunity for people of differing nationalities to spend time immersed in each others' cultures, and feel the enrichment rather than focusing on different-ness.

A further driver came from a playgroup Peri had joined when her daughter – who's now chief designer for Untouched World – was a baby, and the seven mothers still meet once a month. "They are all teachers, curiously," she said. "So I'm in this space where I'm hearing a lot more about what's going on in schools and families than most business people – and it scares me, really scares me. I have a passion for all children, for everyone, having the opportunity to reach their full potential. So that's just really why I set out to do something about these things. And that's the thing: it's very hard to have a concern about something and not do something about it, isn't it? And if you can, you do".

The Untouched World Charitable Trust was set up to make a difference beyond the reach of the business. It has been running since 2000, and funds action-learning based programmes for teenagers working on real-world projects across New Zealand, including conservation, urban sustainability, kiwi recovery, waste and recycling. The week-long projects bring together young people, teachers and business, central and regional government.

"It's about giving the students skills to become action competent," explains Dr Barry Law, an expert on experiential and education for sustainability at Canterbury University in Christchurch who advises the Untouched World Charitable Trust. One project involves a week of conservation work on Blumine Island in the Marlborough Sounds, at the top of New Zealand's South Island, and Barry says he remembers on the first trip how sceptical the Department of Conservation (DOC) people were that the students could set up and monitor a snail plot on their own. "By the time they'd completed two snail plots the kids were really good and very savvy when it came to organising the data. When the students got back to camp they didn't like the DOC data forms, so they used the computers to develop new forms. In a follow-up trip the following year students organised to download the data, including the GPS site of each snail plot, onto a map of Blumine Island. The map was sent to DOC as a record of work completed and work in progress. It demonstrated the action potential of our students and the impact of the programme."

Seven.

The Untouched World Charitable Trust sponsors three trips a year to Blumine Island. The third trip was completely designed by Blumine student participants for special needs students, and involves one-on-one mentoring.

Other projects include a sustainable cities programme in Auckland issues in urban areas, a kiwi recovery programme with schools on the Central Plateau, and the Tiromoana consumption and waste programme in Canterbury. At the end of each project, the students present their findings with recommendations for further action, and they also look at how they can take their learning back into their own schools.

Barry says the results have exceeded expectations. "We see the students standing up and presenting their ideas in front of adults in their community. They certainly shift adults' thinking and make them reflect on the need for a change in behaviour. I had a parent come up to me at the last presentation in Christchurch and say this is the most awesome experience my daughter has had, and I'm just so rapt she's had this opportunity, and it's really going to make us rethink what we do at home. I quickly recognised that what we wanted to achieve was not only a shift in student behaviour, but a change in thinking of the adults connected to these students (parents, relatives and teachers)."

The Untouched World Charitable Trust programmes have also had a profound effect on the company. In 2008, the Trust's work plus the extent of the sustainability ethos built deep within the DNA of the company helped the company win the right to put the UN Decade of Education for Sustainable Development Education logo on its Untouched World products – an enviable marketing boost to the company's global profile.

And for many of Snowy Peak's stakeholders, says Peri, the Trust is the icing on the cake. "There's a great sense of being part of something very big and very worthwhile. When there's a huge shared commitment like this company-wide, a tremendous passion is unleashed, a passion that pulls out the last 10% of effort. And it is that 10% that can make the difference between success and failure."

Snowy Peak remains a family-owned business, and employees are a valued part of that family. Peri is adamant that it's not 'her' company; it belongs to everyone who works with her. The same goes for the commitment to sustainability.

With sustainability an integral part of Snowy Peak's business model, the company has set up a sustainability team of volunteers from across the company and set up a recycling scheme where staff bring in to work items they no longer want for other staff members to take away for a couple of dollars. The money goes into a project to enhance sustainability within the company. The idea of sustainability has taken off: "We've just been through the whole company with reviews – nearly all of the staff were doing stuff at home, families were involved and people are just thinking about sustainability all the time," says Peri.

Shared ownership of the commitment to sustainability is crucial, she says. "The first thing is to get really clear on what that word means to you and your business. And share it with everybody. Make sure that everybody owns what you mean by that. I think that is the most important thing, and that is a process that took us a long time."

It's also important to create a structure that ensures that principles don't get lost in the day-to-day running of the business. "The thing about sustainability is that you can always do it tomorrow. Whereas if a machine breaks down, you've got to fix it today or if the customer rings sales for an order you've got to do it today, or if you're designing you have to work to this deadline. And all those tomorrows add up."

Snowy Peak has also influenced the companies that it works with, – its printer has been persuaded to switch to more environmentally-friendly inks, and the wool spinning and knitting contractors have rethought their processes and inputs. Recently Snowy Peak has re-reviewed its approach to waste and switched thinking within the company to explore the concept of recovered materials. Currently approximately 90% of unused materials are being recovered with less than 10% of factory materials going to landfill. A full circle recovery process collects all cardboard, paper and plastic material, with the cardboard and paper being recycled into new cardboard, which is then purchased back through the collection company in the form of new cardboard products.

In the end, Peri told us, it's the values that matter. "You know, I have no interest whatever in having a fashion company or having a lifestyle clothing company that didn't have these sort of values, I just wouldn't be interested. It wouldn't inspire me; it wouldn't get me out of bed in the morning. The core passion is about the values."

Seven.

For Peri, the issue of financing Snowy Peak's expansion is also about values. She has kept the company in family hands from the beginning, and although she's been courted by innumerable investors she says it's been hard to find one that fits the company's profile. "All the way through the company has been constrained not by the growth it can achieve but by the cash that it can flush out of the growth into the next phase. I always knew that once we'd got Untouched Word to a certain point I would have to find a way to leverage it, but I also knew that I needed to retain control."

Reflections

By this stage of our Sustainable Enterprise odyssey we were experiencing and even anticipating familiar patterns. Peri as activist and enterpriser bringing inspirational leadership to the potential for creating value, through brand and innovation, from merino wool traditionally exported from New Zealand as commodity raw material. Philosophy, purpose beliefs and values underpin the organisation's choice of activities and ways of conducting business. Quality is paramount. Fostering a family-like environment creates the context for performance. Peri and Snowy Peak are in business to make a difference for people and the planet and are rewarded profitably by so doing.

We appreciated learning about how the Untouched World Charitable Trust strives to make a difference by educating the next generation of inspirational leaders for sustainability. The need for succession beyond the founders is of vital importance in any enterprise, and all the more so in sustainable enterprise where values are parmount. We noted in this context that Snowy Peak is fortunate in having Peri's daughter Emily Drysdale as Design and Marketing Director to provide succession as and when Peri decides to step down.

How to finance expansion is an issue that emerged through the Stonyfield Farm story and the Body Shop, and was again encountered at Snowy Peak. We resolved to explore this in the theory development phase of the project.

Eight.

Comvita

"For me, it's about people; it's about the dynamism and enthusiasm generated by a community of people around business ideas that can have positive outcomes on society and the environment. That is the thing for me that makes our business successful. Yes, it's about making and selling products for profit, but we've tried to model behaviour in the business world that's different. Our employees say there's something special about working at Comvita and that's why we work here. It's around our heritage and the sense of shared purpose and values. Seeing people energised and achieving great results through this process is fantastically exciting for me."

"Comvita is committed to acting in a manner that preserves and helps improve the quality of life and environment for generations to come".

— *Alan Bougen, co-founder of Comvita*

From a handful of hives tucked away in a rural backwater, Comvita has grown to become a New Zealand success story, exporting its high quality natural health products around the world. It has achieved that success because of, not in spite of, its founders' passionate commitment to help others.

Although there's exactly forty years between them, Claude Stratford and Alan Bougen exude a comradeship borne of shared inspiration, persistence and sheer optimism. We could see that bond clearly when we caught up with Claude and Alan at Comvita's headquarters at Paengaroa in the lush green of the Bay of Plenty in New Zealand's North Island.

Claude is now in his late nineties, but he still takes his daily tablespoon of bee pollen and olive leaf extract. He's stepped back from the day-to-day running of Comvita, but armed with a cut lunch he heads off daily to take care of business in the bee pollen processing factory now owned by his charitable trust. He's also set up a little shop at the retirement home where he sells natural health products to his fellow residents.

Claude was one of the pioneers of the health food movement in New Zealand in the 1940s. In fact, in 2005 he was awarded the NZ Order

Eight.

of Merit recognising his service over the years. Claude started beekeeping as a boy during the 1920s, sparking a life-long interest in the health-giving properties of bee-based and other natural products. After a string of business failures and health problems, he started investigating the properties of bee pollen. "I didn't know what health was until I was introduced to pollen's nutritional values," he says. At 98 years young, he still swears by bee pollen, a spoonful a day -- 'nature's Viagra', he calls it.

Claude also started developing formulations for natural skincare using the herb comfrey and manuka honey – some of which made their way to Japan to help treat the burn victims of the Hiroshima nuclear bomb. And that, says Claude, was the origin of the company name Comvita – comfrey and vitamins together. In Latin, it means 'with life and vitality', which became the company's tagline up until the 1990s – a fitting testament to a business dedicated to positivity and wellbeing.

During the late 1960s Alan Bougen had been travelling the world and experimenting with alternative lifestyles. "I was part of a generation that was thinking deeply about preventative health, the environment and doing business in less traditional ways, you know; why can't business be fun and help people in the process?" He says it took him just five minutes to decide when Claude offered him a 50-50 stake in Comvita at their first meeting in 1976. He explains why:

> One of the things that impressed me about Claude when I met him was that he spoke constantly about 'being in this business to help improve people's health and to benefit the community'. As a 26-year-old idealist, I was Immediately drawn to Claude's entrepreneurial spirit and his unique values-driven approach to business, so I said, why not? Here's a business opportunity aligned to my own philosophies, and so it was like wow, yes, let's go!

And go they have. Alan joined Claude in producing and marketing a range of bee-based natural health and wellness products, writing columns in newspapers challenging commonly held beliefs about what constitutes good nutrition and promoting the benefits of natural health products. They were at the forefront of New Zealand's 1980s regulatory debate on natural health, and their activist zeal also drew the ire of the traditional honey industry. Alan explains:

> People kept inferring Claude was a bit of a 'nutcase' because he was

promoting honey and bee pollen based on their 'nutritional' values. At the time, the New Zealand honey industry was shipping most of the New Zealand honey crop in bulk to Germany and the UK. In contrast, Comvita was packing and marketing a shelf-ready product and openly promoting its health-giving attributes. This high 'added value' approach still underpins Comvita's business and export strategy today.

It's a value story that's paid off. Today, Comvita employs 250 people around the world, turning New Zealand-sourced bee-based and other natural ingredients into functional foods, skincare products, nutraceuticals and medical-grade woundcare products. Along the way, the company has created significant value around exclusively New Zealand-produced UMF® Manuka honey which has in turn added value to the local beekeeping industry.

Comvita operates out of a state-of-the-art processing plant in the Bay of Plenty which began life as a pub. The company bought the old building in 1997, but Alan says when they sat down to plan what was needed for the next 10 to 15 year programme, "we ended up building a GMP-certified[29] manufacturing facility three times the size with a multi

million dollar price tag which stopped me sleeping at night!"

They had to find some outside capital. Mortgaged to the hilt in order to fund the building of the factory and a rapidly expanding export business, and needing to attract professional managers to take the business forward, Claude and Alan sold around one-third of the company to a group of private investors. From there, Comvita moved onto New Zealand's alternative board (NZAX), then, in 2003, listed on the New Zealand Stock Exchange (NZX). At each stage, it was their philosophy to offer staff shareholding in Comvita. Far from compromising on Comvita's founding beliefs, going public has had the reverse effect, says Alan.

It's actually given us a bigger platform from which to tell our story. We never really saw Comvita being a family empire, it was bigger than that. We said, let's make sure that Comvita can be adequately funded, properly managed to maximise shareholder returns and continue to promote the values that this company has been built on. Now with more than 1,300 shareholders it's a matter of making sure we continue to communicate well with all stakeholders and produce

Eight.

satisfactory returns. For the majority of our shareholders I think Comvita is considered a solid ethical investment opportunity with high medium to long-term growth potential. Our cornerstone shareholders realise that the best returns won't be immediate but that there are exciting opportunities up ahead in the burgeoning global wound care and natural health markets.

Going public has enabled Comvita to focus on and expedite the growth of its offshore business. In 2004, Comvita acquired Apimed, a small company that had developed breakthrough wound dressing technologies using UMF® manuka honey, a concept pioneered by Professor Peter Molan of nearby Waikato University.

Professor Molan's research had discovered that UMF® manuka honey contained antibacterial properties significantly higher than those of other honeys. Comvita was able to take the product through the time-consuming and expensive international medical registration process, and today the honey-based wound dressings are being successfully used to treat burns and ulcers in hospitals across the world. They have proved particularly effective against superbugs such as MRSA[30].

Comvita's Medihoney™ wound care products are a perfect example of how a company can do well by doing good – building on its philosophy of wellbeing, Comvita transformed a natural product into a hospital-grade dressing which can be used anywhere from third world villages to state-of-the-art medical facilities. Comvita's medical grade honey and its product applications return a high margin, and provide long term profitable growth potential and a new product development pipeline. Federal Drug Authority (FDA) approvals in the USA and UK drug tariff listings for a number of Medihoney products have enabled Comvita to move into territory traditionally owned by large global pharmaceutical companies.

The medical honey story also enables Comvita to make a difference to its 'global community'. The company has donated shipments of Medihoney™ products to US military personnel to help prevent infections in Iraqi burns patients. Clinicians have applauded the effectiveness of the Medihoney™ dressings as "nothing short of extraordinary" in the treatment of these burns. Comvita also donates its wound-care products on an ongoing basis to a leprosy treatment centre in Vietnam, a charitable Christian foundation aiding orphans in India, and together with its US woundcare partner Derma Sciences to DebRA, an international charitable organisation supporting the 'Butterfly Children' – sufferers of epidermolysis bullosa (EB)[31].

Alan Bougen puts Comvita's purpose succinctly: "We are in this business to make a difference and to make a profit. We've said that we believe that profit has to be fair and reasonable, and we have no problem being transparent about that. We aim to find the most effective natural health products that have the least environmental impact and take them to the world. Manuka honey in all its various forms including medical dressings epitomises this approach."

Comvita's purpose is to care for customers through the marketing of natural products, and the company has successfully used story telling and word of mouth to sell its products into more than 20 countries around the world. In 2007 export sales exceeded domestic sales for the first time, and there are solid plans to grow the current NZ$55 million business into a NZ$100 million business by 2010.

The keyword or idea that goes to the heart of the business is wellbeing. Alan says Comvita is all about the customer: caring for its internal and external customers and stakeholders and promoting wellbeing through its range of natural health products.

The two big success stories have been the UK and Hong Kong/China market. Scott Coulter, Comvita's Chief Marketing Officer explains: "The UK was our first export market. Our distributors visited Comvita in New Zealand, filled up their suitcases with products, and 20 years later they had a multi-million dollar business in the UK, which Comvita subsequently acquired." As part of its marketing strategy, Comvita has now also acquired its Hong Kong distributor, but in both cases the original owners remain closely involved with the businesses.

Hong Kong businessman K.C. Butt was Comvita's distributer before the buyout, and Scott Coulter describes him as the Chinese version of Claude. "K.C. has set up a charitable trust with the money from the sale of his company Greenlife to Comvita, and he's going to spend it on promoting organics and facilitating overseas educational opportunities for less privileged people in China. It's an amazing philosophy of life, doing well and giving back to your people."

Scott credits K.C. and his son Ronnie with Comvita's success in China to date. "We've found people there who have very similar shared beliefs around sustainability, healthy products and the New Zealand

Eight.

brand, and that has enabled us to start quite positively in China."

As Comvita expands its exports, the company's CEO Brett Hewlett says the challenge will be to ensure that Comvita continues to connect with its people overseas. "It's all very well to have a company based on strong values, but if those values can't be translated to the team and end consumers overseas as well as they are being communicated here in New Zealand, it all quickly loses steam and falls apart. So it's really about engaging those employees, making sure they are familiar with where the company came from, what is good about it, what we are here for, what our purpose is, and making sure they are translating that into the way they behave in their roles."

For Alan Bougen, it's that shared passion that's been all-important. "Part of our success has been communicating our heritage story, our values and our premium brand through people that understand and are passionate about it. That's why today we've established wholly owned subsidiaries in our key offshore markets to allow a closer direct relationship with our customers and end consumers. Our best results have been achieved by employing people who share our core values and who have a close connection with New Zealand.

Whether they're in Hong Kong, Britain, Japan or Australia, Comvita people become part of what's known as the 'Comvita family'. It's a notion that has been picked up by Brett Hewlett, who's made a point of projecting the concept in corporate circles. "People don't work for this organisation because they agree to our objectives; they buy in to it because of the sense of purpose. I've referred to the organisation as an 'army of believers', and I've deliberately trIed to encourage that and endorse it, so I think success would be when we see our products out there around the world enhancing people's lives. And that's basically what drives people here."

Alan Bougen believes family is a key element of what makes Comvita special.

Family has always been an important value to us. In fact we had a time where we used the words extended family a lot because we had people that had come along and there was something about Comvita that they identified with and made them want to be part of it. As the company was headquarterd in a rural area, there weren't enough houses for them so they ended up living in semi-detached houses and in caravans. In those early days it wasn't so much about the external business drivers, but rather an internal sense of mission and shared values being outworked by a very committed group of people.

The caravans have long gone, but the shared values and sense of community remain within the Comvita family. We asked Alan what he saw as the spirit or energy that makes the business buzz.

I think it's the sense of shared purpose; it's about doing good things that are of value to the wider public. For example, Jason Cobb, a naturopath who used to work here 15 years ago, went off to work in Northern India developing orphanages. Comvita has continued to support him financially every month, and he's achieved some absolutely incredible things during that time. It's the barefoot doctor approach of using natural products in a third world environment, effectively healing childrens wounds using manuka honey and propolis based natural health products.

When Jason last visited Comvita and gave a talk to staff in our cafeteria, there was an absolute hush over the room when he talked about what he was doing in India. Later people said, wow, we

just love working for a company like this. Of course everybody needs their salary at the end of the month, but this added social and philanthropic dimension provides the inspiration for those at Comvita to do more.

Family is also about looking after those close to you. For Alan, it's about "believing in people and giving them the opportunity to aspire to greatness, to do things that perhaps they wouldn't believe they were capable of, to give them the encouragement and the opportunity to achieve their goals and dreams".

There's also a focus on wellness within the company – for example, Comvita offers a financial prize to the person that makes the biggest changes in their lifestyle, whether it's losing weight, giving up smoking or running a marathon. Alan says the aim is to ensure that Comvita lives its dream. "We try to provide opportunities right throughout the organisation for people to align themselves fully with our values; we really try to encourage that."

The wellness education extends outside the company too. Corporate Affairs Manager Pip Buckley is literally a hive of energy. She's part of a team that oversees a school curriculum programme called Birds, Bees, Kids & Trees, sports sponsorships and a

Eight.

tree planting programme to restore a local wetland area. It's good for the environment and future generations and a great way to engage the Comvita family in giving back to their local community. "We donate money and trees, and a couple of times a year our staff are given the opportunity to plant native trees. We planted two and a half thousand trees one Saturday afternoon, and then the 60 or 70 staff, families and friends had a barbeque at the end."

Pip is also involved in the company's initiatives on sustainability, wellness and what's called 'sharpening the saw' – an internal initiative aimed at increasing workplace productivity and efficiency. These are cross-functional teams with representatives from all levels of the company charged with coming up with initiatives to present to the Board. "We've got teams of people that are very passionate about sustainability," says Pip. "The company is not just aligning with global trends and getting on the 'green band-wagon' – it has a wonderful heritage with ingrained sustainable values, and there have been some effective and inspiring environmental and corporate social responsibility (CSR) sustainability initiatives in place for some years, all run by a cross-departmental sustainability committee. Our

challenge today from a business perspective is to channel the passion and achieve a higher degree of rigour around our sustainable processes and measures."

Comvita has adopted 'The Natural Step' (TNS) framework to guide the company and provide rigour in setting and achieving its future sustainability objectives. TNS is an international non-profit organisation that has been working since 1988 to accelerate global sustainability. The TNS framework is based on science, systems thinking and practical business decision making. TNS assists companies, non-profit organisations, individuals and communities to lead the transition to an ecologically, socially and economically sustainable future.

Comvita is a quintessential sustainable enterprise, with its eyes firmly on the big picture. Alan Bougen puts that down to the high expectations customers have of Comvita. "I think our company has been fortunate in that we are in an industry where players are expected to operate sustainably. If we are not aligned with our customers' philosophical values, then we could easily drop out of the game. So we've got an advantage in the sense that our customers, particularly European-based customers, are driving us in a direction we believe we must go."

But the road ahead is long, says Alan. "We are committed to continued improvement and to further integrating environmental, social and economic best practices into our business. We see sustainability as an opportunity to innovate and to simplify what we do whilst providing tangible benefits for all stakeholders. We are on a journey that has only just begun."

Part of looking at the bigger picture involves identifying what Comvita can do to further enhance environmental sustainability throughout its supply chain, and the company has recently taken on a supply chain management expert. Alan Bougen explains: "Our idea is to assist our suppliers to develop a framework to measure and monitor their environmental performance and thereby become an integral part of our total sustainability performance."

Security of supply of high quality UMF® manuka honey remains a top priority for Comvita. In late 2007, the company acquired Kiwi Bee Distributors Ltd, New Zealand's leading producer of medical grade manuka honey. Former owner Bruce Stevenson has been retained in a consultative role to expand and improve the medical grade honey

supply programme, introducing it to the growing family of Comvita's approved medical grade suppliers. In 2008, Comvita announced a partnership with Kyoto Forests New Zealand which will provide income from carbon credits and further secure supply by reverting marginal bushland and eroding back country land into profitable blocks of high-yielding manuka. This initiative will positively impact the environment and see an increase in the areas of UMF® manuka honey producing land available to beekeepers.

Comvita has a strategy of growth through carefully chosen acquisitions that are consistent with its philosophy of sustainability, and purpose of enhancing wellbeing through natural products. For example, in 2007 the company acquired Olive Products Australia Ltd, a Brisbane-based company which according to Pip Buckley "has founders and a wonderful sustainable heritage and ethos very aligned to that of Claude and Alan".

Olives are the world's oldest cultivated trees, and olive leaves have been used by healers dating back to ancient times. Comvita Olive Leaf Complex™ uses technologically advanced extractive processes to provide a daily health tonic which supports the body's natural defences

Eight.

for year-round health and wellbeing. This new product line moves Comvita beyond its bee-based origins, but in a way that is entirely consistent with the core focus on natural wellbeing.

As well as moving into non bee-based products, Comvita has also extended its core bee-based ingredients into an entirely new category – the competitive beauty market, based on its natural, sustainable and wellbeing beliefs. The natural segment of the global US$200 billion beauty market is only 1%, but is growing at 20% annually. Comvita's natural skincare range – huni® is based on its core UMF®20+ manuka honey ingredient with its moisturising, anti-oxidant and anti-inflammatory properties, and founded on a powerful set of sustainability beliefs.

Comvita takes its commitment to authentic natural ingredients very seriously, as Pip explained to us. "Ingredients must be extracted directly from nature, free from 'incidental' ingredients, not knowingly carcinogenic, mutagenic, toxic or sensitising, from sustainable, renewable sources, GMO free, not tested on animals, microbiologically safe, appealing, have a reason for being present, and must not include parabens, artificial colourings/fragrances, mineral oils, aluminium and sodium lauryl sulphate detergents." She was passionately precise about these requirements, and insists on honesty and transparency in all their communication. Greenwashing is seen as the ultimate crime.

We asked Comvita CEO Brett Hewlett to identify the three biggest insights for aspiring ethical, sustainable entrepreneurs.

Absolute clarity of purpose that you can articulate in a simple way to the whole organisation so others can connect with it, that's number one. Focus I guess is the second one, and that is a real challenge for us because there are so many opportunities out there. The third one is probably to be really generous with everything that you do. You know, be generous with your time, be generous with the people that work for you, be generous in the way you operate as an organisation, it is based on a fundamental philosophy – whatever you give comes back tenfold.

Reflections

Comvita was one of the last enterprises that we met with. We were privileged to be able to run a workshop with their senior leadership team during which we were able to feed back to them sustainable enterprise theory and practice as it was emerging. This enabled us to fine tune the process of developing a sustainable enterprise to enable others to fast track the learning process of the sustainability pioneers whose stories are recounted in this book.

Comvita exemplifies the technical expert plus enterpriser combination that gave rise to the inspiration for the enterprise (in the same way, for example, as at Stonyfield Farm). Philosophy and purpose drive the business. The story of the enterprise is the primary mode of marketing. Wellbeing is at the heart of the business, and Comvita wants to make a difference through products and services that enhance the wellbeing of people around the world while striving to protect the natural environment from which their products emanate.

Comvita is a stock exchange listed company and as such subject to stock market expectations of profit and performance. It is the only one of our set of enterprises that is listed. The company believes that listing with a strong sustainability positioning and as an ethical investment has provided them with another platform to tell their story, and has enhanced rather than inhibited their business. We will have more on this in Part 2.

Nine.

Patagonia

"Build the best product, do no unnecessary harm, use business to inspire and implement solutions to the environmental crisis. I go back to that every single day. When I'm wondering what I'm doing I think of that mission statement, and like Yvon [Chouinard, founder of Patagonia] says, I leap up the stairs two at a time going (clap, clap) what are we going to work on today?"

— Casey Sheahan, CEO of Patagonia

Bobby Troup wrote the classic 'Route 66' in 1946 as a dedication to the romance and freedom of cars on the open road. His song celebrated the 'Mother Road' highway that started in Santa Monica CA and concluded its trans-American journey in Chicago Ill. Chuck Berry and The Rolling Stones amongst many others produced hit covers of this famous saga and many a Harley fan has made the pilgrimage along this most famous of roads. Route 66 is no more now on the maps, but its mythology lives on in people's souls. Romance and freedom seemed a fitting spirit for this stage of our sustainable enterprise story.

We found ourselves heading along Route 66 through Santa Monica, then heading north along Route 101 and the Pacific Coastal Highway. This magnificent stretch of coastal scenery seemed tired with the weight of population and Los Angeles pollution pressing on the ocean's beauty. We were headed for Patagonia. Not the Patagonia of South American wilderness fame, but the outdoor apparel company of the same name, based in Ventura CA.

The atmosphere lifted as we got alongside the ocean, but then became weighed down once more, this time with the black smoke of out-of-control bush fires that had already claimed several homes. In Ventura itself we found a fleet of fire engines and a steady stream of fire fighters going backwards and forwards to the fire front. We reflected on this phenomenon in the light of the environmental activism that characterises Patagonia, an iconic pioneer of sustainable enterprise. Perhaps it is the long term availability of resources that is the biggest challenge companies must face up to.

The CEO for the thirty-six-year-old outdoor clothing company is Casey Sheahan, and when we met him at the cluster of low-rise buildings that is Patagonia's headquarters, he shared his thoughts on the future. "Looking at the issues that seem to be facing us right now, I'm not really concerned about our business success. I think our momentum is really strong. We are growing at a nice pace. I am concerned about global warming being a major impact, and I'm concerned about the end of oil and what that means to our business. Everything else seems so trivial; we talk about market conditions, about fashion whims and vagaries; it all seems so short term."

Yet Casey – like the company he now runs – is an optimist. Soaking up Patagonia's relaxed family-like atmosphere, we began to experience how passion, a clear sense of purpose and fun combine together to energise their enduring enterprise success. The day's surf report posted at reception, the surf boards stacked ready to run, the chatter of children playing outside, the open-plan workspaces all created a laid-back ambience that is simultaneously energised with an evident passion to do everything better all the time.

When he's not riding his bike or out on his surfboard, Casey Sheahan directs his considerable energy and enthusiasm towards doing just this.

> I walk around the building and go, wow, look at that fabric that has a great look to it. It might be recycled wool or our recycled cotton sweatshirt material. It's both a fashion statement and an environmental statement, and that in turn raises all kinds of questions. Are we going to recycle industrial cotton or just organic cotton? And why wouldn't we recycle industrial cotton? It's already been made, the damage has been done, and it's clean. These are the kinds of things we think about. It's fun!

Patagonia has set itself the goal of achieving recyclable or fully recycled product by 2010. The company has already pioneered recyclable fleece, it has been using recycled-content paper for its catalogues

Nine.

since the mid-1980s, and it's made environmental responsibility a key element of everyone's job.

In the process, it has set new standards for sustainable business success. By holding to his values, Patagonia's founder Yvon Chouinard has built a company that continually seeks to reduce its environmental footprint whilst simultaneously enhancing quality. On top of that, 1% of all Patagonia's sales go to fund environmental activist groups.

The Patagonia story all began with 'clean' climbing. In the 1960s, Yvon was part of what was called the Valley Cong, a free-spirited rock climbing fraternity in the Yosemite Valley that devoted all their time to climbing the Valley's towering rock walls and icefalls, evading rangers and living on next to nothing. Yvon eked out a living forging pitons on a junkyard forge. Hammered into small cracks, these were used by climbers to secure their ropes to the rock.

In his inspirational book *Let My People Go Surfing*[32], Yvon calls himself a 'reluctant businessman', but demand grew for his simple, but functional gear and by 1970, his company Chouinard Equipment led the field in supplying climbing hardware in the United States.

Despite this success, Yvon had more affinity with the natural environment than with sales spreadsheets and profit projections. On a climbing trip back to his old Yosemite haunts, he was horrified at the impact pitons were having on the fragile rock walls of ever-more popular climbing routes. In 1972, he made the decision to replace the company's top-selling product with a more environmentally-friendly alternative, aluminium chocks that could be wedged in cracks and then removed by hand.

It was a shot in the dark, but with the help of a 14-page impassioned plea for 'clean' climbing by top climber Doug Robinson in the first-ever Chouinard Equipment catalogue, the gamble paid off. Sales of pitons tailed off as climbers embraced the concept of 'clean' climbing.

Kris McDivitt joined Yvon and Melinda Chouinard at Chouinard Equipment in 1972 when the company was just a handful of people. As a skier she realised the need for enduring, protective and aesthetic outdoor clothing. This proved a catalyst for the creation of Patagonia climbing and skiing clothes. She subsequently became CEO, a position she held for twelve years until 1993. Kris remains associated with Patagonia as a board member of the parent company, The

Lost Arrow Corporation, and through Patagonia's involvement with the Chile wilderness conservation projects that she and her husband Doug Tompkins (founder of the North Face and Esprit) instigated.

The company grew rapidly under Kris' leadership until in 1990 she and Yvon decided that they wanted to try doing different things. They appointed a team of senior executives and handed over day-to-day management to them with only limited oversight. Patagonia went off the rails. The new leadership team took on significant debt financing and opened up markets and sales to the point where the company over-reached itself. In a period of less than two years the hitherto conservatively managed company hit serious financial difficulties.

Kris returned as CEO, and she and Yvon had to work extremely hard to bring the company back from the edge. They had to fire 120 people in order to keep the business afloat. It was a terrible experience for this family company which prided itself on its family-like working environment. Having turned the company around, Kris resigned as CEO in 1993 to pursue ambitious conservation initiatives in Southern Chile, along with her now husband Doug Tompkins.

In 1994 Yvon took the decision to switch to organically grown cotton across the entire product range within 18 months. Like his make-or-break decision more than twenty years earlier to stop making pitons, this was the sort of gamble that Yvon was to take again and again in the quest to reduce the environmental impact of his business operations.

"It was a big risk, and we could have lost a lot of business if we had failed," CEO Casey Sheahan recalls. "The price of the product was more expensive, the supply chain was infantile." Patagonia had to go direct to organic cotton farmers, and negotiate with the mills to process the raw product separately – a costly exercise.

Yet Patagonia's customers responded by buying more cotton garments. "We were hoping to create a market that would cause more farming and more agriculture to move toward pesticide-free manufacturing of cotton. And we did it, and that success has pushed us to keep finding more and more ways to reduce waste in the waste stream, to reduce pesticide use, and to find ways to recycle clothing."

It hasn't always been an easy choice. Patagonia abandoned work with a supplier on a promising odour control process based on silver

Nine.

anti-bacterial technology because of environmental concerns. The decision was very painful, says Rick Ridgeway, an old climbing partner of Yvon's and now Vice President of Environmental Initiatives in the company. "That was a choice guided by our mission statement," he said. "The mission statement is something that many people in this company use on a daily and weekly basis to always remind ourselves what our larger goals are." Patagonia now uses a product derived from crushed crab shells to do the same job.

Rick explains Patagonia's view of sustainability like this:

> There is no way around causing harm when you're a manufacturing business, and if you think it through it also means there is no such thing as sustainability in a business like this. We view sustainability as the horizon line that you are always walking towards. That is your goal: you are always trying to get there, but you can never arrive at it. Every time you take a step forward, it goes that little bit further away. So what you really want to do is always try to cause no unnecessary harm in every action you take.

This philosophical approach was typical of the business thinking we found at Patagonia. Yvon

Chouinard brought to his company a lesson he learned from risk sports: Never exceed your limits. He has also brought to business his Zen philosophy – focusing on perfecting the process rather than achieving an end goal. His model of stewardship and sustainability comes from yet another, Native American tradition. The Iroquois people had a seven-generation system of planning, and every major decision included input from a person who represented the seventh generation.

Rick told us that the environmental consciousness of Patagonia was rooted directly in Yvon's ability to foresee trends.

I suspect that talent is probably held by most successful entrepreneurs, but he is very talented in foretelling environmental trends especially. He's done that in partnership with his close friend Doug Tompkins. Those two together sitting down at a table or around a campfire on climbing trips and fishing, just comparing notes, sharing their own views, reinforcing each other, consequently had a huge influence on the direction this company has taken.

Doug Tompkins was also responsible for putting Yvon in touch with some key individuals who helped shape Patagonia's ethos. These included author and deep ecologist Jerry Mander, who subsequently joined Patagonia's first board of directors. Jerry had been the creative genius behind the hugely successful 1960s ad campaign by the Sierra Club to prevent the construction of dams in the Grand Canyon. "Jerry's thinking was most directly responsible for the mission statement that we have for this company today," Rick told us. "It still guides all of our actions and decisions."

Environmental activism is written into Patagonia's purpose and there's a palpable sense of that throughout the company. CEO Casey Sheahan came to Patagonia in 2004 after a career in the outdoor sports industry. He'd just spent four years as president of the Conservation Alliance, set up by Patagonia and three other outdoor equipment firms to donate 1% of sales to environmental activist groups. "At that time of my life, it was much more important to me than having a successful backpack business. I was in my early 40s, a time when some of us going through a mid-life crisis buy red sports cars. In my case, I felt this need to start giving back to the industry and the sports that had given me so much in my life."

Coming in to Patagonia, Casey found a whole set of likeminded people.

This is a private company owned by the Chouinard family, but in a greater sense the company is owned by its employees because they are so passionate and so imbued with this drive to save what's left of our planet. That is a greater and stronger ownership than even the owners themselves. Because we provide our employees with opportunities to do internships and to take time to work on these issues, that's what they do. They feel it deep: this is who they are, this is what they are about.

Lu Setnicka is married to a park ranger and used to work for the US National Park Services. She now handles HR for Patagonia, and she shared with us her experiences when she spent three weeks in Chile working on a Patagonia project with Doug and Kris Tompkins to set up a national park there.

It's basically a sheep ranch that's being converted to a national park, so the fences have to come out. So we are out there pulling fence in this magnificent landscape with mountains all around and the wind blowing and it's very dramatic. And I realised this is what John Muir, one of the founding fathers of the US national parks, must have felt when he went to Yosemite Valley that first time, when he started

Nine.

thinking we need to talk to Teddy Roosevelt about making this a national park.

The creation of a Patagonia National Park in Southern Chile and across the border in Argentina is Patagonia's most ambitious environmental initiative to date. And it's a way for the company to give back something durable to the region that inspired the development of its clothing line.

Casey Sheahan told us how it all started:

[Patagonia's first-ever CEO] Kris McDivitt Tompkins and her husband Doug Tompkins, in a philanthropic gesture, bought a tremendous amount of acreage in Argentina and Chile in the Patagonia region which they have donated to governments to create national parks. While we are not giving a lot of our company's money to the acquisition process, we are sending four groups a year down there to work and to do field work, tear out fences or support them in building a volunteer centre at the main park HQ. It is a paid internship programme for our employees that happens as many as four times a year. And of course we provide publicity through the website and catalogues, which we think is very exciting. Not very many companies are actually

trying to create national parks around the world!

Lu Setnicka also explained to us that the Patagonia internship programme, which every Patagonia employee can apply for, is a way to make the brand real. "We always talk about the heritage of the brand, and the story behind the brand, so for employees that have been hearing this for years and years, to actually have the opportunity to go down to Patagonia is really good."

The project also connects Patagonia employees from Ventura to Reno to Japan – Lu talked about the camaraderie built by the experience: "By the end we are just all having a blast together and it just emphasises the respect and the fun we have with the people we are working with."

The Patagonia internship programme isn't the only way Patagonia employees get involved. Sustainability and environmental care are written into everyone's job description, and are reviewed regularly. One retail manager did an internship watching primates in Thailand, while the company's print manager has been a volunteer on-board naturalist on commercial whale watching boats.

The company also offers training workshops for activist groups, and that ties back in to the internship programme, as Lu Setnicka explained:

When we started giving money away in 1985, we started spending time with activists, and we found what they really need is to learn how to market themselves better. So the next step might be a marketing conference, where we teach activists how to be better marketers, and now we are working with them more on a regular basis, maybe they need more than a cheque, maybe they can use a PR expert or a design person. So it keeps opening all these doors, and that's how the internship programme has grown. It's always about listening to what people need and then building programmes around that.

These initiatives build on Patagonia's belief that activism works, and that it's the job of business to help drive positive environmental change. From the early 1970s, when the company helped campaign for the successful restoration of the local Ventura River, Patagonia has dedicated resources to educating people about a different environmental issue every year. In 2001, building on the concept of the Conservation Alliance, Yvon co-founded 1% For the Planet, whose member businesses pledge to contribute 1% of annual sales to environmental organisations. Its slogan is 'keep earth in business'; today membership across the world has reached 930 companies.

At Patagonia, grants under the 1% programme are made twice a year, and recipients help to inform the company's annual environmental campaigns. Lisa Pike, who's in charge of Patagonia's external environmental grants, gave us an example: "We had a wild salmon campaign, and during that time the National Salmon Planning Act was going through the legislature, so we had several grantees who focused on that issue. In partnership with them we were able to generate 15,000 letters on behalf of healthy salmon recovery and work with them on ways to educate the public on the issue."

In keeping with Yvon's belief, that the most important agents for social change are the people, Lisa stressed that education has to be tied to actions.

You need to ask: What can I do about it – can I write a letter to my Senator? Can I look at a seafood watchcard and choose with my consumer dollars a different type of fish, one where stocks are regenerating? Whatever the action might be, the two have to go hand in hand. And when I took the job, I

Nine.

remember Yvon saying to me: when you think about creating a public environmental education campaign, you should remember two things: one, it has nothing to do with our product, it's not tied to selling our products; and two, you have to give people a call to action because of that activism component.

In a hugely competitive industry with cheap products continually nibbling away at the bottom, Patagonia has managed to stay ahead by continuous innovation. We asked CEO Casey Sheahan what the secret was: "Well, it's really driven by our Patagonia ambassadors, by all the athletes who are striving for certain performance characteristics," he said. "Yvon is still our top ambassador. He's not climbing as much as he used to, but he's fishing and still skiing, so he's always pushing us to find solutions to problems. Over time he has been supported by as many as 20 Patagonia ambassadors who are also providing that same input."

These ambassadors – top paddlers, climbers, fishermen, surfers and skiers across the world – test and provide feedback on new products. They also help to project Patagonia's environmental message.

Timmy O'Neil is one of the company's top climbing ambassadors, but on Patagonia's website and in its promotional video, instead of posing on top of an impressive mountain peak with an ice axe in his hand, he's goofing around in a green Superman bodysuit on the streets of Tokyo trying to persuade shoppers to recycle their underwear. It's to promote Patagonia's Common Threads Recycling Program, which encourages customers to return their worn-out underclothing (and now fleece and cotton clothing) so it can be made into new garments.

"[Timmy's] a great personality," says Casey. "And he's having fun with this. It doesn't have to be all gloom and doom. We need to be excited about this initiative, because we have a dwindling amount of raw materials to work with in the world, and it's only going to get worse."

Patagonia also forges strong partnerships with its suppliers. US-based Malden Mills and Japan-based Teijin make Patagonia's Synchilla fleece fabric; Casey explained to us how the symbiotic relationship works.

All the development is done here, and we work with fabric mills like Teijin and Malden Mills to develop innovative knits and wovens – solutions to keep people warm and dry primarily. They bring us what they think is the best new product first, because of our long-standing partnerships, and they give us some time exclusivity to market and promote those products, and we help them in turn, we push them forward to develop more recyclability or recycled content.

The partnership idea works throughout the company. Take the Patagonia catalogue, for example: the paper used is 40% recycled and certified to Forest Stewardship Council (FSC) standards. "The way we achieved that was by pushing our mill," Angela Weidman in the Creative Services department told us. "When we first started talking to them, they said well maybe we can get to 25-30% recycled content, and then before we knew it we were at 40%. Then they said what about FSC, we have all these small land owners supplying us, and next thing we knew they were at FSC, so I think we've been moving them forward. And as soon as they give us something we say OK, what's the next thing to move on."

Patagonia's commitment to sustainability has had a knock-on effect right through the supply chain. Casey Sheahan told us a great story about what happened as a result of Patagonia's licensing partnership with footwear manufacturer Wolverine World Wide.

I said there are going to be some requirements of this contract beyond your normal royalty arrangements. First, we're going to ask that you join 1% For The Planet. And the second part is, that we're going to ask you to build highly functional beautiful footwear that is as environmentally sensitive as possible and that uses the least toxic manufacturing processes. And they said OK, we think we can do that.

This is a billion dollar-plus footwear manufacturing outfit with factories all across China. So we get recycled outsoles, the highest quality leathers, recycled materials in the uppers, we use latex from the avea tree, and all these technologies and all these learnings from the Patagonia footwear are being translated over to their mainstream.

Casey told us that the changes at Wolverine went even further.

They used to have this pond behind their big corporate buildings in Grand Rapid, Michigan, that they used to poison every year because it was full of tadpoles and frogs and other animals and they realised we can't do that anymore. This has to be a natural sustained living environment. We can't have it just look blue because we dyed it a chemical blue – this has to be a real pond.

Patagonia has always made a point of sharing its technologies with other

Nine.

companies, and Yvon Chouinard is a sought-after speaker at top business schools. He's helped create awareness about sustainability that's touched companies ranging from small family-owned businesses to retail giant Wal-mart. "Yvon Chouinard is really one of the greatest ambassadors for this concept that there is," said CEO Casey Sheahan. "When Yvon speaks at Harvard Business School or at a university lecture somewhere, there is this whole connectivity chain that starts."

Casey told us that Patagonia gets about three calls a week from companies interested in purchasing the business, but the answer is always no. "We don't want short term thinking being applied to a company that is trying to be here for another hundred years," he explained. "It's just not us. I go back to conversations I've had with Yvon about if you do the right thing you will be profitable. You will be profitable because consumers will appreciate the effort you made to build a better, more sustainable product, and will pay for it."

And they do, all over the world. Outside of the United States, Patagonia has a presence in Europe, Japan and South America, due in no small part to the company's environmental stand, according to Casey:

Our environmental positioning has resonated hugely in both Europe and Japan and that has really given us a leg up. We didn't pander to them, we didn't dilute the product itself or the image of the brand; we wanted them to buy into the southern Californian mountain surf lifestyle for what it was. The environmental side of it is key; elements of Japanese society really relate to that.

But growth is not a key driver for Patagonia. Ever since the 1990 financial difficulties, Patagonia has kept the lid on growth and borrowing. Casey again: "We think natural organic growth is achievable through our direct channels and through some wholesale, and that should be just fine. The demand for the brand right now is as strong as it's ever been, and it's interesting: this is truly one of those cradle-to-the-grave kinds of brands. There's a psychographic around the consumer that is more important than the demographic."

Looking forward, Casey sees the company's major concerns as environmental: global warming and peak oil. "We are thinking about everything involved in our supply chain, whether it's going to be feasible to keep building products, sourcing fabrics in the US and Japan and sending them to China, shipping them there and to El Salvador, or whether we should be getting more into a local manufacturing scenario again."

Casey Sheahan believes Patagonia's response to the environmental challenges ahead has to be to spread the word:

> We really have an obligation to help educate. I think there is this feeling that because it has been on the news, because of the movie *An Inconvenient Truth*, in some ways it's becoming a mainstream belief. I don't believe that at all. I think that only 5% of the population is actually aware of what a hugely and powerful environmental crisis this could be. And the other 95% of the population has no idea and won't know until the water is rising around their ankles!

Reflections

Along with The Body Shop, Patagonia is the longest established and best known of our enterprise set. They are the quintessential sustainable enterprise with origins in and an orientation towards environmental activism. The importance of sustainability philosophy as an underpinning for the purpose of a sustainable enterprise became clear to us at Patagonia. Their philosophy was carefully crafted with wide involvement and became a guiding light for enterprise development.

We admired their constant attention to innovation, efficiency and cost minimisation in everything they do, and the way they bring partners into their innovation process both by pressure of expectation and by demonstrating mutual benefits. Innovation is enhanced by their network of high performance ambassadors who test the products under extreme conditions and provide honest feedback. We enjoyed the way they use new and up-and-coming designers to keep the designs and products fresh, and this too is a source of innovation.

The spirit of positivity was perhaps the stand-out experience, created and nurtured through a family-like environment, symbolised by the onsite kindergarten. At the heart of the enterprise is environmental activism, and it is here that they seek to make a difference through campaigns, stories, the products themselves and the work of their foundation. We believe that their approach to running the foundation and their donations to environmental organisations constitutes best practice. Staff are directly involved in making the decisions on what to fund, and are actively involved in environmental projects as participants themselves.

Ten.

Dilmah Tea

"We say that business is a matter of human service, and we believe that in all things we do in business. Sometimes you see a tree with an orchid growing on it, it's a beautiful flower, it doesn't kill the tree, they exist in symbiosis. As a business, we need to grow and develop like the orchid. If the community in which we exist doesn't develop with us, then we become a parasite. And we never want to be in that situation."

— *Dilhan C. Fernando, Marketing Director of Dilmah Tea, and head of the Dilmah Foundation*

We were stopped seven times by soldiers of the Sri Lankan military on the way from Colombo International airport to our city hotel. Each time our vehicle was carefully checked for explosives before we were sent on our way with a friendly wave.

For more than 25 years, the country was wracked by a bitter civil war fuelled by ethnic tensions between the majority Sinhalese and the minority Tamil population, which is largely based in the north and east of the country. But in May 2009, government forces took the last remaining stronghold of the rebel Liberation Tigers of Tamil Eelam (LTTE), and declared victory. The military defeat of the Tamil Tigers signalled a possible end to the violence which is thought to have claimed the lives of more than 80,000 people[33].

It is against this background of developing nation unrest that the improbable story of Dilmah Tea has unfolded. Dilmah has become one of the top ten international tea brands in the world, occupying a unique position in a global industry dominated by first world multi-national corporations and British colonial era brands. With more than $500 million in revenue from 93 countries, Dilmah has doubled in size since 2000 and enjoys annual 15% growth in profit and revenue.

Sri Lanka remains the world's leading exporter of tea by value, though Kenya and now China export higher volumes. Tea represents 25% of Sri Lanka's exports and is of vital importance to the economy. Until Dilmah, Sri Lanka's tea exports were predominantly bulk based for first world nations to extract the value through packaging and brand. This producer nation was relegated to commodity production, at subsistence-level returns.

Founded in Sri Lanka in 1988, Dilmah Tea has transformed an industry once a byword for first world exploitation of developing countries into a vehicle for adding value to the local communities that produce tea. For founder and owner Merrill J. Fernando, ethics are the cornerstone of his business – and, he believes, the driving force behind his company's success. "The more I share, the more I give, the more I have received," he told us as we took tea with him on the porch of his colonial era villa in Colombo.

Tea turned to the ritual G&T[34] as we listened fascinated to the tale of the origins of Dilmah. Born in 1930 in what was then the British colony of Ceylon, Merrill Fernando was one of the first Sri Lankans to be selected for training in Mincing Lane, London, as a tea taster. He subsequently worked for British-owned tea companies before setting up his own bulk tea business at the age of 32, supplying the world's major tea brands. His company, Merrill J. Fernando & Co, was the only Sri Lankan company to become one of the top 10 tea exporters in the country.

Merrill's son Dilhan shared with us a glimpse of the spiritual bedrock on which his father built the business:

> Many of the values that my father built into his business, which he shared and taught my brother and I and which he fulfils through his business today, are those that are rooted in the values inculcated in him by his parents and by his Christian beliefs. This is important since he was born to middle class, rural parents and he is very clearly a product of that environment in that his mother, my grandmother, was noted as a philanthropist. This was not in any significant way or scale but rather a gently benevolent form which I recall was mainly in sharing food, sharing medicines, taking care of neighbours. All essentially simple values of family and what differentiates us as humans.

Sri Lanka's tea plantations, including those belonging to multinational corporations and those belonging to Merrill, were all nationalised in the 1970s, after the election

Ten.

of a socialist government. This proved a disaster for the nation as planters left, many for Kenya where a competitor tea industry was established that now rivals Sri Lanka's in size. Plantations were split up. Production dramatically declined. But Merrill was undeterred by the nationalisation of his estates. He launched Dilmah, named after his sons Dilhan and Malik, using his expertise as a tea planter and tea taster to select the finest Ceylon teas and in this way offer consumers a choice of a quality, single origin and unblended tea. The prevailing trend was towards commoditisation and cost cutting with quality of tea as the primary victim. Merrill took a directly opposite course in spite of the opposition of the government, bulk tea customers and vested interests in the tea industry. Positivity and determination rebuilt the enterprise.

Merrill first observed the dysfunctionality in the industry in the 1950s, when he was doing his training in London.

When I learnt tea tasting and trading in tea, I could not understand why we were exporting our original tea to England and all these countries for value addition, for creating wealth in those countries by branding and marketing. We could have done

that very well, to great benefit for the country. But industry – which was owned by the British at that time – said you grow and we'll make the money!

I saw an opportunity to bring real Ceylon tea to the consumer. I knew that if I marketed my own Ceylon tea, I would cut out all the middlemen and take my crop direct to the market – fresh packed at source like no other tea.

Merrill understated the enormity of this challenge as he told us the story. The commitment to '100% pure Ceylon, single origin, garden fresh, unblended tea' calls for tea, fresh picked, to be packed within a few days. By contrast, for most other tea brands which are usually packed offshore from where the tea is produced, it takes three to seven months from harvest and production on the estate to packing and supply to supermarkets. Moreover Sri Lanka suffers from a creaking infrastructure, antiquated labour laws and, until very recently, a civil war that imposed frequent military disruption to supply lines. Undeterred, Merrill steadfastly built Dilmah's own infrastructure, manufacturing plants and transport fleet to be in control of his own destiny. Some shippers abandoned Sri Lanka because of concerns about safety as the civil war conflict extended to sea battles and piracy. Freight prices increased by up to 50%. Dramatically increasing volumes and price premiums through a leading brand positioning enabled Dilmah to live its purpose despite these difficulties.

And the purpose is to bring back single-origin, quality tea. The challenge is global leadership of quality tea. Today, Dilmah exports its single-origin Ceylon tea to 93 countries, and has set up subsidiary companies in New Zealand, where it's the number one brand, and in Australia, where it's the number two.

Dilmah was the first global consumer brand to be developed from any tea or coffee producing country, and the first brand to be owned by farmers in a producing country. "The significant difference between all other brands of tea and Dilmah is that we are farmers taking our crop to the market, and we take it with pride," Merrill told us. "This is our tea: we care for it from the tea garden right up to your cup."

"The idea is to create a win-win-win situation", says Dilhan, who with his brother Malik has followed his father into the family business.

When he started the business, my father set out a covenant to benefit the community, to benefit the industry and to benefit the consumer. To some people it seems a very difficult proposition, but to us it's the most simple thing on earth. We are producers: we should be able to take our produce to market to the customer, we should have the ability to explain because we grow it, and so we know about it. We love it, so we like to talk about it. It's like my father, when he starts talking about tea – non-stop!

It may be a simple proposition, but it's not been an easy road to success. When Merrill imported the first teabagging machine into Sri Lanka, he faced huge opposition from the Sri Lankan Tea Board and his old clients. "It took me 35 years to launch my own brand of tea," quips Merrill. He had the dream but simply could not get past bureaucracy and an industry that saw its role as raw material producer for overseas packers who apparently held the keys to the consumer market.

The government and my colleagues in the tea trade said you are mad: people with big companies which are buying our bulk tea and branding and marketing will stop buying our tea. Four years later, when they saw the results, everybody else was trying to do the same thing.

The benefits flow in many directions. Doing away with the middleman means that all profits remain

Ten.

with the local developing nation producers instead of flowing into the pockets of multinational company shareholders. Merrill has seen at first-hand the results of shareholder pressure to increase profits and reduce margins. "The multinationals buy raw materials as cheaply as possible and squeeze the producer flat to the ground. Their profits grow out of the misery of the producer."

Dilmah does things differently. Merrill strongly believes that a sustainable tea industry must look after the interests of the producers. And he counts it as a strength that he lives alongside his community.

I see every day what happens to producers as the multinational big companies get bigger and bigger, making more profits. The farmers might be starving or they might be unable to educate or clothe their children, but that is not their concern. Unless you live in that environment, you don't feel for it.

Merrill says Dilmah's single-origin 100% pure Ceylon tea is his antidote to the multinational, multi-origin blends which line the supermarket shelves. "What do the big multinationals, big brands, big traders do? They bring the quality of tea down and they make it a commodity." He points out that a multi-origin product can contain tea from up to 35 different places of origin. "Origins are selected not for quality, but for price," he says. "So countries which sell their crop at 10 cents per pound, it's their tea that goes into those teabags." Just like fine wine, the finest teas are grown on their own estates.

Real Ceylon tea is the most expensive tea in the world, often 20-40% higher in price than teas from other regions. So when you walk into a tea aisle anywhere, you will see all the brand names. What's inside, the origin of the tea is never clear. They cannot buy quality tea, so they sell the brand. And they can bring prices down by dropping their quality substantially, so their brand will become a monopoly player in the market. It is almost impossible to buy fine quality tea in supermarkets today. Tea has become a commodity. One pays for brand names, not for quality!

Even the production of tea has changed. Most producers have been switched to a new manufacturing system called CTC (cut, twist and curl) which brings out the colour of the tea quickly, without having to wait for it to brew in the traditional manner. Dilmah teas are produced using traditional orthodox methods. They are handpicked with just the two leaves and the bud where the full flavour is concentrated. Merrill abhors CTC teas which he describes as 'soulless'. We learnt to distinguish these subtle flavours with a tea tasting experience of more than 100 teas in the heart of the Dilmah Colombo factory. We will never drink CTC tea again!

The big losers in all this, says Merrill, are the consumers. "We have unhappy customers, because whatever brand they switch to tastes just the same, and they have no opportunity to drink real Ceylon tea."

Dilmah's response to commoditisation of the tea industry has been to go back to the traditional, authentic heritage of tea-making. "When you drink Dilmah, you drink real tea," explains Merrill. "It is a little bit more expensive than multi-origin blended or commodity tea because it is pure Ceylon tea – after tasting Dilmah, people often tell me that is the tea my grandmother raised me on. For the consumer, instead of going from one brand to another, all the same damn tea, they now have the traditional quality Ceylon tea. So that is what has made a difference to the tea trade. And that is the success of Dilmah – the quality and the integrity of the brand."

Merrill described to us how his multinational competitors put pressure on governments to create regulatory barriers to his tea, and how they sought to drive Dilmah out of the market by price cutting. "One of the rumours the big brands spread when I started out, was that this is a third world country product and unhygienic, don't drink Dilmah tea, reject it," Merrill told us. "Yet our factory is probably one of the best facilities you'd see anywhere in the world." We can attest to that following our comprehensive factory visit[35] where each step of the process was carefully explained.

Merrill told us a story about standing up to the big players.

> When Bob Hawke was Prime Minister of Australia, they told him this third world country is dumping cheap tea in the market and we've got thousands of people employed in the industry and they will lose their jobs. So I sent a note through a friend to Bob Hawke, saying these are the facts: We are bringing back the number one quality tea that Australians enjoyed 25 years ago, our conditions are very hygienic, and the industry in Australia doesn't employ more than 200 people in the tea packing industry, so there's no question of losing jobs. So Bob Hawke told the multinational that if the consumer was going to benefit he'd have no objection.

The pressure however continues. Recently, one New Zealand

Ten.

supermarket chain stopped stocking Dilmah tea because of pressure from the big first world brands. The result was unexpected. "Store managers found their customers were going elsewhere to buy Dilmah tea and they also bought other goods at the same time," says Merrill. "So they persuaded the supermarket to let them stock Dilmah again, and they are doing well. But it's not a level playing field," he adds.

Merrill's son Dilhan takes a reflective approach to the ways of multinational corporations, but wonders whether the philosophy that underpins them is simply incompatible with sustainability:

> We also understand that you cannot blame multinational corporations and their employees for their often misguided and unsustainable actions. No one is born good or bad but rather a product of their environment. The environment in which these people operate is one which respects profit and profit only. Taking into consideration the average lifespan of a CEO (in Europe I understand it's eighteen months to two years), the significance of performance on that narrow benchmark becomes even more apparent. Business as defined by capitalist theory and so simply encapsulated by Friedman in

his famous statement 'the business of business is business' externalises social and environmental aspects. The individuals that compose these corporations therefore simply do not have the means to internalise these aspects since the system in which they operate is not geared to doing so.

> It takes therefore a very different – many would say more primitive and definitely more human – approach to embrace that wider responsibility as part of the business process. I think this fundamentally sets family business and owner operated business apart from corporations.

Integrity has been fundamental for Dilmah, it is part of the company's commitment to caring for its stakeholders. "The most important rule I followed is absolute honesty in what I said and in what I did," explains Merrill. "If I told you this is the freshest tea in the world, then it IS the freshest tea in the world. I did no marketing talk. Consumers are my best friends and support me. They keep me in business and they let me do all this charity work I am doing. I owe them a lot and I will never tell them an untruth."

Merrill's commitment to telling the truth has prompted him to speak out against the fair trade movement.

He sees fair trade labelling as simply another way to enhance the brands and brand premiums of first world multinational corporations. He contrasts Dilmah's independent, value-added operation, where the benefits of marketing and branding are shared with the producers, with the dependency engendered by so-called fair trade. "Fair trade is a marketing gimmick," he says. "There are about four or five middlemen between the farmer and the consumer. All of them take money. What is left to go to the producer? There is nothing fair about that trade."

He believes the fair trade movement, like aid, simply reinforces the disempowerment of poor and underdeveloped countries. "Foreign aid has taught us to submit," he says. "We don't raise our heads. I raised my head and I'm in a very different position today."

Fair trade certification by the FairTrade Foundation guarantees that estate owners pay tea pickers at least the local minimum wage, while maintaining safe working and living conditions. We support the intent of fair trade and any attempt to safeguard the human rights of the people of producer nations. Yet we also understand Merrill's passionately held reservations. His philosophy of marketing Dilmah tea direct to customers and consumers is designed to ensure that the company and its people are free from post-colonial exploitation. Dilmah reinvests in the tea gardens and the country to benefit the workers and the economy of Sri Lanka through wages, taxes and charitable activities. For Dilmah this is truly ethical trade.

Some 500,000 people in Sri Lanka depend on agriculture for their living, mostly in the tea and rubber plantations. It's a difficult life for low pay. Sri Lanka has the highest costs of any tea producer nation, twice as high as Vietnam, 75% higher than Kenya and 50% higher than India. Some 60% of costs per kilo are for labour. By contrast with some other tea producer nations, Sri Lanka has strong welfare and labour laws, legislation outlawing child labour and environmental protection laws. Wages are set at a national level by agreement with the trade unions.

During our visit we drove to the middle of the island to stay for a few nights at the tea gardens on the Tientsin Estate. Our home was the plantation manager's bungalow from the bygone colonial era, literally and metaphorically at the heart of where the tea story begins. The gardens exhibit an almost surreal calm, harmony and beauty that dates back more than 150 years. The

Ten.

tea plants spread as far as the eye can see for 187,000 hectares across the country. Purposeful rows of harmonious shades of lush green roll up and down the hills and valleys in manicured symmetry.

This harmony stands in stark contrast to the political landscape contested by the minority, mainly Hindu Tamil population and the majority, mainly Buddhist Sinhalese. And at the time of our visit the hillsides were bare of the colourful sari-clad women tea pickers due to a national strike of mostly Tamil pickers that threatened the industry.

Merrill wants disputes like these settled as quickly as possible. He knows how quickly in a commoditised industry the major manufacturers will switch their choice of supply to the lowest cost, lowest wage economy. He sees the best solution to this low wage commodity trap is for Sri Lanka to follow the Dilmah example and add value to its commodities through brand, marketing and supply chain, rather than exporting raw materials for others to reap the benefit. The strike was uneasily resolved before we left and picking resumed. The low wage problem endures.

A family business located within the community, Dilmah's philosophy is summed up by Merrill: "I have a conscience; I have a commitment to improve the life of the planters, producers and farmers."

"We refer to them [the planters, producers and farmers] as the Dilmah family," adds Dilhan. "We have a very flat organisation structure in our office, and except for my father whom by tradition every staff member wants to call Sir, everyone else is called by our first names. And it works well, because that's more natural. So when we go down to the factory, we see our passion and commitment reflected in the work of the humblest worker, even the person who puts the barcode on the pack. If they don't do their job, we are sunk. So there is no them and us, it is all us. And I think they understand that it's not just words, but we really mean it."

Dilmah backs up this sense of family kinship with its tradition of paying the school clothing and books expenses for the children of any of its employees who cannot afford it. The company has also helped to cushion the spiralling cost of living in Sri Lanka by offering staff subsidies on basic foodstuffs such as rice, and it provides in-house medical care with free or subsidised medication.

Dilhan expands on this philosophy to emphasise the importance of simplicity in business:

An attribute that we believe to be fundamental to sustainable enterprise, in addition to the independent spirit, activist orientation, clear set of beliefs and passionate commitment to the consumer is 'simplicity'. To explain, in observing my father and the example that he has set for us, simplicity and, associated with that, humility, in our approach to business is essential for us to remain a sustainable enterprise. That is simplicity not in a general sense, but in terms of adherence and a belief in human values, rather than those that are acquired as the business becomes more successful and one's image and status grow. I think there is a dehumanising influence that business success has on the beneficiaries of that success.

A parallel in politics would be the reality that 'power corrupts'; that parallel is also applicable to business, because 'powerful' businesses seem to confer upon their leaders a sense of irresponsibility that often ends in disaster. This is a generalisation, but it is also something we observe in varying degrees and hence determines that everything from the type of car we drive, the publicity we allow ourselves, is strictly regulated to maintain the simplicity and passionate commitment to our business, humanitarian and environmental objectives without any distraction.

Merrill strongly believes that companies have a responsibility to share their success with the wider community. To this end, he has set up a charitable foundation, the MJF Charitable Foundation, chaired by Dilhan who personally supervises the Foundation's work. A minimum of 10% of the company's pre-tax profits goes into the Foundation to fund scholarships and community health, education and development projects. Merrill also contributes substantial funds personally to these projects. In 2005, the Foundation made four and a half million dollars available for self-sustaining projects in isolated communities devastated by the December 2004 tsunami. Amongst thousands of projects are micro-credit schemes to encourage villagers to switch to growing more profitable cash crops, such as vanilla, the provision of breast screening facilities in Colombo, building schools and hospitals, and the establishment of homes for elderly people.

The wartorn north-eastern region of Sri Lanka was the worst hit by the tsunami. Whilst aid agencies were reluctant to send assistance into the conflict zone, Dilmah saw the need

Ten.

and sent in a fleet of its trucks with emergency supplies to Mullaitivu in the north, as well as to other affected parts of Sri Lanka in the east and south. Dilhan led the project, including personally leading some of the convoys.

During our visit we were privileged to be part of the Fernando family's frequent and favourite weekend activity of visiting their various community projects to inspire and encourage. We celebrated the annual Christmas gift-giving with the people of Negombo, Merrill's home village. We were touched by the reverence in which the family is held as we participated in the blessing and opening of a home for elderly people at Sadhasarana. Such homes were never needed in the past because the elderly were cared for through the extended family tradition. But this is now breaking down with the extensive emigration that Sri Lanka has experienced. The Dilmah philosophy is to respond immediately to emergent needs that are not being met by government.

We were energised by the pragmatic business clarity that the Foundation brings to its grassroots enterprise development. We visited the little fishing village of Idhiwara, the scene of much tsunami damage. Local inshore fishing has been damaged by the tsunami and by overfishing of local waters by overseas vessels, so the villagers have to go further offshore to catch their fish which means only a short fishing time before the catch spoils in the sultry heat of summer. Then local middlemen make most of the profit by taking the fish to market. The fishermen struggle for a subsistence living; an experience that is close to Merrill's heart from his tea industry experience. The solution was an ice maker and a refrigerated van to take the catch to market. The components of the ice maker were supplied by Dilmah together with project supervision, while the villagers supplied the person power and Dilmah micro-credit energised the process. All was undertaken in careful consultation with the villagers so that they owned the project and process.

All these projects have one thing in common: they must be sustainable. "For the Foundation, success is first of all to operate within a community and to leave it self-sustaining, so not dependent on us for further aid, but a community that regains its pride, and we want them to have clear focused goals," explains Dilhan. "It's like when you spin off a business, you want it to take on a life of its own. The point is, they must be sustainable thereafter."

Dilhan runs a deliberately no-frills operation. The Foundation shies away from what Dilhan calls fanfare, although the company has recently revised its policy of not talking about the work of the Foundation and has produced a booklet for customers containing Dilhan's own photographs and his own account of the projects undertaken. He showed us the photo album, pointing out himself and his team of four, all in simple white t-shirts, helping to build a free hospital and centre for abused women.

"They're not fantastic shots, but I have a little Nikon D70 and it's my hobby," he apologises. "We don't follow the model of most aid agencies, because if they get a dollar they spend 40-50% of that on infrastructure and administration. Our prime criteria are, to get help to the people who are the most isolated, who really have no other options."

Dilhan tells of a Foundation project to build 900 houses in a war-stricken part of Batticoloa, the largest tsunami resettlement area in Sri Lanka. "Eleven NGOs had promised to build these houses, but nobody did it, so by the time we came on the scene two years later nothing had happened and these people were still in temporary shelters in 40 degree daytime temperatures."

The Foundation decided to work directly with each of the 900 families, providing the equipment, materials and guidance to build new houses. "It's called an owner driven housing scheme," explains Dilhan. "When the first family started up, they waited for an auspicious day and you could see the father, the mother and the grandmother all out there measuring and building their own house."

Dilhan pointed to a picture of a little boy carrying a tray of bananas.

> We had just finished building the roads, and we came to meet the first families and I got out of my vehicle to talk to them, and this little boy turned up out of nowhere with this tray of bananas. And I was thinking they've been affected by the tsunami, they've been messed around by all sorts of agencies, and he brings me bananas. I believe I've become enriched by seeing what I have had the privilege of seeing.

Contributing to building communities like the one in Batticoloa is a way to ensure that Dilmah remains a beautiful orchid, rather than becoming a parasite. Dilhan is convinced that his personal involvement in Dilmah's community outreach work enables him to

Ten.

connect better both with the communities that benefit from the work of the Foundation and with the customers who make that work possible.

It's actually a delight to talk directly to customers, when I have the opportunity to talk to them about variety in tea, the ethics in tea and the fact that there is a lot more behind your cup of tea than just your $1.99 or $2.99 on the shelf, and how it impacts on lives of others. When I see people transforming their understanding of tea then step by step, by word of mouth, others get to know about it – and that is really our objective – to enthuse and involve consumers in tea by sharing with them the beauty and artisanal values in tea, you could say a producer's perspective on tea.

It was fascinating to realise how the MJF Charitable Foundation is not simply a charity that exists for the purpose of fulfilling the Dilmah humanitarian service commitment. Rather, the specific emphasis is on using Dilmah's expertise and networks as a successful business to assist marginalised, underprivileged communities in Sri Lanka and beyond. Dilhan explains:

Each of our projects is guided by the principle of sustainability, in relation to the project itself and its long term viability, the environment, the dignity of the beneficiaries. This is achieved by applying learnings we gain through our business, you could say by applying the same techniques we use in our business, with the same commitment and energy, to solving humanitarian problems.

The growth and success of Dilmah implies similar expansion of their humanitarian and environmental commitments, consistent with the commitment of 10-15% of profit. More recently they have expanded the horizon of these contributions beyond Sri Lanka to assist other developing nations. For example one project is to assist the fledgling and heavily exploited Nepal tea industry, as Dilhan told us:

For decades Nepal has been trying to make something of its tea industry although it has suffered at the hands of competing producers and international brands which would rather see Nepal remain a cheap source of raw material. At the recent meeting in China of the FAO Intergovernmental Group on Tea, I met with a representative of the Himalayan Orthodox Tea Producers Association in Nepal. We designed a plan whereby Dilmah would assist the industry, to gain an identity and begin to add value at origin. Currently most of the production from Nepal is sold as raw material to either Indian or European buyers.

Consumers merit a special place in the Dilmah 'family'. Merrill explains Dilmah's philosophy like this:

> If we as family companies do not demonstrate business ethics, corporate responsibility and social justice, other people who work for shareholders will not and cannot practise that. We need profits to sustain our business, but we need to share the success with everyone associated with our business, not only those who work for our business but those who keep us in business and they are the consumers.

Success for Dilmah means spreading the message that there is another way to do business. Whether it's improving the lives of the least fortunate through the work of the Foundation, or ensuring tea producers get a fair share of the proceeds, or bringing excellent tea at a fair price to consumers around the world, Dilmah imbues its work with integrity and passion for the product.

Merrill says he receives hundreds of letters from customers, traders and companies which have been inspired to change their views on business because of Dilmah. "I've had so many people and consumers saying we love Dilmah, not only because of the quality of tea, but because of what you do."

Dilmah has recently established a ready-to-drink iced tea factory, the first of its kind in a tea plantation, and has plans to build a decaffeination plant to reduce the company's reliance on overseas suppliers. Merrill's aim is to grow Dilmah to cover every segment of the tea industry, while retaining its core values of integrity and honesty. The company has recently opened 65 'T Bars' around the world, with a view to bringing the experience of 100% pure Ceylon, single-origin, garden fresh, unblended tea directly to consumers, and to tell the Dilmah story and to strengthen the brand.

Merrill concludes:

> My greatest success is I have out there very happy consumers who enjoy the quality of tea and equally my philosophy behind Dilmah. And the greatest success in my business area up to now is to see people around who have benefited from the Foundation, and that satisfaction never came from my money or profits.
>
> When we come into this world we bring nothing with us and we take

Ten.

nothing with us. Therefore the wealth we acquire while we serve here, must be given to those who work with us, to the needy and towards alleviating poverty.

There is a palpable harmony, calmness and determination of spirit that infuses Dilmah Tea, reminiscent of the aura of the tea gardens themselves. To be there is to feel the authentic power of the story of origin. The challenge of global leadership in truly ethical, single-origin, quality tea is only part of the story. Dilmah is role modelling to developing nations what can be achieved through vertical integration and to the world what can be achieved through a humbler, more sustainable way of conducting business.

Reflections

A passion for quality was the departure point for Dilmah as it has been for all the enterprises in our set. The development of the brand story, construction of efficient production and distribution facilities, and the careful creation of win-win partnerships and channels to market grew the business. To grow a family business to the global scale and brand recognition of Dilmah from a developing nation base is extraordinary. To do so in the face

of the exceptional lengths to which multinational first world competitors went to ensure they failed puts Dilmah in a class of its own. Social activism in health and education and a commitment to nation-building are the focus of Dilmah's performance. Social activism contributes to workforce wellbeing and to the brand story and therefore to the company profitability. But this is not the reason for the focus. The Fernandos simply believe this is the right way to do business.

2.

In **Part Two** we explore the nature of Sustainable Enterprise success and develop a theory of Sustainable Peak Performance designed to enable enterprises to maximise their performance for profit, people and the planet.

Chapter 11

In Chapter 11 we explain the overall theory, and then in the following six chapters we explore each of the Principles of Sustainable Peak Performance by reference to practical examples from the stories in Part One.

Final Chapter

In the final chapter we argue the importance of just doing something. We conclude with brief stories of some of the lessons we learned while implementing Sustainable Peak Performance ideas in a variety of companies.

Eleven.

Sustainable Enterprise

In the introductory chapter we used the term 'sustainable enterprise' to refer to new, innovative or pioneering ventures that create value for entrepreneurs, their people, society and the environment through addressing unsustainability challenges and opportunities. Sustainable enterprise is about how business can do well financially while at the same time contributing to making the world a better place. By studying successful enterprises founded on sustainability principles from around the world we expected to learn lessons for entrepreneurs (Figure 1). We hoped that a pattern of attitudes and actions would emerge that could be formulated as a theory of sustainable enterprise success. Theory is simply an explanation of cause and effect and an understanding of the relationships between concepts. A theory of sustainable enterprise success will be based on a set of interrelated concepts that will explain how to build an enterprise based on sustainability principles to global success. Great theory should be simple. There is nothing so practical as great theory because it predicts the most likely path to success and provides a basis for action.

When we embarked on this sustainable enterprise odyssey we had no idea whether a generalisable theory would emerge from these lessons, or whether the process of enterprise development would prove as individualistic as the iconoclastic founders. It was therefore thrilling to us to observe a consistent pattern of characteristics from the first few interview visits. You will have sensed that pattern in reading the stories in the preceding chapters.

Beyond a theory of sustainable enterprise development for new sustainable enterprises, we also hoped for two more outcomes from the project:

1. That a theory of sustainable enterprise success formulated from companies founded on sustainability principles could also be applicable to more traditional companies that seek to transform towards a sustainability agenda.

2. That through learning about the characteristics of successful sustainable enterprises, people will be able to make more informed choices about which

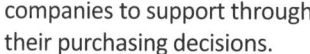

companies to support through their purchasing decisions.

In this chapter we explain our philosophy of sustainable enterprise, upon which sustainable enterprise success can be built. Sustainable enterprise is about economics, equity and the environment, or more colloquially – profit, people and the planet. This trilogy is common language in sustainability circles.

However, the intertwining of these elements is the subject of some controversy. 'Weak sustainability' thinking calls for a trade-off between all three, closely associated usually with calls for environmental concerns not to impact significantly upon economic outcomes. Such outcomes are typically measured in conventional terms through the medium of historic cost accounting. The fact that the externality costs in lost natural capital and societal degradation are entirely ignored by conventional accounting is discounted. Real sustainability thinking spurns the idea of trade-off and seeks outcomes that benefit or

Figure 1 – Sustainable Enterprisers

1 **Anita Roddick**
The Body Shop

2 **Tim Smit**
Eden Project

3 **Alan Bougen &
Claude Stratford**
Comvita

4 **Peri Drysdale**
Snowy Peak

5 **Gary Hirshberg**
Stonyfield Farm

6 **Yvon Chouinard**
Patagonia

7 **Jonathon Porritt**
Forum for the
Furture

8 **Dan Storper**
Putumayo

9 **Merrill J Fernando
& Dilhan Fernando**
Dilmah Tea

Eleven.

do no harm to all three elements. Sustainable enterprises seek to make substantial profits, while contributing to societal wellbeing and enhancing the environment.

Sustainable enterprisers know that sustainability is about economics as much as it is about the environment and equity; they know this personally and profoundly through putting everything they own on the line for the sake of their sustainable enterprise dreams.

Equity is about fairness, human rights and social responsibility. It can be summed up simply in the time-honoured American declaration of human rights – "life, liberty and the pursuit of happiness". Happiness is an important component of sustainability and will be revisited later in this chapter (and will be revisited in chapter sixteen). Equity is in the eye of the beholder and is time and context contingent. For example, the British and European

Figure 2 – Sustainable enterprise dynamics

colonists of the 18th and 19th centuries saw it as their God-given right to appropriate by force the resources and even the people of their subjugated colonies. Some corporations appear to have a similar agenda today. What is seen as socially equitable today remains a function of culture, political and religious credo, and increasingly, popular reaction. Sustainable enterprises develop a point of view on where they stand on the social equity issues of our time – for example fair trade, health and safety, child labour, GMOs[36], animal rights, third world debt.

Environmental sustainability is often confused with sustainability taken as a whole; or sustainability is regarded as being just about the environment. Former US Vice-President Al Gore's[37] overwhelmingly successful publicity on the challenges of climate change has tended to exacerbate this emphasis. Sustainable enterprises realise that climate change is but one dimension of environmental sustainability, and that the environment is but one of four dynamics of sustainable development. They realise that social and environmental issues are irrevocably intertwined, and that it is invariably necessary to approach their resolution in an integrated way such that the needs of people and

opportunities for enterprise are met ethically and economically, and in a manner that nurtures or does no harm to the natural environment.

In Figure 2 we add ethics to economy, equity and the environment. Ethics is the branch of philosophy that deals with choices about how to live. We see sustainability as being about ethical choices.

Economic value is created through ethical business activity. The environment is protected or enhanced while at the same time creating equitable outcomes for people, organisations and society. In the long term, economic value will only be created and sustained through the creation of social value. If social value, however perceived, is not created, people will simply stop buying. Traditional economic and accounting models ignore environmental costs as 'externalities' unless priced in through legal or contractual means (which most are not). An increasing number of consumers are well ahead of business and legal norms in this regard, and are voting with their wallets away from brands that are seen as risking their health and well being or sense of social justice.

These four dynamics create four concepts of sustainable enterprise

Eleven.

action illustrated in the model in Figure 2.

Ethics and the environment combine to form the concept of environmental ethics – a consideration of the moral relationship between people and the natural environment.

Ethics and equity combine in the form of human rights – the fundamental rights and freedom to which all people are entitled, often considered to include the rights to life, liberty, freedom of thought and expression, and justice.

Equity and economics combine to form the concept of social responsibility – organisations should embrace the interests of society by taking responsibility for the effect of their activities on customers, employees, shareholders and communities. In this way their own long-term profitability will be maximised through protecting their right to operate, through enhanced brand and through motivated people.

Economic value and environment combine to form the concept of eco-effectiveness – emulating nature by ensuring the 'cradle to cradle'[38] use of resources such that the concept of waste does not exist; the outputs or unused resources from one process become the inputs for the next. This concept stands in contra-distinction to eco-efficiency (creating more goods with fewer resources and less pollution) which can be seen as simply slowing down the process of pollution and environmental depletion. Eco-efficiency is a stepping stone towards eco-effectiveness.

This model of sustainable enterprise provides the macro context within which enterprises operate. Each of our case studies exemplified these four dimensions, whilst usually emphasising one. For example, the emphasis at Patagonia is on environmental ethics; the emphasis at The Body Shop is on human rights; the emphasis at Putumayo World Music is on social responsibility; the emphasis at Stonyfield Farm is on eco-effectiveness. The model provides a framework within which to analyse how enterprises can minimise business risks and take advantage of opportunities to achieve strong economic outcomes and enhanced wellbeing for people and the planet. For a comprehensive set of stories and concepts to enrich each of these dimensions we invite you to read 'Our Views' at www.sustainableenterprise.org

Peak Performance

The earlier *Peak Performance*

project looked outside the mainstream for insights about how to create successful enterprises. We observed that in all the team-based global sports codes with which we were familiar there were one or two organisations that had been continuously in championship contention for a decade or more. Over such a period the explanation could not just be the players, because they come and go. So we concluded that there had to be something special about the enterprises to enable them to keep on winning. The research with twelve of the world's best sports organisations across different sports codes, cultures and countries focused on discovering the formula. This formula became Peak Performing Organisations theory, which has now informed the peak performance turnarounds within such iconic global corporations as Procter & Gamble in the fast-moving consumer goods industries and Saatchi & Saatchi, the world's most famous advertising brand[39].

We defined peak performance as continuously exceeding an organisation's best performance in pursuit of a shared inspirational purpose. Peak performance theory was presented as the best way for enterprises to achieve peak performance. Over the last ten years we have developed a series of techniques, web-based tools and stories that enable organisations to implement peak performance theory, and have worked with more than 100 different enterprises around the world, both large and small. Peak performance is applicable to any organisation that is significantly dependent on people and ideas for its success. We have engaged with companies across most industries and have found the principles and concepts to be generalisable. But we have not to date conducted further original research beyond the sports enterprises to expand our understanding of peak performance theory and practice.

Sustainable Peak Performance

We commenced our sustainable enterprise project with the intent of discovering how enterprises could be instigated and grown to global success, based on sustainability principles. It quickly became apparent that many of the concepts of peak performance were also illustrated within our sustainable enterprise stories along with additional insights. As a consequence we concluded that we may be able to develop a theory and practice of Sustainable Peak Performance, which we define as

Eleven.

"continuously exceeding enterprise best performance in pursuit of a sustainable purpose".

Over the next few pages we sequentially construct Sustainable Peak Performance theory, building on the list of characteristics with which we concluded Chapter 1. We set the context within the sustainable enterprise model as described above. We take it as axiomatic that enterprises should strive ethically to create both economic and social value, whilst nourishing or doing no damage to the natural environment.

There are six principles of Sustainable Peak Performance theory (Figure 3). These principles relate to but are not the same as those for peak performance theory. This relationship derives not from prior intent, but rather from a confirmation of some of the theoretical insights in this different organisational domain.

Conclusion

We develop each of the principles in more detail in the next six chapters, with illustrations from the stories in Part 1.

Sustainable Peak Performance Theory

Principles	Concepts		
People	Activist	Enterpriser	Inspirational leader
Potential	Inspiration	Opportunity	Spirit
Philosophy	Purpose	Challenge	Focus
Practices	Sharing the purpose	Value creation	Family
Positivity	Wellbeing	Flow	Making a difference
Performance	People	Planet	Profit

Figure 3 – Sustainable peak performance theory

People
who are passionate about
what they do are at the heart
of a sustainable enterprise.

Potential
is about the genesis of the idea
or insight that gave rise to the
enterprise.

Philosophy
explores the set of ideas and
beliefs that underpin enterprise
activity.

Practices
relate to the way the enterprise
conducts business and creates
the context for performance.

Positivity
is about attitude of mind that
creates confidence, optimism
and progress.

Performance
is concerned with what is to be
achieved, in terms of enterprise
outcomes, role modelling a
better way of doing business and
philanthropic engagement.

Twelve.

People

It is axiomatic that enterprises are all about people. How many times have you heard business leaders say "people are our most important asset"? And what does the typical traditional organisation do when confronted with a cost or profitability problem? Their most important assets become instantly expendable!

Sustainable enterprises have a different point of view, illustrated through these principles. Sustainable enterprise founders are energised by a deep commitment to sustainability principles across all four dimensions explained above.

In this chapter we explain the three concepts related to the people principle, and illustrate how this principle relates to the Sustainable Peak Performance action model (Figure 4):

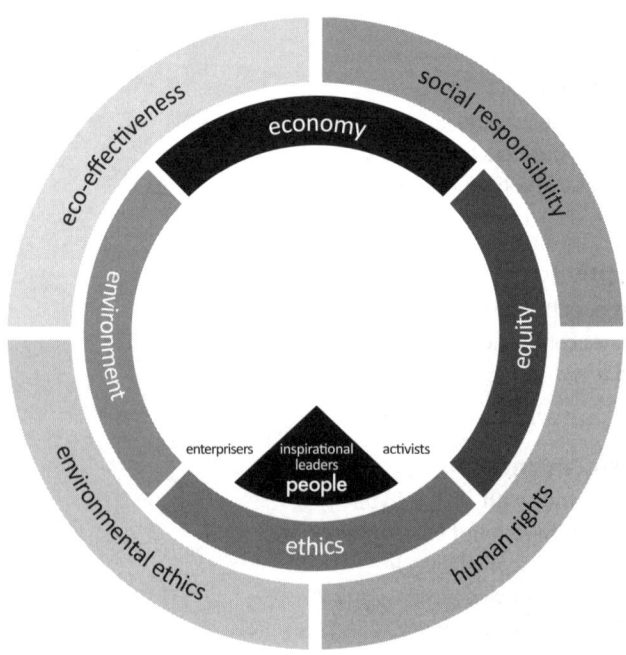

Figure 4 – People

Activist

Enterpriser

Inspirational leaders.

Activists

Activists promote direct, often vigorous action in support of or opposed to controversial issues or causes. The founders of our featured enterprises are activists. They believe passionately in causes that they consider are for the betterment of people and the planet. Jonathon Porritt, co-founder of Forum for the Future, was also a leading light in Friends of the Earth in the UK and formerly a leader of the UK Green Party. Anita Roddick explained that she and her husband "were activists; we were both active in the anti-war movement, in the civil rights movement, in the student union – we were activists." And she explained that their activism morphed into the company -- "we are an activist, an advocacy company, we are a company that stands up". She explained The Body Shop approach to finding staff: "We looked for activists, teachers, we looked for people who were in civil society, who were in the care business." As well as being activists, sustainable enterprises engage with other activist groups.

CEO of Patagonia Casey Sheahan said, "The more profitable we are, the more money we have to give to the various environmental activist groups that are desperate for our support." Stoneyfield Farm's Carmelle Druchniak told us "we are an environmentally activist company, yes and I think it's tied certainly to the brand, it's tied to Gary [Hirshberg, the co-founder and CEO]."

The activist ideal is about making a difference. Activists identify with a cause and the purpose of their enterprises becomes intertwined with that cause.

Enterpriser

The term 'entrepreneur' is used to describe people who instigate new enterprises and assume some responsibility for the inherent risks and ultimate success. 'Enterprise' and 'entrepreneur' derive from the French verb 'entreprendre', meaning to take in hand or undertake. The word entered the English language in the 15th century, and the person conducting the enterprise was originally called the enterpriser. This term eventually lost out to the current and more cumbersome 'entrepreneur'. We like the older and simpler word enterpriser (which remains extant in the English

Twelve.

language) and use this in the development of Sustainable Peak Performance theory.

The majority of new ventures fail. The majority of those that don't fail remain small. It is a special group of individuals that have the talent, foresight and tenacity to create a global business from an initial idea. It is an even smaller group that do so based upon sustainability principles. It is to these pioneers that this book is dedicated.

Enterprisers have strong beliefs about a business or market opportunity and often take on significant personal or financial risk to make them happen. They are the lifeblood of capitalist society; without them business does not happen. They reveal an independent streak and a need to be autonomous and in control of their own destiny. They tend to be confident, self-assured and natural inspirational leaders. In every case in our study the enterprisers were passionate about their cause and profoundly optimistic about their ultimate success. They exuded levels of energy, enthusiasm, mental toughness and fortitude in adversity beyond all normal levels of human endeavour.

Enterprise is a way of life for the iconic founders in our study. Sustainability is intrinsic to who

they are. Their personal beliefs and philosophy become intrinsic to the business. In many cases, enterprise experiences prior to that featured in this book paved the way for ultimate success. Dan Storper had previously run a successful chain of ethnic clothing and artefact stores before discovering world music. He compiled ethnic music collections to play in his stores to be consistent with their brand image. People loved the music. Whereas most people would have missed this opportunity, Dan as enterpriser seized it and drove it towards the creation of a successful global business.

Usually a dyad of founders with complementary technical and entrepreneurial skills provided the catalyst for the enterprise idea. Dan teamed up with musician Michael Strauss to bring the world music dream to life. Alan Bougen teamed up with bee expert Claude Stratford to create Comvita, the wellness enterprise specialising in the health benefits of bee products. Gary Hirshberg teamed up with Samuel Kaymen, a yoghurt making expert, to create Stonyfield Farm.

Sustainability is intrinsic to who the founders are. Their personal beliefs and philosophy became intrinsic to the business. This philosophy both forms and is formed by the development of the business. For Yvon Chouinard, it was the sight of the damage his beloved sport of rock climbing was doing to the mountains that inspired him to the idea of equipment and clothing compatible with the environment, which formed the business model for Patagonia. For Merrill J. Fernando, the experience of unethical trade at the hands of large global corporations led to the creation of Dilmah Tea with its foundation premise of single-origin, premium quality, ethical tea, and subsequently a holistic health and education agenda for his Sri Lankan developing nation.

Inspirational Leadership

Inspirational leadership deriving from a shared sense of purpose was evident throughout the research. The word Inspiration derives from the Old English word 'inspirit', which means to infuse with spirit; spirit in turn literally means 'the breath of life' or life-force. So an inspirer is someone who infuses life and energy into those around them, projects and places. Everywhere we travelled on our sustainable enterprise odyssey we experienced a sense of energy and joy. We took this spirit to be of the essence of sustainable enterprise. Multiple inspirers were spread throughout the enterprises. Two examples serve to illustrate.

It was impossible not to be inspired by the infectious enthusiasm of self-styled Stonyfield Farm 'yoghurt fairy' Carol Chapman as she shared stories of the early days of establishing the brand. She would convert people to the cause wherever they lived, worked and played. Free yoghurt sampling in supermarkets dressed in a person-sized yoghurt cup as the 'yoghurt fairy' was a favourite; the 'yoghurt run' unannounced and uninvited up and down the floors of city office blocks was another. Her enthusiasm was unabated some 20 years on during our visit to Stonyfield when we were treated to a passionate explanation of the joys of the most comprehensive array of yoghurt options imaginable.

Our first introduction to the Patagonia passion came the moment we stepped in the door. Receptionist Chipper Bro was running the show like a DJ, choreographing calls and visitors, managing the fleet of corporate bicycles, and waving friendly messages to Patagonia people as they grabbed their surfboards to race down to the beach and catch the waves; surf was up. Patagonia is no ordinary company and the passion was contagious as we learnt more about their fascinating business model; each Patagonia participant is passionate and inspirational in their own ways

Twelve.

and roles, all with their shared purpose in mind and commitment to environmental activism.

The word 'leader' itself derives from the Anglo-Saxon word 'laed' meaning a pathway, so a laeder (subsequently leader) was someone who took others on a pathway or a journey to a known or unknown destination. The journey is a common metaphor used within the organisational development literature and practice. There are two forms to this metaphor, the journey as destination (see Albrecht's *the Northbound Train*[40]) and the journey as exploration (for example see Capparell and Morrell's *Shackleton's Way*[41]). The traditional view of leadership is of the leader setting a vision (the destination) and then gathering the people, the resources and the plan of action to achieve it; leadership as destination.

The following model (Figure 5) portrays a richer set of perspectives of leadership accomplishment based on human needs[42].

At a base level of leadership is the need to survive. The Shackleton story perfectly exemplifies this mode of leadership. For the individual this manifests as satisfying physical and economic needs; for the organisation survival is about covering costs, profit and shareholder returns.

The leader has the responsibility for developing and sharing a clear and viable enterprise model to start the play. Beyond survival, the leader's role is to enable relationships of trust and mutual understanding to be built as the foundation for successful lives and successful organisations. Empathetic and engaging communication is the leader's essential attribute. From effective communication and positive relationships a sense of self-worth, recognition and confidence can be developed amongst organisation participants that can lead to productivity, quality and performance at the organisational level. This in turn can engender respect and esteem for the organisation internally and externally. In the past this has been enough for business leaders to build successful companies and successful careers.

In a climate where businesses are only as good as their next idea, the transactional leadership perspective thus far described is no longer sufficient to attract and retain the most able people and to secure their full passion and engagement to imagine and create the future. The inspirational leader focuses on co-creating meaning and a shared sense of purpose and beliefs, and engaging the hearts and minds of the enterprise's people. As Bill Gates

Leadership perspectives	Organisational development	Individual
Sustainability	Sustainability, CSR, ethics	Service to people and the planet
Making a difference	Engagement, involvement	Make the world a better place
Renewal	Opportunities, success, innovation	Adaptability, openness, continuous learning
Meaning	Shared purpose, values, passion and harmony	Purpose and direction: mind, body and spirit
Esteem	High performance productivity, quality	Personal self-worth; recognition; confidence
Relationships	Communication	Love, friendship valued
Survival	Profit and shareholder value	Physical and economic needs

Figure 5 – Leadership perspectives

explains "when people come to work it's important that they be connected to a dream[43]". Inspiration does not exist in the abstract; it energises people towards the achievement of a meaningful purpose – to live the dream.

Meaning is a starting point for inspirational leadership and renewal or transformation is the outcome. The inspirational leader will engender opportunities for individuals to continuously learn and grow through new challenges and opportunities. Innovation and invention are the consequence, leading to ongoing success. The organisation is a fun place to be because of the new ideas, products and experiences that are being created and personal growth being achieved. Shared organisational success can lead to confidence and the foundation for ongoing peak performance. This virtuous cycle can continue so long as nothing happens to undermine any one of these stages of leadership; they are all important. Loss of inspirational leadership can cause the whole cycle to unwind rapidly and dramatically. For example, a change in leadership in 1999 at Procter & Gamble from the inspirational John Pepper to the more transactional and directive style of Durk Jager contributed to a crisis of confidence which in turn contributed to a

Twelve.

halving of the share price in a few months. Jager was replaced within the year by the inspirational and charismatic A.G. Lafley, who set as an immediate priority the restoration of relationships, spirit, self-confidence and a shared sense of purpose[44]. Jager focused successfully on renewal, but in the process some key aspects of what led to successful communication, relationships, confidence and meaning were lost.

Inspirational leadership for the 21st century must go well beyond the creation of meaning and renewal. There is a flood of research that demonstrates people want to make a difference in their work to the lives of others; to make the world a better place. In his book *Happier*[45], Tal Ben-Shahar of Harvard University explains that "we often enhance our happiness to the greatest extent when we pursue activities that provide us with meaning and pleasure *and* that help others". All the sustainable enterprises featured in this book encourage their people to make the world a better place and to provide service to people and the planet. Sustainability leadership is the new inspiration, because people want to make a difference and are inspired when provided with the opportunity to do so. Inspiration leads to engagement and commitment which in turn leads to

ideas and productivity in a virtuous cycle. Beyond an enterprise's people this inspiration is extended to customers, users and partners, and all who share in the dream. And sustainable enterprises do well by doing good. As Yvon Chouinard explained, "every time the company invests in the environment, it shows up in its bottom line"[46].

Conclusion

Activism to make the world a better place sets founders and their company in the direction of a cause. Enterpriser skills enable the confident pursuit of complex projects with expansive scope, potential and risk that create value for the enterprise, people and society. Inspirational leadership attracts others to the cause, and secures and retains their maximum engagement and commitment in a virtuous cycle of Sustainable Peak Performance development. Inspirational leadership needs to extend throughout the organisation to ensure that the sustainability commitment is sustained when the founders depart.

Thirteen.

Potential

Sustainable enterprisers have a special ability to identify potential for enterprise opportunity. In each case the enterprises derive from an inspirational insight from world social, cultural or environmental movements, the recognition of a unique enterprise opportunity, and

the spirit to seize the moment.

In this chapter we explain the three concepts related to the principle of potential and how this principle contributes to the Sustainable Peak Performance action model in Figure 6:

The three concepts in the principle of potential are:

- Inspiration
- Opportunity
- Spirit.

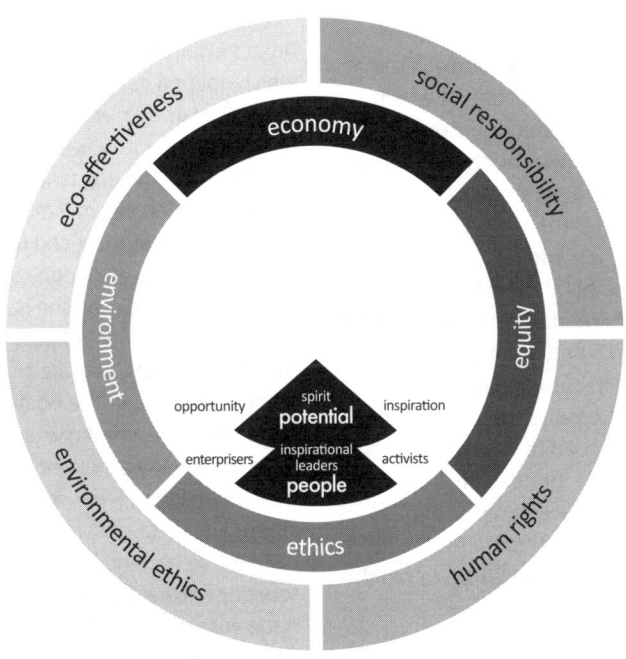

Figure 6 – Potential

Thirteen.

Inspiration

Enterprisers seek and embrace significant challenges, create opportunities and seize on serendipitous events. They pursue these with overwhelming persistence, prescience and positivity. This enables them to prevail through major setbacks.

Tim Smit, enterpriser and CEO of the Eden Project achieved acclaim through his work in instigating the Lost Gardens of Heligan, a romantic tourism experience and nature lover's paradise in west Cornwall, England. From the excitement of this initial project, he perceived that they had created a context which helped re-build people's connection to the land, reveal our dependence on plants and emphasise that we are part of rather than apart from nature. Eden was 'a glorious tilt at a windmill' to expand this idea into a larger-than-life environmental education theatre, that could stand as an icon of the relationship between people and the planet around the world. What better way than to take that symbol of industrially induced environmental crime, the disused quarry, and re-create a beautiful natural environment within which to tell the story of people and plants?

Tim runs his life by two theories: 'Tinkerbell', which holds that if you can get enough people to believe in something it will happen, and 'Last Man Standing' which holds that if you have enough charm and people know you won't go away, they will eventually pay you to do so! It was his inspirational ability to network and tenacity to get people to believe his impossible dream that instigated the multimillion pound funding to create a new Eden. More than a million visitors now share this dream every year. This echoes Anita Roddick's belief, that to succeed you have to believe in something so passionately that it becomes a reality.

Anita's inspiration for The Body Shop, which opened its first store more than 30 years ago, was economic necessity to create a livelihood for herself and her young family. During her early travels she had experienced the traditional farming and fishing lives of pre-industrial peoples from around the world. And she had grown up in an environment of post-war frugality, recycling, reusing and refilling everything. The Body Shop environmental activism was instigated from these early experiences at a time when Europe was starting to 'go green'. For Anita, activism and good business went hand in hand. Through sourcing natural ingredients by fair trade with indigenous communities, The Body Shop created a distinctive brand and enterprise model.

Dan Storper's youthful travels and adventures in South America and other more remote cultures of the world led to a successful chain of ethnic stores in the USA selling clothes and artefacts. On a tour of his stores, he was hit by the discordant notes struck by the random choice of music of the store assistants, often completely off brand with the ethnic cultures that the stores sought to portray. This insight led him to develop compilations of music on brand with the cultures of his stores. Visitors loved the music and wanted to buy it. This inspiration led to the sale of the ethnic stores and the birth of Putumayo World Music.

For Yvon Chouinard, the inspiration for action was the site of his beloved mountains pockmarked with scars from the overuse of traditional hammered in pitons that both despoiled the pristine rock faces and progressively eroded the natural environment. From this insight he developed a range of climbing equipment that was in harmony with the environment and this was the first step towards the Patagonia project.

Opportunity

These initial inspirations would have come to naught without the recognition of the opportunities and the translation of those opportunities into clear, simple enterprise models and value propositions. An enterprise model is different from a strategy. It is a simple statement of the logic of how an enterprise creates value. Six steps to enterprise model creation that we have found to be valuable in practice are:

1. What is the fundamental sustainable value proposition (how does the idea create economic, social and environmental value)?

2. What markets or market segments is the enterprise aimed at (be as focused as you can)?

3. What network of relationships will the enterprise rely on to find its customers and new ideas to drive the business?

4. What is the enterprise's place in the value cycle (the sequence of events from research and development, sourcing of materials, design, production, marketing, distribution logistics, wholesale, retail, recycle)?

5. What is the basis of revenue generation (how do you make money? – eg a margin on cost, market based pricing, royalties from an idea or patent, a stream of income from a franchise business)?

Thirteen.

6. What are the value drivers or bases on which the enterprise will compete?

So, for example, for Stonyfield Farm the illustrative enterprise model is as follows:

1. Value proposition – the best-tasting natural and organic yogurts, without any preservatives or artificial flavours.

2. Market segments – healthy eaters, initially in North America, now Europe.

3. Network of relationships – partnerships with organic farmers; users via website and regular giveaways and consumer interactions; Danone for technology, resources and channels to market; retail customers; sustainability enterprises; philanthropy recipients.

4. Place in the value cycle – early philosophy of grow your own milk has changed to contract supply; manufacturer; brand developer; logistics; wholesale to the trade, no retail other than factory shop.

5. Revenue generation – margin on manufactured price.

6. Value drivers – excellent product, strong brand, emotional engagement with users through education about healthy food and sustainability activism.

The essence of enterprise is deep engagement across multiple dimensions:

• Understanding the current and intended usage patterns, needs and aspirations of the users of your products and services.

• Foresight to anticipate what is becoming or what could be; this takes us beyond user needs and aspirations. As Henry Ford explained, if he had asked users what they needed at the time he introduced the Model T, they would have said faster horses!

• A network of relationships through which the enterprise idea can be technically developed, funded and taken to market.

• As Steve Jobs said "Creativity is just connecting stuff". Deep knowledge of unusual technology, skills or culture can lead to creative insights across domains of activity. Knowledge of world ethnicity and world culture led Dan Storper from ethnic artefacts to world music; experience of natural remedies and body treatments from her global travels led Anita Roddick to natural body lotions.

- An absolute focus on creating value for the customer and end-user.

In Chapter 1 we introduced a set of issues that together can be seen as leading to unsustainability. They are reproduced here, categorised as environmental ethics and human rights (Figure 7).

They are fully explained on our website www.sustainableenterprise.org.

Environmental Ethics	Human Rights
Agriculture	Aid
Animal ethics	Child labour
Biodiversity	Conflict
Climate change	Corruption
Deforestation	Debt – Third World
Desertification	Demography
Eco-footprint	Education
Energy	Fair trade
Fisheries	Health and safety
Genetically modified organisms	Malnutrition Obesity
Industrial pollution and waste	Poverty
Transportation	Urbanisation
	Water
	Women's rights

Figure 7 – Unsustainability issues

Both the categories and the issues within them are inter-connected in that ethical determinations drive both society and its impact on the environment. Social issues invariably have environmental impacts and vice versa. So for example, adequate access to fresh water can be seen as a fundamental human right – the right to life; it is also an environmental issue because of the increasing pollution of diminishing fresh water supplies which are becoming inadequate for the burgeoning global population and for the survival of other species with which we share the planet. In turn, changing climate patterns are leading to changing rainfall patterns and desertification of hitherto productive agricultural areas[47]. Fresh water is demanded for irrigation leading to fresh water shortages. Planet Earth is one integrated living system or Gaia[48].

It is however helpful to study these issues discretely as well as to understand their inter-connectedness, because focusing on sustainability issues gives rise to opportunities. An organisation's ethical choices about sustainability issues can create both risk and opportunity.

Risk abounds when organisations ignore or are unaware of the issues, or when they make ill-conceived ethical choices which bring them into

Thirteen.

conflict with the law or public and consumer perception.

Opportunities arise when organisations understand sustainability issues, have the foresight to imagine their implications, and the insight to develop sustainable enterprise solutions. Economic value can be created through embracing eco-effectiveness and social responsibility (see for example Simon Zadek, 2004[49]).

The sustainable enterprise well understands and anticipates the sustainability trends impacting on its industry and uses this foresight to create and sustain value. Traditional businesses (and politicians locked into old style short term economic thinking) meet sustainability issues with denial of the science, the practices, the outcomes and responsibilities; for example, tobacco, climate change, pollution, child labour – you will be able to list many of your own examples. But in the age of the blog and NGO activists dedicated to the pursuit of truth across every walk of life, it's becoming much harder to hide. And consumer reaction can be swift and devastating to a brand.

Nike's original denial of the sweat shop practices used by contract manufacturers put on trial one of the world's most famous brands[50]. It was a battle they could not win.

The only course of action was and is to investigate, acknowledge, sincerely and repeatedly apologise, immediately rectify and compensate. Nike may have been no worse than its competitors, maybe even better. But it was the most famous brand, and activists know about the power of brand recognition, so they attack the most famous brand first, not the worst offenders.

A gentler approach was adopted by Greenpeace in its chiding of Apple through the 'Green My Apple' campaign[51]. "I love my Apple, but please can it come in green". Within weeks of the launch of the campaign, Steve Jobs went public on his blog announcing a review of their component and production methods to make disassembly easier and avoid the use of the most toxic elements.

Sustainable enterprises understand this phenomenon. Their motivation to do well by doing good comes from a deepseated belief in social and environmental equity and an awareness of the growing significance of this for economic success. They are proactive. They know that defensiveness on a sustainability issue will ultimately prove counter-productive and lead to the need for a more expensive response later. They have already embedded basic sustainability issue identification and actions into their managerial processes.

More significantly, they embed sustainability issues at the core of their business models. The stories in the preceding chapters reveal how sustainability lies at the foundation of the purpose and business models of these iconic organisations.

Figure 8 illustrates the areas of activism that each of these enterprises focuses on:

Enterprise	Activism
Patagonia	Environmental degradation
The Body Shop	Human rights and animal welfare
Stonyfield Farm	Healthy food
Comvita	Wellbeing
Snowy Peak	Sustainability leadership
Forum for the Future	Sustainability policy & education
The Eden Project	Environmental education
Putumayo World Music	Cultural understanding
Dilmah Tea	Ethical trade

Figure 8 – Activism

Some sustainable enterprises, including those in our study, choose to take global leadership as activists and advocates for sustainable

enterprise. For example, Ray Anderson and his company Interface have become icons of sustainable enterprise notably through Ray's book *Mid-Course Correction*[52]. Interface has as its purpose:

To show the entire industrial world what sustainability is in all its dimensions: people, process, product, place and profits.

Sustainable enterprises create value for their founders, shareholders and their people through sustainability issues leadership.

Sustainable enterprise is about how companies can embrace sustainability as a strategic option, embed it into their business models, and for some, incorporate it into their brand positioning such that they contribute sustainability leadership in thought and action.

One such company with whom we worked on Sustainable Peak Performance during 2008 was Gazeley Ltd, a construction company engaged in the development of distribution centres for the supermarket industry around the world. We had met Gazeley's then chairman John Duggan at a sustainable enterprise seminar we gave in London earlier in 2007 for 50 chief executives from various companies. Gazeley is no ordinary construction company. They are

Thirteen.

exceptionally sophisticated thinkers on sustainability issues at the leading edge of sustainable construction. Their goal is the construction of zero emissions facilities that people actually want to have in their neighbourhoods because of the benefits that the developments bring. For example, one centre was built underground in such a way that a park was constructed on the roof bringing much valued facilities to the community. CEO Pat McGillycuddy explains their sustainability philosophy:

> At Gazeley we recognise that being a profitable business, protecting the environment and making a difference in our communities are compatible.

> Our customers drive our business, and our colleagues and Virtual Team partners are aligned to deliver the best quality service in a sustainable way.

> There is now a growing recognition that we must do everything possible to sustain and enhance our wonderful planet. For our business to thrive, society must thrive. We are pioneering the way to sustainable development and sharing our learning with customers and competitors alike. We have inspired others to take this path and we continue to look for new ways of making our developments welcome in and beneficial to the communities we work in.

> We are passionate about our business, from developing our people to be more than they believed they could be, to leading our industry peers on the route to complete sustainability.

> We work in a transparent way with our customers and partners as part of our effort to co-create a better world and a better way of doing business.

> We are exploring how we can work with others on the complex issue of system change – improving economic, political and social systems in ways that promote the wellbeing of people and the planet.

> Some years ago we recognised that our industry had an obligation to tackle the issue of sustainable development. Now we feel that system change will become an increasingly important component of the broad and rapidly growing sustainability movement.

> System change is the means by which we can reach out beyond our current capability and leverage the goodwill of people everywhere.

Sustainability is at the heart of Gazeley's business model and is its point of competitive differentiation.

Spirit

It is common in business literature and practice to refer to 'values' as the accepted set of principles, standards or tenets by which an enterprise or group operates. Values such as accuracy, agility, integrity, honesty, quality, reliability, speed, and teamwork would all be typical of the sort of commitments which find their way into many companies' values statements. Such values sets often derive from moral or religious philosophy and are undoubtedly an important foundation for a successful business. The typical values espoused by companies are often little more than 'table stakes'; characteristics that are necessary simply to be in business.

The driving force behind the sustainable enterprises we visited was much more compelling. It was about passion, energy and character, which we sum up in the word 'spirit'. The initial inspiration and opportunity recognition would not have been sufficient without spirit as the all-important third concept of potential. The concept of spirit was not included in the original *Peak Performance* book, because it was not recognised in the research, although it ultimately proved to be evident in the data. It was from implementing peak performance in practice that we realised the importance of spirit as energy for the enterprise. This proved to be even more the case within the sustainable enterprise research.

The etymological origin of the word spirit is from the Latin 'spirare' meaning 'to breathe'; spirit is the breath of life or the animating principle in living beings. The word spirit has both metaphysical and metaphorical meanings. From a metaphysical perspective, spirit is a ubiquitous but not visible energy that is present in all living things and which grows and develops as an essential aspect of the intelligence and consciousness of human beings. Spirits are sometimes seen as inter-connected through a life-force which transcends individual consciousness. The experience of such connectedness forms the basis of spirituality. The metaphorical meaning draws on this connectedness and refers to the experience of loyalty or being part of a collective experience within a group, an enterprise or a social movement; for example, the spirit of the 'green movement'.

We can take it literally then that all members of an enterprise will have spirits, but whether there is a collective spirit or a shared spirit of connectedness will vary from

Thirteen.

enterprise to enterprise. In the sustainable enterprises we visited, the sense of collective and connected spirit was palpable. That spirit was founded in the boundless energy and attitude of the enterprisers, and developed through the inspirational leaders with whom they had surrounded themselves. For Patagonia, the spirit is aptly summed up by the memorable title of Yvon Chouinard's book *Let my people go surfing!*[53], which explains his unique and successful model for business. For Dame Anita Roddick and The Body Shop it is "commerce with a conscience". In New Zealand, Peri Drysdale's Untouched World brand is all about "freedom of spirit, go anywhere, do anything, be you". For Stonyfield Farm the spirit is *Stirring it Up!*, the title of Gary Hirshberg's 2008 book[54]. Spirit is what motivates and energises.

One word that was common across all the sustainable enterprises was 'activist'. They are activists for the causes they stand for; the environment for Patagonia, human rights for The Body Shop, wellness for Comvita and healthy food for Stonyfield Farm. In the development of more than 100 spirit sets for different companies, no two have been the same. Spirits are unique.

The essence of spirit derives from the original enterprisers. So for example the spirit of The Body Shop remains substantially embodied in Anita Roddick although she sold the company and it is now part of the large global cosmetic company L'Oreal. When The Body Shop announced the opening of a chain of shops in India, it was Anita who fronted and L'Oreal were nowhere to be seen. This spirit will live on, despite Anita's tragic and untimely death in 2007.

Spirit defines the character of an enterprise, its energy and attitude. Enterprises with a strong spirit will achieve whatever challenges they set themselves. Those with weak or disconnected spirits are unlikely to be sustainable. It all starts with spirit; first with the spirit of the enterprisers which is then infused through their enterprises and touches those who choose to be a part of the dreams that they create.

Spirit can be for good or evil. Inspirational leadership designed to energise others can be for good or evil. History is riddled with examples of leaders who inspired others to their deeply flawed or evil causes. By contrast sustainable enterprises are built from an ethical foundation, respecting the environment and human rights.

Conclusion

The purpose of an enterprise starts with its spirit. Spirit energises enterprisers in particular directions. Anita Roddick's spirit as enterpriser, traveller and social activist led to her experiences with indigenous peoples in remote regions of the world, and the inspiration that natural ingredients could be far healthier for the body than the synthetic products of the traditional cosmetics industry. Tim Smit's experiences in enabling people to reconnect with the spirit of the land through the Lost Gardens of Heligan inspired the impossible dream of creating an environmental theatre and educational experience on a grand scale in a disused quarry. It is this spirit that energises the development of an enterprise philosophy discussed in the next chapter.

Fourteen.

Philosophy

In this chapter we explain the three concepts related to the principle of philosophy and how this principle contributes to the Sustainable Peak Performance action model in Figure 9.

The three concepts in the principle of philosophy are:

- Purpose
- Challenge
- Focus.

Philosophy

For sustainable enterprises, language is of the essence. Language is used to create clarity of shared understanding, to create distinctiveness, to tell the story and to engage people emotionally within and outside the enterprise. Anita Roddick expressed it in this way:

Language was major. We used poetry, we used metaphysics, and we used philosophy as our language. We took more language out of the poetry of Walt Whitman than anybody else, and so our language was an economic language. Our language was a language of joy; it was a language

of wonderment and amour.

This is what I've found: I've found that people get incredibly motivated and excited when enthusiasm comes straight from the heart, when it's not the enthusiasm of a corporate CEO saying we will be the biggest and talking about business as if it's war and sport!

It is through the thoughtful use of language that each enterprise has developed and expresses a distinctive philosophy which continuously evolves. 'Philosophy' derives from Greek, and means "Love of Wisdom". Philosophy embraces ideas about how we should live, what is the essential nature of existence, what counts as knowledge, and what are the primary bases of reasoning. So in that sense we see Sustainability as a Philosophy: a way to be.

Tim Smit of the Eden Project explains:

The philosophy... is a dynamic constantly evolving thing in relation to both the trajectory and the organisation our social past and the nature of the opportunities which determine our collective futures. And being at that pivot point is the place where we draw energy and have our meaning.

The philosophy of each enterprise

is based on answering the deep questions of "Why are we doing this? What are we doing? What are we trying to achieve? How are we going to achieve this?"

The enterprise philosophy is energised by the activist and optimist spirit of the founders and grounded in ethics. This is how Merrill J. Fernando, founder of Dilmah explains it:

If we as family companies do not demonstrate business ethics, corporate responsibility and social justice, other people who work for shareholders will not and cannot practice that. The purpose is naturally commercial, but that is not the only purpose. We need profits to sustain our business, but we need to share the success with everyone associated with our business. Everyone associated with our business is not only those who work for our business but those who keep us in business, and they are the consumers.

Central to sustainable enterprise philosophy is the idea of more than

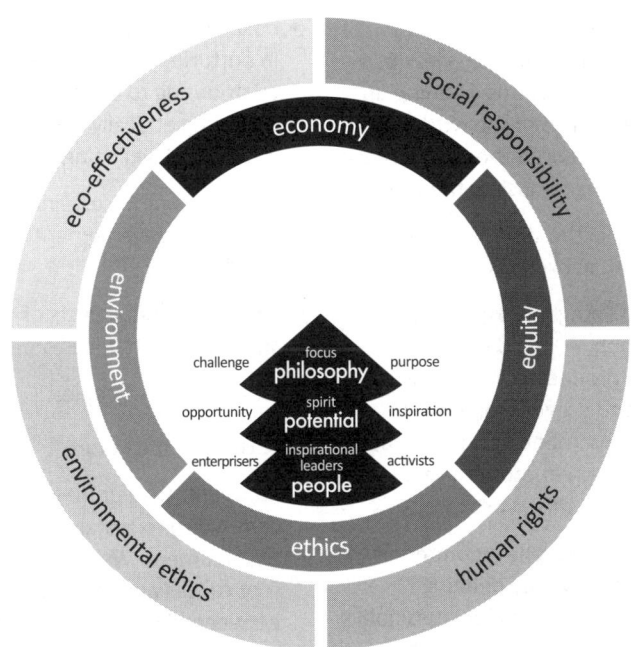

Figure 9 – Philosophy

Fourteen.

just profits. Jacob Edgar of Putumayo World Music explains this eloquently:

> In terms of what Putumayo's underlying philosophy is, I mean it's a business. We are trying to sustain ourselves and make money, but at the same time, there is a social purpose underlying what we are doing, underlying Dan [Storper]'s passion, and its music that we sell, but really the product so to speak is culture. We are a company, whose product is basically introducing or supporting the notion of cultural diversity and supporting the learning and understanding and appreciation of other cultures, putting a positive face on diversity and opening up people's minds to the world, to learn more about the world. Music is the vehicle, music is the tool.

At Patagonia the story is similar. Casey Shehan explains:

> Look at Patagonia's grounding philosophy – "Build the best quality product with the least harm and provide solutions to the environmental crisis." Great products, great profits, great for society and the environment.

The term philosophy is commonly used to describe the defining principles of business for sustainable enterprises beyond those that feature in this book. For Whole Foods Markets, philosophy embraces a declaration of interdependence, core values, quality standards and sustainability. Grove Mill Winery, the world's first carbon neutral winery, uses the term philosophy to describe its approach to producing premium quality wine with minimal environmental impact.

A philosophy of sustainability comprises:

- a viewpoint on what constitutes sustainability and its fundamental importance;

- belief in the role of enterprises in nurturing the environment, contributing to equity in society, operating ethically and generating wealth and wellbeing;

- commitment to sustainable enterprise development as a way of living;

- choice of what aspects of sustainability to focus on.

Here are some examples:

Forum for the Future[55]

Forum for the Future is a charity committed to sustainable development. We focus on the root causes and connections between big issues such as climate change, social inequality and environmental degradation.

We believe sustainable development is the big idea for the 21st century. Learning to live sustainably is not an option: it's vital for our long-term survival.

We want to see businesses and communities thriving in a future which is environmentally sustainable and socially just. It can be done. In fact we believe it's the only way businesses and communities will prosper in the long run.

That's why, since 1996, we've been working in partnership with world-leading businesses, cities and public sector bodies to bring about change. We offer advice, research, inspiration, capacity building, support and constant challenge.

We focus on key sectors including the built environment, finance, retail, transport, tourism, the public sector and with cities, with the long-term goal of transforming each sector.

We take a practical, solutions-based approach. We believe change will come not by threatening people with ecological doom and gloom but by showing how their lives will be better, and where there are opportunities for responsible wealth creation.

Comvita[56]

We respect our communities and the environment. This is our source of inspiration and commerce. We embrace sustainable thinking and action, caring for the future of people and nature.

We believe that business has the potential to make the world a better place across all dimensions of sustainability – economically, socially, environmentally and culturally.

Sustainable living starts with happy, healthy people. Our wellness philosophy promotes work-life balance through flexible working arrangements, subsidies for health and fitness and health education.

Our product donations are supporting communities in need around the world – burns clinics in Iraq, Leprosy clinics in South-East Asia and orphanages in India.

We are committed to designing product packaging that minimises our environmental footprint, with a vision of taking nothing from the earth that cannot be reused by nature.

We aim to use only ingredients from sustainable and renewable sources around the world. Through

Fourteen.

Manuka planting programs we are actively ensuring a sustainable resource.

We can learn to mimic nature's ability to heal. What we take from the natural environment we must replenish and nurture.

Saatchi & Saatchi the global communication company, is a long time peak performance partner. Early in 2008, Saatchi acquired Act Now, a sustainability consultancy based in San Francisco founded by Adam Werbach, a former president of the Sierra Club and green activist. Act Now was rebranded as Saatchi & Saatchi S with a view to spearheading the development of Saatchi & Saatchi as a leader in communication and sustainability. Act Now's primary service is workforce engagement through their Personal Sustainability Practices™ (PSP). Their foundation client is Wal-Mart. More than one million associates at Wal-Mart have experienced PSP training with sometimes dramatically positive effects on their wellbeing. In the PSP programme people learn key elements of wellbeing and how the adoption of personal sustainability practices can enhance their wellbeing and that of their family, friends and workmates. Saatchi & Saatchi S has a clear philosophy statement illustrated in Figure 10.

The enterprise philosophy is enacted through:

The purpose, supported by a set of beliefs which define what the enterprise stands for;

- A clearly articulated significant challenge or goal to be achieved;

- A determined focus on how the challenge is to be accomplished.

Purpose

Purpose defines an enterprise's reason for being. It clarifies meaning, intent and direction, provides a unifying agenda and explains how the enterprise will make a difference. In an age when passionate people who are good at what they do can choose where they work, the primary means to attract and retain the best people will be an inspirational purpose.

We do not use the traditional business terms 'vision' and 'mission', partly because of a wish to move beyond the often confused and confusing language of business. Visions are sometimes presented as an attitude or what we have described above as spirit, sometimes as a big goal for the future of the business, and sometimes as an aspiration for why the company is in business. Vision as a metaphor is a mental image of the future; as such,

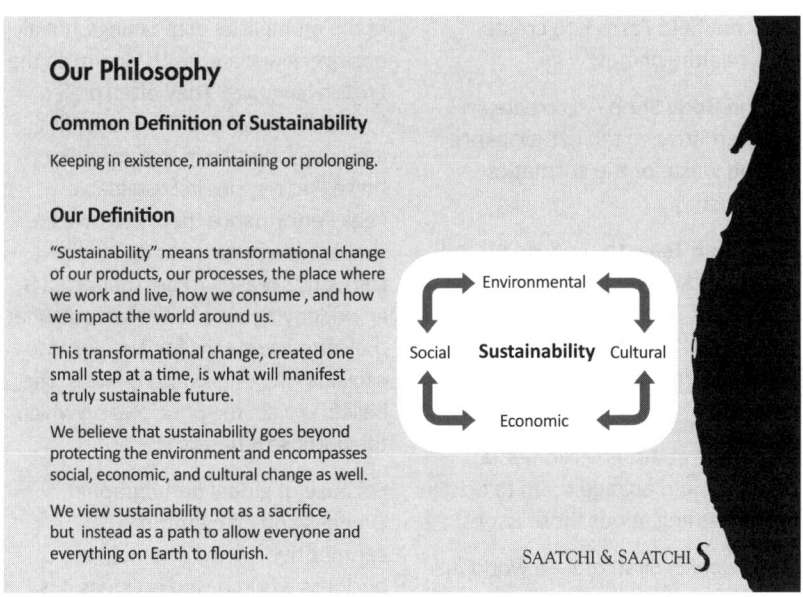

Figure 10 – Saatchi & Saatchi S sustainability philosophy

visions illustrate where to go, but not why.

Peak Performance uses the concept of an inspirational dream, a passionate aspiration or reason for being. An inspirational dream should be emotionally engaging, provide meaning, and inspire people to want to belong and to give of their best to pursue the dream. One of the most famous speeches in all of history is Martin Luther King's 'I have a dream' speech, a dream in which one day all men will be free. Inspirational dreams are about changing things; about making the world a better place, as Robert Greenleaf explains:[57]

Not much happens without a dream. And for something to happen there must be a great dream. Behind every great achievement is a dreamer of great dreams. Much more than a dreamer is required to bring it to reality, but the dream must be there first.

Each sustainable enterprise started with a dream:

Fourteen.

Stonyfield Farm – to create a healthy planet;

The Body Shop – to create an alternative to the extravagance and waste of the cosmetics industry;

Dilmah Tea – to produce ethical tea 'picked, perfected and packed' at origin in the producer country to guarantee consumers a fresher, better cup of tea;

The Eden Project – to educate people about environmental issues and engage them to do something about those issues;

Saatchi & Saatchi S – a world full of happy people contributing to a healthy planet.

We have found the *Peak Performance* concept of inspirational dream to be powerful in the process of helping people to think deeply about why the enterprise exists and how it will create value for people and society. However, we did not hear the term used in our research into sustainable enterprise. Instead, the term purpose was used, or the traditional business ideas of vision and mission. We have also found that enterprisers often find it difficult to use the inspirational dream concept in everyday communication to those who have not been exposed to *Peak Performance* thinking, because

of the multiplicity of meanings, not all positive, associated with 'dream' in the English language. They often prefer to use the simpler and more explicit, if more prosaic, term 'purpose'. For these two reasons in Sustainable Peak Performance theory we use the simple term purpose to define the company's reason to be, supported by an underlying set of beliefs about what the company stands for. The purpose explains why the company exists. The beliefs explain the principles on which the purpose is based.

Because of global demographic changes and an ever more competitive environment, in a business world based on ideas it is essential to be able to attract and retain top talent. The best people are able to choose who they work for, and increasingly they are doing so based on what the enterprise stands for and its contribution to making the world a better place. When people find meaning in their work, they are much more likely to develop the passion that can lead towards sustainable peak performance.

Beliefs define what is important to the company and how it creates value for people, enterprises and the environment; they are a set of principled choices by which the enterprise lives. Sustainable enterprises create their purpose and beliefs informed by environmental and social issues and ethical commitment. Beliefs will be determined by a careful consideration of the evidence and by consistency with the spirit of the enterprise and its participants. There is consistency of action with these beliefs, come what may.

Beliefs are sometimes seen within the business literature as synonymous with values. However, there are at least ten definitions of 'value' in common use, the most common of which is utility or economic value of goods or services. Value is what businesses seek to create; in traditional businesses value is seen as purely economic, whereas sustainable enterprises aspire to the creation of environmental, and social and economic value. Beliefs relate to ideas that are believed to be true and important. By contrast, the term 'values' is often used to embrace both the ideas and attitudes [which we describe as spirit], which people value.

To avoid the risk of confusion we use the term 'beliefs', rather than 'values' to define the principles upon which the enterprise builds its business, what it believes in and stands for, and how it creates value.

Sustainable enterprises are knowledgeable about and develop a point of view on the issues and emerging issues of our times. They are thoughtful and ethical and speak out about what they believe in.

Below are two examples of beliefs sets.

Comvita

- We care for the future of people and nature.
- We apply integrity and sustainable principles in everything we do.
- We are passionate about the quality and effectiveness of the products we make.
- We believe that nature holds the key to a better quality of life.
- We aim to change perceptions of natural health by applying science and innovation.
- Our New Zealand origin and culture drive new thinking.

Saatchi & Saatchi S

- In moving from limits to possibilities.
- In the power of consumers to change the world.
- In working at the scale of the problems we face.
- Sustainability is fundamental to personal and business growth.
- Sustainability is about connecting the dots.
- Sustainability comprises four integrated streams.
- No sustainability, no Lovemark[58].

Fourteen.

Challenge

The purpose and beliefs are not measurable; they are lived rather than achieved; a state of being rather than a destination. By contrast the next concept of philosophy, the challenge, is a tangible, measurable outcome to be achieved within three to five years. This time horizon is sufficient to provide for trajectory towards something truly significant, but not so far into the future that it becomes remote and un-motivating. The challenge must be a simple, preferably singular, significant and stretchy achievement that can be feasibly and sustainably accomplished within a three to five year time horizon. And it must be measurable.

The challenge concept can be compared with the traditional vision, or Collins and Porras' BHAG or Big Hairy Audacious Goal[59]. The challenge is 'What do we want to achieve?'; 'Where do we want to go?'. A vision can be seen as a picture of a desirable future, in the same way as the challenge. However, the challenge has a stretchy connotation, a big achievement, whereas by contrast visions are often nondescript, or confused with mission statements or spirit. For example, 'self-proclaimed Disney experts' Bill Capodagli and Lynn Jackson in the *Disney Way fieldbook*[60] explain "How to Implement Walt Disney's Vision of 'Dream, Believe, Dare, Do' in Your Own Company". This is more spirit and attitude than vision or direction. Challenges are strategic and primarily for internal use. They provide a compass and cause for celebration when accomplished. Supporting the challenge will be a series of goals that will provide way-points for navigating the future.

Challenges are at their best when they are simple and memorable. Peri Drysdale of Snowy Peak established the challenge of creating a global fashion brand, Untouched World, based on a unique spirit and sustainability principles. Dilmah Tea based their company on the creation of a global, ethical single-origin tea brand to rival those from long-established first world multi-national corporations. Anita Roddick wanted her naturally sourced body lotions to be accessible throughout the world. Interface have set the challenge to be "the first company that, by its deeds, shows the entire industrial world what sustainability is in all its dimensions: People, process, product, place and profits – by 2020 "[61].

For sustainable enterprises, challenges are not only about the typical corporate goals of being the biggest, or beating competitors. They emphasise making their sustainable products and services widely available, and telling the story as compellingly as possible of the causes and beliefs to which they are committed.

Focus

The final concept within enterprise philosophy is focus. Focus is the main emphasis or concentrated effort and attention that the enterprise chooses to make in order to live the purpose and achieve the

challenge. Stonyfield Farm focuses on educating people about the benefits of organic. Patagonia focuses on 'inspiring and implementing solutions to the environmental crisis'. The Eden Project focuses on human interactions with plants. Putumayo focuses on 'making you feel good'. Focus helps everyone in the enterprise to understand what is really important and how they contribute. A focus should be actionable, short, memorable, and go to the heart of how the enterprise creates value.

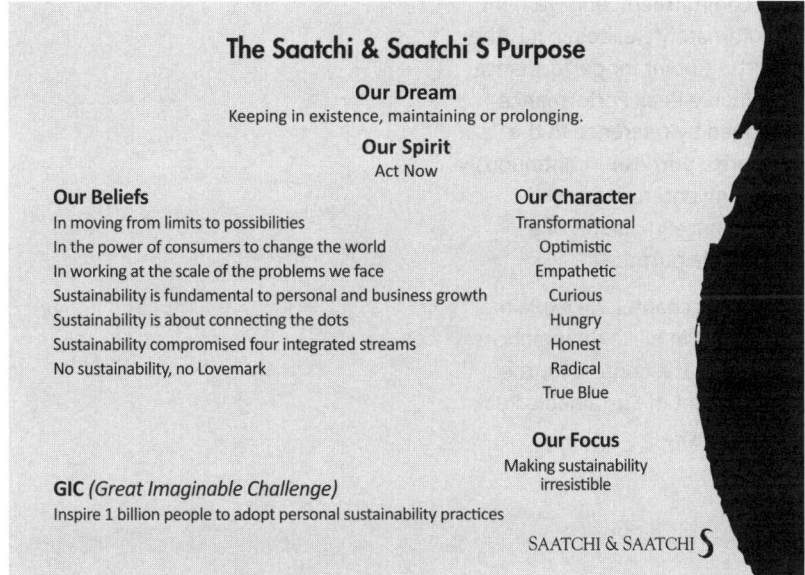

Figure 11 – Saatchi & Saatchi S Purpose statement

Fourteen.

Purpose example

By way of illustration, Figure 11 provides an example of a complete purpose statement for Saatchi & Saatchi S.

Conclusion

The enterprise sustainability philosophy, and its spirit, purpose, challenge and focus provide clarity of direction and enables everyone associated with the company to determine why and how they can contribute. This enriches the meaning they derive from their work, and therefore enhances their commitment, engagement and ultimately wellbeing. It is the departure point for performance. Sustainable Peak Performance is defined by reference to the enterprise purpose – continuously exceeding enterprise best performance in pursuit of a sustainable purpose.

In the next chapter we explain how to put in place the practices that create the context for the achievement of Sustainable Peak Performance.

Fifteen.

Practices

Authenticity is everything for sustainable enterprises. It is not sufficient for enterprise leaders to proclaim sustainability and to incorporate sustainability claims into their purpose and marketing material. Sustainable development must be incorporated authentically and progressively into everyday actions.

Practices create the organisational context for everyone to achieve their best performance. In this chapter we explain the three concepts related to the principle of practices and how this principle contributes to the Sustainable Peak Performance action model in Figure 12:

- Sharing the purpose
- Value creation
- Family.

This chapter is a lengthy one because it contains comprehensive practical

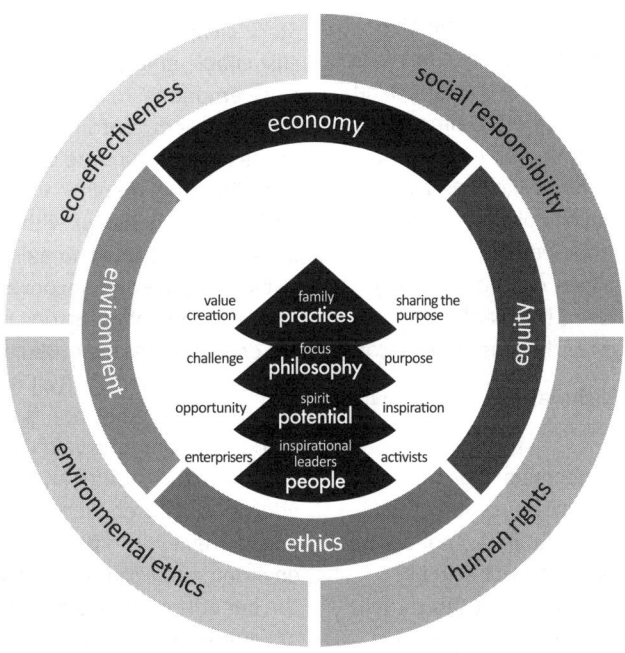

Figure 12 – Practices

Fifteen.

suggestions for what is involved in the development of sustainable enterprise.

Sharing the Purpose

Sustainable enterprise philosophy and purpose are shared through stories that emotionally engage people internal to the enterprise and externally. This is how Tim Smit explains the success of the Eden Project:

> It is because of what lies behind it in terms of the philosophy. Actually, there are other greenhouses, for example, the National Botanic Garden of Wales had almost exactly the same kind of money spent on it, almost at the same time. And it was shot because nobody goes as it was only about the plants. I don't think the fact that we hold the million people a year coming [to Eden] is because of the plants and the buildings. It's because of the story.

Anita Roddick was the consummate storyteller.

> Another subliminal plus was our consistent education of the human spirit. So it was not about educating on how to sell the product, it was about this is the story of Amnesty, this is what happens, this is the story of Native American farmers, this is the story. And I remember saying to staff years ago I looked at what the Celts used to say because they are prominent storytellers, if it doesn't go through the heart, it's dangerous, and that's the way they should live. Poets should be there. …. And we did this in a very institutionalised way because we trained storytellers in the company, they went to a specific college and so every two years they gathered all the storytelling, all the anecdotes, every two years, into a booklet *Our Stories*.

Storytelling is central to how the sustainable enterprises develop close emotional relationships with their suppliers, customers and users. These relationships are based on deep listening, humility and respect. Enduring relationships with users[62] are achieved through imaginative public relations and unconventional, inventive marketing. Strong brands are developed based on exceptional quality and sustainability. Customer and consumer education is central to market and brand development. The approach to customer and consumer education is based on authentic engagement with significant social or environmental issues within which the benefits of enterprise products or services are contextualised, shared through stories.

The sustainable enterprise philosophy is shared across all touch-points:

- partners,
- place,
- promotion,
- products,
- people.

Sustainable enterprises **partner** with people and enterprises that share commensurate purposes. For example, Stonyfield Farm developed a network of organic farmers throughout New Hampshire, USA and in so doing made a significant contribution to the transformation of the economic, environmental and social life of the region. The Body Shop partners with Oxfam on human rights and with Greenpeace on climate change and with a range of community-based suppliers around the world in order to practice ethical trade by going to the source. Patagonia partners with hundreds of environmental groups around the world to help preserve the wild and wonderful places that the company and its people cherish. Sustainable enterprises are careful about their choice of partners, eschewing suppliers, manufacturers, distributors and retailers that are inconsistent with their brand. They take this to extremes. At Putumayo, 'storebusting' got them started. They would land with their bicycles in some new city and scoot around to find stores to stock their music that were consistent with the brand. They quickly got a feel for the place and appearance of potential partners, such that a quick look was all that was needed to know whether further investigation was warranted. A company is known by its partners. Many companies have been destroyed or come close to destruction through not checking out their partners with sufficient care; Arthur Andersen and Enron, and Nike and Asian sweatshop manufacturers are two well-known examples.

The physical premises or **places** of operation of sustainable enterprises provide tangible experience of the enterprise philosophy. At Patagonia the surfboard racks in the entrance exemplify the spirit – 'let my people go surfing'; the 'corporate bicycles' exemplify the commitment to low environmental impact; the wilderness pictures on the walls illustrate the purpose. All Body Shop stores have their beliefs writ large – *Against Animal Testing, Support Community Trade, Activate Self-Esteem, Defend Human Rights, Protect our Planet*. The beliefs are illustrated and explained. The shop managers and assistants are both

Fifteen.

passionate and knowledgeable about the beliefs and the stories that underpin them. You don't just see the beliefs, you experience and feel them.

Care is taken to share the philosophy consistently throughout all **promotional material** including web sites, blogs and other interactive media. Digital media are preferred to print because of the limited environmental impact. Interactive media are preferred because of the greater propensity for emotional engagement and shared understanding. Activism, education and information sharing about sustainability issues are prerequisites for understanding why the sustainable enterprise product is to be preferred. The emphasis is on making the world a better place. The benefits of the product or service are set in the context of this greater good. Public relations is the preferred mode of promotion because of the greater authenticity it can generate.

Stories are the preferred vehicle; stories about their beliefs, stories about the source of origin of materials and products, stories about people, stories about everything they do. Through stories they create emotional engagement and convey facts in a memorable way. The stories are quirky, or funny, or outrageous,

or serious and fascinating. 'Moos from the Farm' at Stonyfield Farm captivates kids with its quirky humour, and educates in the process. Patagonia features stories about its campaigns of cause-related activism; for example, protecting the Arctic National Wildlife Refuge or oceans as wilderness. The enterprisers and inspirational leaders from throughout the companies are active as speakers to community groups, educational institutions, industry groups, NGOs – anyone with whom they can share the philosophy; they write books, blogs, articles, stories; they appear on TV, radio, chat shows. They live and love the brand.

The **products** and services are the primary medium for telling the story. Products that are inconsistent with the philosophy are brought in line or eliminated. Extraordinary care is taken to ensure that the story of origin is authentic and that the products are consistent with all aspects of the enterprise's beliefs. For example, extraordinary care was taken by The Body Shop to ensure all its beliefs, especially their opposition to animal testing of cosmetics, were preserved through the takeover of the company by the traditional cosmetics company L'Oreal. Care is taken from design, through material sourcing, manufacture, distribution and sale.

The **People** of sustainable enterprises are the storytellers. Enterprisers and inspirational leaders ensure that there is transparency and open debate about the philosophy and purpose which are widely shared throughout the enterprise and with partners. The purpose and spirit become the criteria for hiring new employees; people are hired who passionately embrace the organisation's purpose. People are promoted and rewarded based on the extent to which they live the purpose. They achieve personal growth, meaning and fulfilment through their association with the enterprise, and as a consequence become its best champions. Everyone is encouraged and expected to create opportunities for storytelling in the course of their everyday activities. Storytelling becomes a natural way of sharing the purpose within and beyond the enterprise. People are encouraged and given the opportunity and experiences to develop their own stories of active participation in the purpose of the enterprise and to share these with others.

Most sustainability claims by most companies are not authentic[63]. Greenwash is a term coined in the 1990s from a combination of green and whitewash. It is used to describe the deliberate use of green marketing or communication to conceal fundamentally unsound environmental practices, or to persuade users of unjustified green credentials of a company, with a view to persuading them to buy its products. It's serious and widespread, and fraudulent because it creates perceptions and benefits that are untrue. Users could be persuaded to buy products which are not what they are purported to be, or to invest in companies that are a higher risk than they appear because environmental and therefore consumer related risks are concealed.

Greenwash comes in many flavours:

- The use of advertising promoting environmental stories or images which are only a tiny part of the companies' activities, giving a misleading impression of the whole.

- Falsely claiming environmental credentials or associations.

- Publishing incorrect or misleading claims about the scientific attributes or environmental benefits of products.

- Promoting products as natural when they are in fact chemical compounds.

- Spending more advertising

Fifteen.

environmental activities or philanthropy than on the activities themselves.

- Cloaking with green fundamentally unsustainable industries and business models such as fossil fuel exploitation.

- Environmental labelling systems which purport to provide assurances of environmental responsibility, but where weak regulations, oversight or audit requirements fail to live up to their commitments.

Shell, BP, HP and other leading global companies have been singled out by leading NGOs such as Greenpeace for perpetrating greenwash. It's much harder to hide now. Blogs and NGOs combine to highlight greenwash abuse. Often high profile companies are deliberately chosen for attack, not because they are necessarily worse than others in the same industry, but because their renown better highlights the issues of concern. Making inappropriate environmental claims now comes with a serious risk of exposure. This damages credibility about their products and product claims, and worse. In a world of much greater sustainability awareness, it makes the perpetrators look ignorant and out of tune with changing consumer preferences and values.

The message to sustainable enterprises is to keep sustainability claims simple, clear and authentic. If you do not, consumer and NGO backlash can be profound.

Value Creation

All aspects of the enterprises are carefully and systematically constructed taking a long-term perspective. It took at least a decade to build the businesses featured in this book to global success. Sustainable enterprises integrate sustainability throughout their organisational structure, infrastructure, systems, processes, technology and policies.

The emphasis is on sustainable value and value creation. We consider 3 approachs to value creation:

- A value creation model

- Sustainable enterprise practices

- Lean enterprise.

- **Value Creation –
  A value creation model**

Figure 13 illustrates a model of value creation[64] that can be used as a lens through which to assess existing practices. The north-south dynamic features on the one hand creativity (or great ideas and design) and on the other hand operations (or great

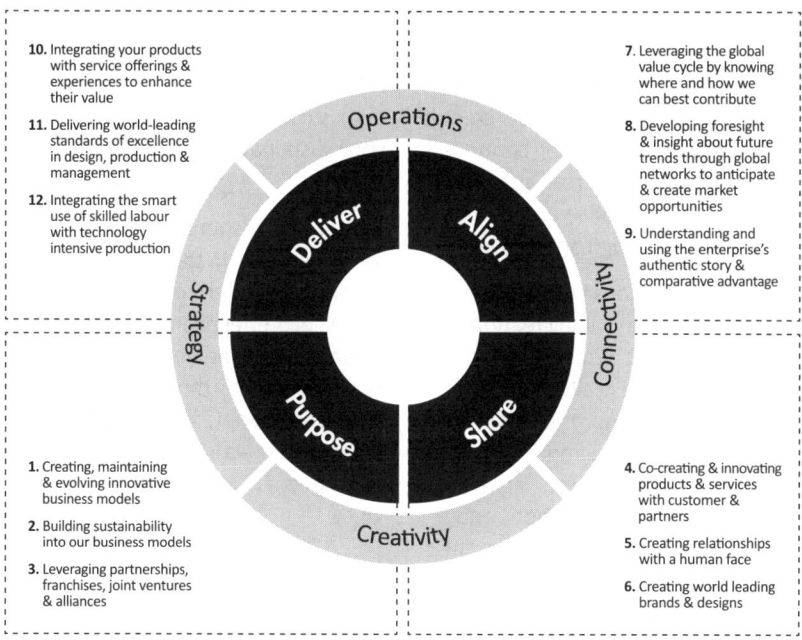

10. Integrating your products with service offerings & experiences to enhance their value

11. Delivering world-leading standards of excellence in design, production & management

12. Integrating the smart use of skilled labour with technology intensive production

7. Leveraging the global value cycle by knowing where and how we can best contribute

8. Developing foresight & insight about future trends through global networks to anticipate & create market opportunities

9. Understanding and using the enterprise's authentic story & comparative advantage

1. Creating, maintaining & evolving innovative business models

2. Building sustainability into our business models

3. Leveraging partnerships, franchises, joint ventures & alliances

4. Co-creating & innovating products & services with customer & partners

5. Creating relationships with a human face

6. Creating world leading brands & designs

Figure 13 – Value creation model

execution). The west-east dynamic features a clear strategy on where to play and how to win (we use the term strategy in the sense of choice of action), combined with close connectivity with markets, customers and users. The combination of strategy and creativity yields an innovative purpose and business rationale differentiated from competitors. The combination of creativity and connectivity yields brands, products and services designed to delight customers and users through shared co-creation and experiences. Sustainable enterprises get close to their customers and end-users to understand their hopes and needs, to share ideas, create rewarding experiences and educate them about enhanced wellbeing for people and the planet. The combination of connectivity and operations yields excellent alignment of the enterprise with emerging trends, comparative advantage, and an understanding of in which parts of the global value cycle the

Fifteen.

enterprise can create the most value. The combination of strategy and operations focuses on world-leading standards of delivery. Value is created and sustained by ensuring continued peak performance across all four of these domains of value creation – purpose, share, align and deliver.

To what extent does your business model emphasise value creation? How many of the 12 concepts above is your enterprise really good at? In our work with more than 80 companies using this model the most successful are strong across all or most of these concepts, and significantly differentiated from their competitors in several. A complete explanation of the theory and practice of the value creation model can be downloaded free from http://www.sustainableenterprise. org/publications.aspx.

• Value Creation – Sustainable enterprise practices

Sustainable enterprises embed sustainability practices throughout everything they do. Sustainability is not just an add-on extra, or something nice to do. Sustainability is everyone's job and is integral to how the enterprise creates value. Here is a taxonomy of the main issues that should be considered, set in the context of our sustainable enterprise

model. This taxonomy should be seen as an overview to prompt reflection about progress to date, or as a catalyst to get you started on your sustainability journey[65].

The taxonomy is presented in four sections corresponding to the four quadrants in the sustainable enterprise model – environmental ethics, eco-effectiveness, social responsibility and human rights. Each section has three concepts and for each concept, four sustainable enterprise practices are listed and explained. This is illustrated in Figure 14.

Section 1 Environmental ethics

1 – Resources

a) Maximising the use of renewable resources

Renewable resources are resources that through management, treatment, development or other means, can be replenished or regenerated by ecological processes that operate on a time scale relevant to their use. For example, biomass, solar, tidal, wind, geothermal resources, hydroelectric, plants (eg forestry) and animals (eg fisheries). The opposite of renewable resources is natural capital, resources that have no substitutes and a market

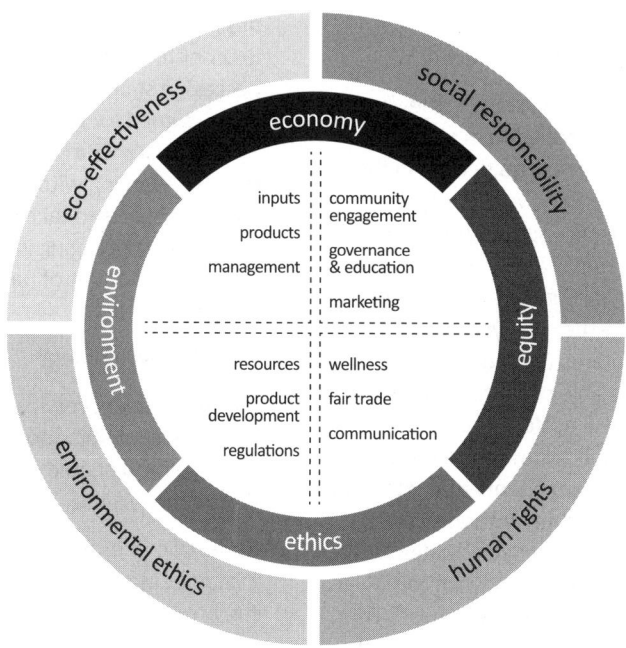

Figure 14 – Sustainable enterprise practices

value that does not account for all social and environmental costs.

b) Practice nature restoration and create programmes for replenishing the environment

Nature restoration is the rehabilitation, reclamation, re-creation, recovery, conservation and/or maintenance of sites of natural ecologies such as forests or rivers. Other programmes for replenishing the environment include support of environmental community projects, 'brownfields' redevelopment and educational workshops. Brownfields redevelopment refers to sites/areas that are under redevelopment, expansion or reuse after environmental contamination. It is a term usually used to describe underutilised or abandoned sites within urban areas. For example, the Eden Project.

Fifteen.

c) Take action to limit the global reduction in bio-diversity

Bio(logical)-diversity is the variety of life. A reduction in global bio-diversity means a decline in the variability and variety of living organisms – species/populations and genes – and the ecosystems which they generate. The more diverse the eco-system and its inhabitants the more likely they will be able to survive change. The ideal ecology is one that is in equilibrium with a diverse array of inhabitants that interact in sustainable methods. For example, Patagonia's 2006/7 environmental activism campaign was 'Oceans as Wilderness'. The company spent 18 months with marine scientists and writers, surfers and fishermen, to teach themselves and their customers just how close the connection is between the vitality of human life and the marine environment, with the aim of becoming better stewards of the ocean in our daily lives.

d) Design packaging for recycling and/or take-back

The dispersal of packaging and its rapid disuse after production makes it hard to enter into producer take-back cycles. Therefore careful packaging design needs to be implemented. In order to avoid waste, the packaging should be minimal and designed for easy recycling by the consumer in their local context. Working with retailers and distributors to take back and recycle packaging is also an important element of packaging design.

2 – Product Development

a) Design products/services to minimise contamination of materials and enable easy disassembly/reuse

Material comprises everything that goes into the production of the product/service, ie the coal used to create the necessary heat to melt a product component, the cotton used to make an item of clothing or the petro-chemicals required to transport a product/service. Enterprises that are sustainable champions are designing their products and services to use fewer materials, especially raw materials, to save costs and enhance product/service performance.

b) Continuously review and disclose the eco-characteristics of products/services

Reviewing eco-characteristics of products/services involves

understanding the different environmental flows that products/services are involved in and making this information available to shareholders, business partners and customers. The common types of flow that need assessing are energy, water consumption, material use and ecological wellbeing. These need constant measuring in both physical and economic units to identify true costing and benefits. Eco-characteristics of products/services include:

- effective energy use by facilities, materials and products/services – particularly limited use of non-renewable energy and maximising renewable energy,

- low harmful emissions – with the aim of the product/service generating nourishing emissions during the entire lifecycle, or neutralising emissions such as carbon dioxide by planting trees,

- compliance with health and safety regulations,

- efficient use of water,

- durability,

- modularity [for ease of repair, re-use and multiple use],

- adaptability to local context,

- efficient distribution/transportation methods including manufacturing close to distribution outlets to minimise the impact of transportation,

- design for easy efficient recycling and/or remanufacture at end of use,

- avoidance of waste.

c) Ensure that GMOs are eliminated from your products/services (does not apply to pharmaceuticals)

GMOs (Genetically Modified Organisms) are organisms that have had their genetic make up (DNA) changed by methods that do not occur naturally. Genetic modification transfers traits – genes that produce proteins – that are advantageous from one organism to another. One of the most common forms of GMOs is plants with resistance to pests, such as soybeans, so as to minimise the use of herbicides. There are many consumer and scientific concerns about the long term effects of GMO use, especially as there is no 100% foolproof method of predicting what will happen when GMOs interact with other naturally

Fifteen.

occurring organisms and cause environmental contamination.[66]

d) Do NOT test products/services on animals (does not apply to pharmaceuticals/ legal requirements)

Now that there are alternatives to testing products/services on animals with the aid of advanced technologies, it is no longer ethical to pursue animal testing. Methods such as test tube studies can be carried out on human tissue cultures, or computers can be used to model statistics on effective alternatives. By law some pharmaceuticals require animal testing, but products/services such as make-up or cleaning products/services should not need animal testing if they are sustainably made with non-toxic materials.

3 – Regulations

a) Lobby to change laws and regulations to support sustainable commerce

Many laws and regulations – taxes, policies and subsidies – provide incentives for people to pursue unsustainable enterprise. Lobbying to support environmental ethics and natural capitalism rather than continuing distortions in the economy benefits the environment, equity and your enterprise. Much damage to sustainability comes from unethical subsidies on, for example, fossil fuels, agriculture, forestry, fishing, waste, coal, toxins/pesticides and mining. These subsidies damage the environment and equity by encouraging unethical practice and hiding the true costs.

b) Sustain an excellent record of compliance with environmental legislation

Does your environmental record have zero occurrences of failure to meet regulations? Do you voluntarily make process and material changes by setting your own high sustainable standards before regulations require costly upgrades? Do you have an excellent relationship with regulators and permit providers? Is your entire enterprise well informed about current environmental legislation? Are you registered with appropriate organisations, such as The Natural Step, that help enterprises to attain sustainable enterprise and compliance with environmental legislation?

c) Review the environmental sustainability practices of suppliers and business partners

The reputation of your enterprise as a champion of sustainability is influenced by what and who you endorse – suppliers and business partners must match your standards. Environmental sustainability practices include careful monitoring and efficiencies in water, energy and material consumption, effective waste management and avoidance of harmful substances and emissions. It is important to stimulate healthy connections to encourage innovation and market opportunities through collaboration. By working with suppliers and business partners to jointly look for the cheapest, most efficient and sustainable resources and systems, your ability to discover and implement these findings will be increased.

d) Offer environmental expertise to other enterprises

The techniques and information you acquire that benefit your enterprise and the environment could also be of use to other organisations, such as universities, NGOs, and enterprises which share similar concerns and purpose. The act of networking and sharing stories builds your reputation as an industry leader and pushes the tipping point for all enterprises to become sustainable. For example, Forum for the Future is devoted to developing educational and practical tools which assist organisations to accelerate their sustainability journey.

Section 2 Eco-effectiveness

4 – Inputs

a) Strive to reduce the intensity and amount of material used in products/services

To completely understand the ecological impact of your products and services, your enterprise needs systems to monitor all inputs and outputs. This entails representing the flow of physical materials, energy and emissions in enterprise accounting. Analysing the entire lifecycle from input to output of physical materials, energy and emissions during the construction of products and services reveals the true costs and where waste occurs. Monitoring input and output is not only about tallying data, it also involves controlling what is required at particular times during the day. For example, the use of sensor lighting in places used less frequently like

Fifteen.

toilets and kitchen areas saves a significant amount of energy.

b) Continuously reduce energy use intensity

Light, motive power, electrical activity and heat are all forms of energy. The amount of energy used to light your offices, fuel your car on business trips, make your computers hum, and heat your hot water cylinder all need regular consumption appraisal. Steps to reduce energy consumption can be simple things from turning off computer monitors when not in use to complex building refits with more efficient sensor lighting and insulation. In our experience most enterprises that have not conducted an energy audit can easily reduce energy consumption by 20 to 40% at low investment, with immediate economic and environmental gain.

c) Take action to minimise harmful waste and emissions, strive to produce nourishing emissions

Harmful emissions are gases, solids, noise, liquids (effluents) or radiation, which contaminate the environment they are released into. One example is the release of carbon dioxide during the combustion of fuel. Minimising the harmful impact your enterprise has on the environment, through minimising damaging emissions, contributes to the wellbeing and productivity of the people working in your enterprise, and the health of the people buying your service/product and the health of the planet. A sustainable champion will have zero harmful emissions and only release substances that nourish the environment by becoming nutrients for something else, as in post-use recycling.

d) Measure, mitigate and offset greenhouse gas emissions to become carbon neutral

It is generally accepted, based on the work of the Intergovernmental Panel on Climate Change[67], that human-induced greenhouse gas emissions such as those created by burning fossil fuels contribute towards climate change and that global warming represents a substantial environmental, economic and social threat to humanity. There is increasing consumer awareness of these issues, and as a consequence increasing resistance to products or services that are seen to be associated with high greenhouse gas emissions. Enterprises should measure their emissions, mitigate them wherever they can, and offset what in the short term they cannot mitigate through appropriate carbon offset actions or the purchase of carbon credits. There can be employee, public relations and marketing benefits from moving towards carbon neutral and ultimately carbon positive; increasingly this will be a legal requirement.

5 – Products

a) Take responsibility for the post-use recycling of your products/services

Post-use recycling, often referred to as product/service take-back or remanufacturing, is a cradle-to-cradle operation. The product/service that the enterprise creates is fed back into the enterprise once the user has finished with it. The enterprise demonstrates responsibility for the collection and reuse and disposal of the product/service components in a sustainable manner.

b) Strive to extend product/ service durability

Extending durability means lengthening the amount of time the main components of the product or service will last and stay in the user's hands. Durability also implies market durability; that the product/service is designed to survive the market for an extended period of time. For example, the product/service is easy to upgrade, is maintainable and is therefore flexible to meet the changing needs of the user. Durable products/services have components that are easy to disassemble and reassemble, the potentially weaker areas are easily accessible for fixing with tools, the product/service is easy to install and the product/service is easy to deliver.

c) Search for and invest in potential disruptive and 'leapfrog' technologies

Disruptive technologies are beneficial technologies that shift the purpose or value propositions of the enterprise and create new markets. They are called 'disruptive' because these technologies change markets. At first disruptive technology products/services may underperform in existing markets and be of interest to only a few customers. But the potential of disruptive technologies is to secure new customers, while retaining past customers, and

Fifteen.

build the enterprise into a leader in new rapidly growing markets or perhaps industries. Leapfrog technology is the ability to use, or jump to, the technology most suited to the development of the product/service and the enterprise's needs. Does your enterprise have research processes in place to search for new technologies and potential forms of competition? Does your enterprise invest in these discoveries by leaping to new technologies that will alter the enterprise's value proposition? For example, the iPod has created a whole new industry of downloadable music and disrupted portable CD players and CDs. This is a win for people through enhanced functionality, experience and reduced cost, for the planet through reduced raw material consumption, and for Apple's profit through industry leadership. The market for such a product did not exist until it was released; it has revolutionised the music industry.

d) Integrate biomimicry in product/service development

Biomimicry is the study of nature to find creative ways to develop products/services. It is the conscious emulation of life's genius. This new science acknowledges that nature has been practising the production of non-toxic products for billions of years, and has already tested and removed trillions of failures. For example, leaves use photosynthesis to produce energy without harmful emissions. Janine M. Benyus, the author of *Biomimicry: Innovation inspired by nature*[68], describes the origin of biomimicry, derived from the Greek, meaning 'bios' (life) and 'mimesis' (imitation). Benyus uses three principles of biomimicry to encourage people to build on ideas from nature's database; nature as model, nature as measure, nature as mentor. Velcro is a classic example of a biomimicry inspired invention. Swiss engineer George de Mestral returned from a hunting trip one day in 1941 with burrs or seeds of burdock stuck to his clothes and his dog's fur. He examined the seeds under a microscope and saw the numerous tiny hooks that enabled them to cling on to anything with a loop such as the clothing on passing people and fur on animals, thereby providing a naural distribution system. George reasoned that if he could emulate the hook and loop system he could create a simple fastening device. It took ten years to perfect the manufacture and successfully apply for a patent. From the inspiration of natural burrs, a new product category was born.

6 – Management

a) Develop a proactive system of waste management

Waste generated by the products/services you use and produce should be managed, reduced, and ultimately reused or recycled into useful resources. A proactive waste management system is one that acknowledges the hidden costs of waste, above and beyond that of simply disposing of it. With a proactive waste management system health, labour, environment, energy and further costs are factored into the enterprise's financial performance and not left for others to clean up and pay for. Sustainable enterprises design their waste management systems with the goal of zero waste and only nurturing emissions.

b) Design your buildings, facilities and equipment for sustainability

The way an enterprise's buildings and facilities are designed and the equipment available dictates patterns of use and are significant influences on people's behaviour. To encourage sustainable patterns of practice, buildings, facilities and equipment need to be highly efficient and considerate of occupant needs over an extended lifespan. Insulation, natural ventilation for cool and hot conditions, landscaping, flexibility of workspace, local renewable or recycled building materials, lighting, efficient use of energy, efficient water and electric equipment and finally non-toxic cleaning and regular maintenance are important aspects of sustainable buildings and facilities.

c) Implement Environmental Management Systems

Environmental management systems (EMS) are designed to help an enterprise perform as a sustainable enterprise. There are a range of standards upon which to model EMS, such as ISO 14001 or The Natural Step (TNS). Each gives guidelines and processes to focus enterprise's efforts to act sustainably, particularly in regards to advice on lifecycle assessment, auditing and labelling. ISO 14001 specifies requirements for an

Fifteen.

environmental management system to enable an enterprise to develop and implement a policy and objectives which take into account legal requirements and other requirements to which the enterprise subscribes, and information about significant environmental aspects. It applies to environmental aspects that the enterprise identifies as those which it can control and those which it can influence. It does not itself state specific environmental performance criteria. TNS uses science and a systems-based methodology to develop strategies to manage environmental, social and economic aspects within enterprises. It offers implementation tools and design criteria to aid enterprises in assessing current approaches and in making sustainable decisions.

d) Use creative and resource efficient transportation and distribution methods

Resource-efficient transportation and distribution is the effective transit of ideas, people, products and services, and their sustainable delivery. It involves guidelines, planning and technologies that assimilate sustainable values. Design plays a vital role in creating

efficient transportation methods, especially in facility/building and city planning to encourage environmental behaviour, such as pedestrian and green zones. Alternative travel options, such as teleconferencing or working from home, aid the development of creative 'enterprise delivery' options.

Section 3 Social responsibility

7 – Community Engagement

a) Establish policies and practice in regard to people diversity

To be a sustainable champion, policies and practice, especially employment practices, should celebrate diversity. Women, men, and people of differing races, religion and opinion will be employed at all levels of the enterprise. Other areas that benefit from excellent diversity policies are consumers, community involvement, shareholders and business partners. People diversity brings diversity of ideas and new insights, from which new opportunities for value creation can derive.

b) Become actively involved in the communities in which you operate

Enterprises that are actively involved in supporting local communities – for example, through employment, donation of time, advice, money or goods – increase the wellbeing of communities and foster engagement and harmony. One term used to describe involvement with communities is local capacity building (LCB). LCB in developing nations, or in underdeveloped areas of developed nations, aims to reduce poverty, increase personal wellbeing and people's ability to access human resources and global markets. It aspires to remove a one-sided financial 'aid' relationship by encouraging enterprise interaction and the sharing of information. For example, the founder of Dilmah Tea, Merrill J. Fernando, through his MJF Charitable Foundation, assists staff and workers and underprivileged people in Sri Lanka through the improvement of medical and educational facilities and support of micro enterprise. Snowy Peak Ltd, commits a proportion of its revenue towards the education of school students as tomorrow's leaders of sustainability. Communities give enterprises the right to operate in their midst.

By exemplifying good citizenship, sustainable enterprises model a better way of doing business and foster community support when needed for their own development.

c) Utilise local expertise, and purchase locally in so far as possible

Purchasing locally involves using resources, such as materials and energy, that come from the local economy and therefore returns value to the local economy. Incorporating local expertise into your enterprise, such as consulting with local experts, is another way to sustain the community in which you operate. Utilising local expertise and resources minimises waste, particularly unnecessary transportation, and avoids detrimental impact to the environment. It involves acting on a local level where accountability can be witnessed and where strong personal connections can be fostered, especially the relationship you have with suppliers.

d) Make regular contributions to relevant charities, both in money and in kind

Charities that are relevant to your own enterprise could

Fifteen.

share a similar purpose, support issues that you also endorse or simply have access to markets that you wish to operate in. Monetary contributions are one form of support, another is in-kind assistance – in other words, offering anything else that would benefit the charity, such as volunteer work, access to technology, education workshops, advice, accounting services, free advertising. Consider the establishment of a charitable foundation.

8 – Governance and Education

a) Embrace sustainability principles within your enterprise's purpose

Your enterprise's purpose should embrace sustainable enterprise, natural capitalism (economy/ environment), environmental ethics (environment/ethics), human rights (ethics/equity) and social responsibility (economy/ equity).

b) Practise world-class governance

World -class governance involves accountability, effectiveness, continuous education on the latest standards and innovation, research and development, evaluation, maintenance, compliance with laws, and voluntary actions to manage

risk and create opportunities. Two globally recognised sets of policies are the United Nations Global Compact and the OECD Guidelines for Multinational Enterprises. The Global Compact is an initiative of the United Nations to bring together enterprises and UN agencies to encourage and implement sustainable development. It is a voluntary compact that upholds responsible corporate citizenship and facilitates a network of enterprises interested in sharing solutions on global problems and demonstrating accountability. The OECD Guidelines are recommendations addressed by governments to multinational enterprises operating in or from adhering countries. "They provide voluntary principles and standards for responsible business conduct in a variety of areas including employment/ industrial relations, human rights, environment, information disclosure, combating bribery, consumer interests, science and technology, competition and taxation".[69]

c) Educate employees, partners and customers on sustainability

Health and safety is an important component of sustainability education. Health and safety education already occurs in most enterprises because of legal requirements, reduction of risk and liability, and increased health and productivity of employees. Educating everyone involved in your enterprise – employees, partners and customers – on all aspects of sustainability will further enhance the innovation, productivity and reputation of your enterprise. Holding sustainability workshops or inviting experts to talk are valuable practices. Most important is to cultivate an environment that promotes continuous education about and a shared passion for sustainability.

d) Engage with external sustainability experts

External sustainability experts are champions in their industry who can offer advice to your enterprise to strengthen knowledge, for example about using biomimicry to enhance product/service performance. Experts could work in NGOs, charities, universities, other enterprises, or any field that is pertinent to the practice of your enterprise. External experts can prompt new ideas

for sustainable value creation through new knowledge or insight, challenges to existing practices and experience from other sustainable enterprises.

9 – Marketing

a) Develop products and services aimed at the 'bottom of the pyramid'

The bottom of the economic pyramid (BOP) refers to the four billion people who exist on less then $2 a day. Developing products and services aimed at this market can be a profitable pursuit if an enterprise thinks outside of conservative service/product sales, and can contribute towards the wellbeing of people who typically fall outside the global market economy. For example, shampoo can be sold in single servings or cellphones can be rented rather than purchased. From the perspective of global social cohesion, it is dangerous to ignore the needs of four billion people for freedom of choice and wellbeing. Experts in this field, such as C.K. Prahalad, author of *The Fortune at the Bottom of the Pyramid: Eradicating Poverty Through Profits*, stress that once you stop thinking conventionally and start thinking practically there are tremendous returns to

Fifteen.

producing products/services for the bottom of the pyramid.

b) Factor sustainability into marketing and communication

The people/enterprises you work with to market and advertise your products/services should be informed about your sustainability successes. As more and more people are looking to invest in the health and stability of our environment and society, providing them with authentic information about your enterprise's achievements can enhance your brand and sales revenues.

c) Implement a process of stakeholder dialogue to identify and integrate stakeholder views into business products and processes

Stakeholders are those people who affect or are affected by an enterprise. To identify and integrate stakeholder views into enterprise products/services and processes, enterprises must open their processes to critique by stakeholders and create vehicles to integrate feedback into the actions of the enterprise. Open stakeholder dialogue encourages employees, suppliers, business partners, investors, insurers and the community to meaningfully connect and be involved with the operation of the enterprise. Open dialogue can contribute to continued relevance of products and services, as well as enhance the enterprise's reputation amongst its publics.

d) Design your products beautifully so that they will continue to be cherished

Love your product/service. If you do not think your product or service is beautifully designed then why are you providing it? In order to decrease the throughput of raw materials, products need beautiful design to encourage the customer to hold onto it for the entire lifecycle. A beautiful product demonstrates care and consideration for materials. It also displays personality and creativity and makes the user fall in love with it.[70]

Section 4 Human rights

10 – Wellness

a) Sustain an excellent health and safety record

The health and safety record of an enterprise indicates the responsibility of the enterprise to employees, shareholders and customers. Champions of sustainability will have minimal incidence of accidents and work-related sickness, stress or injury.

b) Strive to reduce the amount of fresh water that you use

Water is an essential element for every person's life and the wellbeing of the environment. As such, access to fresh water can be regarded as a fundamental human right. Sustainable enterprise champions realise that we need to collectively reduce the amount of fresh water we use to balance the impact of industrialisation, changing lifestyles, climate change and a growing population. Effective water management involving careful monitoring and improvements in efficient conservation will minimise environmental impact and create enterprise value through cost reductions and risk avoidance.

c) Regularly review and disclose the health effects of products/ services

Reviewing the health effects of products/services involves understanding the different social flows that products/services are involved in, and making this information available to shareholders, business partners and customers. The common types of flow that need assessing are energy (such as emission of CO2), water (excessive use restricting others' access to water), material (toxins in material) and health of people. These need constant measuring in both physical and economic units to identify true costs and benefits. Health characteristics of products/services include:

- zero harmful emissions, with the aim of the product/ service generating nourishing emissions during the entire lifecycle,

- efficient water consumption and energy use,

- compliance with health and safety regulations,

- content fully disclosed,

- do not exacerbate obesity ,

- no toxic ingredients.

d) Establish a policy for supporting HIV/AIDS awareness

HIV/AIDS is widely regarded as the world's biggest threat to public health, especially in developing nations. AIDS awareness is especially important to multinational corporations operating in the developing world.

Fifteen.

Policies for supporting HIV/AIDS awareness can be in the form of HIV/AIDS treatment programmes, involvement with communities at the bottom of the pyramid, and aid through donations and in kind. The policy should also include educating people on the transmission of HIV/AIDS and the impact HIV/AIDS has on society and the economy. Workshops or resources for friends and family of people with HIV/AIDS to help cope and support loved ones are also an important policy issue. For example, the MAC global cosmetics company has created an AIDS fund fronted by Pamela Anderson to foster awareness and research.

11 – Fair trade

a) Adopt fair trade practices with all partners, suppliers, customers and users

Fair trade practices are methods of operating that involve transparency, dialogue and respect within all relationships – partners, suppliers, customers and consumers. The purpose of fair trade is to foster sustainable enterprise by creating more equitable circumstances for trade and enforcing human rights, especially but not limited to transactions between first and third world nations. The main aspects of fair trade are: a fair price, transparency, gender and cultural equality, capacity building/social development and provision of healthy/safe working conditions.

b) Monitor the compensation, fair trade and human rights practices of outsource partners

Sustainable enterprise requires accountability for actions performed by outsource partners. Inequitable or unethical practices by partners constitute a significant risk for enterprises, especially those operating in cultures and contexts that are unfamiliar to them. Rigorous scrutiny of the actions of partners minimises risk. Education about sustainable enterprise practices will enhance long term value in the partnership.

c) Uphold fundamental human rights with emphasis on fair compensation and employment practices within all the countries in which it operates

Human Rights are the rights we as humans have to life, liberty and the pursuit of happiness. The Fundamental Human Rights were declared in 1948 by the United Nations to educate and ensure that justice, freedom and joy is upheld by everyone. The key principles of human rights are: every person is treated fairly and equally, work and compensation rights, freedom, right to education, healthy standard of living for oneself and ones family, right to social order which upholds human rights, ability to pursue joy, and security of person and life.

d) Embrace clearly documented ethical principles and processes

Clearly documented ethical principles involve accurate and properly timed financial disclosure to the public and proven compliance with relevant laws. They are designed to remove fraud, demonstrate transparent financial transactions and deliver honest conduct. The global economy is therefore improved by the removal of corruption, such as bribes, and money laundering, and unethical political or charitable contributions are removed from enterprise practice.

12 – Communication

a) Produce a sustainability or TBL report

A sustainability or triple bottom line (TBL) Report is a document that relates to the performance of the enterprise on economic, environmental, equitable and ethical issues. These reports are a valuable means to show stakeholders the enterprise's commitment to sustainability. Sustainability reports aim to raise social and environmental accountability to the standards of financial reporting. A TBL report focuses on the three distinct aspects of sustainable performance: social, environmental and economic. Some authors critique the TBL approach as inappropriately creating silos of these aspects of sustainability, whereas in fact they are irrevocably interlinked.

b) Have an established approach for engagement with relevant NGOs

Non-governmental organisations (NGOs) are cause-related non-profit organisations that do not have the same vested interests as government and for-profit enterprises. They include such organisations as Oxfam, Greenpeace and Amnesty International. They strive for social equity and environmental accountability through political activism, campaigning or direct action, often to create changes in national and international policy and/or consumer awareness.

Fifteen.

NGOs can be a source of helpful advice to sustainable enterprises, and they can be a powerful source of public critique and condemnation to companies and brands that pursue unsustainable practices.

c) Have an appropriate process for screening communications for inappropriate sustainability claims

A familiar term for inappropriate sustainability claims is greenwashing – the dissemination of disinformation to present the enterprise as more environmentally friendly than they are. Greenwashing takes advantage of customers looking for environmentally friendly/'green' products and services. To avoid damage to your reputation and financial liabilities from inappropriate claims, enterprises should have controls to ensure that all marketing, labelling, presentations and employees deliver the correct sustainability information. The web, NGOs, activists and blogs will quickly deconstruct greenwash, resulting in potentially serious reputation risk.

d) Become a member of the World Business Council for Sustainable Development (or its national equivalent) or a similar sustainability network

The World Business Council for Sustainable Development's (WBCSD) mission is "To provide business leadership as a catalyst for change toward sustainable development, and to promote the role of eco-efficiency, innovation and corporate social responsibility." The WBCSD is composed of 175 international enterprises from over 35 countries. National equivalents of the WBCSD endeavour to support sustainable enterprise on a country level. The aims of the WBSCD are[71]:

- Business leadership: To be the leading business advocate on issues connected with sustainable development.

- Policy development: To participate in policy development in order to create a framework that allows business to contribute effectively to sustainable development.

- Best practice: To demonstrate business progress in environmental and resource management and corporate social responsibility and to share leading-edge practices among our members.

- Global outreach: To contribute to a sustainable future for developing nations and nations in transition.

Other education, activist and knowledge sharing organisations committed to sustainability exist in various parts of the world. For example, the European Academy of Business in Society, (EABIS), the Asia-Pacific Academy of Business in Society (APABIS) and the Sustainable Business Network in New Zealand.

To those less familiar with sustainable enterprise the above taxonomy may appear to be a challenging agenda, necessitating the understanding of unfamiar concepts and practices. To those enterprises already well down the quality management and lean business ways of working, the ideas will quickly be seen as a natural progression of this direction. Sustainable enterprise practice is simply good business practice.

Sustainable enterprises are pioneers. They track emerging issues and form a point of view early. Stonyfield Farm commenced the journey to carbon neutral many years before Al Gore's 2006 documentary film on global warming, *An Inconvenient Truth*; they were doing while others were denying. Dilmah Tea practiced ethical tea production long before the fair trade movement came to prominence to bring some measure of responsibility to global consumer brands. Dilmah was founded on a strong basis of ethics not as a means to market or gain consumer support but because the Fernando family believe that is the only sustainable way of doing business. The Body Shop shunned animal testing of cosmetics, a practice endemic throughout the cosmetics industry, long before users started to demand it be banned. As pioneers they come under extra scrutiny, and most of the companies in this book have been criticised at times for not moving fast or far enough or by not living up all the time to their high ideals. Simultaneously, they have been criticised by the Friedman-influenced business lobby that proclaims any actions to enhance social or environmental outcomes beyond those required by law is anti-capitalist and anti-shareholder. Such criticisms are more muted now as consumer expectations have changed and as realisation has grown that companies can do well by doing good. A characteristic of sustainable enterprises is that they remain true to their beliefs in the face of strident criticism, and

Fifteen.

in the process model the way to a better world. They are not afraid to experiment and to take risks because they know that the answers to many sustainability questions are emergent and often complex, multifaceted and sometimes contradictory. Sustainable enterprise involves action. As Anita Roddick asserted at the end of our interview with her, "Just do something; do something!"

● **Value Creation –**
  Lean enterprise

Lean enterprise is an attitude of mind that links long term thinking with immediate action by maximising value to the customer and end-user, eliminating waste (overproduction, waiting, unnecessary transport or movement, unnecessary packaging, over-processing, excess inventory, defects) and maximising efficiency, quality and sustainability.

The concept was instigated as a core aspect of Japanese management systems, in particular by Toyota Motor Corporation. The theory of lean was first popularised by James Womack, Daniel Jones and Daniel Roos in their bestselling book *The Machine That Changed the World: The Story of Lean Production.*[72] Lean had its origins in manufacturing production, but today it is used today in a wide variety of organisations,

including manufacturing companies, hospitals, banks, and government, and across both manufacturing and administrative functions.

The fundamental idea behind lean is value creation for the customer and user. Lean is about process. Any activity in a process which does not create value for the customer is waste and should be eliminated. We have assisted many organisations on their journeys towards lean, with often dramatic impact on cost reduction and profit maximisation through elimination of waste and enhancement of efficiency.

Because of lean's focus on eliminating waste, there is a close nexus between lean and sustainable development. This was underscored for us in one client engagement during 2008 with Stainless Design, a New Zealand based engineering company with a difference. Stainless Design was already well advanced in lean thinking, innovation and quality management systems. During the course of a workshop with them we developed sustainable enterprise practices and strategy as a natural extension of their existing practices and business model.

Lean thinking is a long term process of continuous process flow improvement to eliminate waste.[73] Waste includes overproduction, waiting time, unnecessary transport or movement of products, parts or people, unnecessary packaging, over-processing or excessive features that do not add value to the customer, excessive use of energy, uneven workflow leading to excessive capacity at troughs in the cycle, excessive scrap, excess inventory and quality defects. Stainless Design had introduced lean thinking four years previously and the economic gains had been dramatic.

In our work with Stainless Design, the nexus between sustainability and lean thinking became apparent. Waste is unsustainable. There is no waste in nature, with the output from one process providing the input to another. We realised that lean thinking would minimise the use of natural resources and as a consequence be a win for the environment and for profit. The challenge for advocates of lean thinking and business process reengineering has been that the results can sometimes be devastating for people if as a consequence of lean thinking it is revealed that the tasks they are performing are no longer necessary. However, when lean is combined with innovation, design and smart business models that create vibrant customer demand, the capacity that may be released through lean thinking can be used to

enhance innovation and production.

It became apparent to us that lean thinking is sustainable thinking, and that the sustainable enterprise practices introduced above could very easily be blended with Stainless Design's existing lean processes to gain new insights for continuous improvement. There is huge potential for systems change towards sustainability if industries beyond those in which sustainability champions are traditionally found (such as the several food and apparel manufacturers featured in this book) can learn the benefits of sustainability steps.

Family

Family is the last of the three concepts of Practices. Sustainable enterprises operate in a family-like environment, with high levels of loyalty and investment in people. This is extended to embrace the communities within which the enterprises operate. By family-like we mean creating a context for the achievement of Sustainable Peak Performance, where everyone feels a sense of mutual respect, recognition, trust and confidence to inspire them to be the best that they can be in pursuit of the enterprise's purpose. They are special places.

We use the term 'family' because

Fifteen.

it was the one we encountered most often, both in word and experience, in our research both for *Peak Performance* and for this book to explain the context of the organisations. The term 'family' derives from the Latin 'familia', meaning a household or establishment. One definition of 'family' is 'an association of people who share common beliefs or activities'. This fits well with our usage of the term in sustainable enterprise theory, although the more common usage is to describe a group of people living in one house, parents and children, or people with common ancestry.

Anita Roddick explained that as The Body Shop grew to be a global organisation, they became too big to be a family, and the term 'community was more appropriate. However the family-like environment was preserved at the local level.

Sharing is of the essence of 'family'. Families in all their varieties are the primary building blocks of society through sharing the responsibility for providing:

• food, shelter and clothing,

• emotional and psychological security,

• warmth, love, companionship,

• economic productivity,

• social order,

• rearing of children,

• care for members when sick or disabled.

You will have seen from the stories that the sustainable enterprises do share many of these same responsibilities and take them very seriously, perhaps as a consequence of their origins as family businesses. For example, the Stonyfield Farm family extends its embrace to its farmer suppliers and to its users and their families.

There is growing empirical evidence that family businesses[74] outperform their peer group[75]. The reasons for these differences have not been resolved, but possible explanations include reduced agency costs, a longer term perspective and less frequent turnover of leadership. Aspiring to a family-like environment therefore would appear to be supported by financial data as well as by both the earlier peak performance work and this current research on sustainable enterprise.

Family in this sense is a metaphor in that most companies cannot literally operate like families in the common use of the word. Metaphors are helpful in providing a rapid transfer of insight about a known context (the source domain) to the target domain. The most valuable aspect of a metaphor often occurs at the point it breaks down. How would well-functioning families respond when one of their members is ill, makes a mistake, disappoints, is unmotivated, doesn't perform as well as we know they can? Or what if the family economics can no longer support all the members of the family? The metaphor will inform our thinking about how the family patriarchs and matriarchs could act, and about the likely response of the members of the family.

Abusive families and abusive workplaces and abusive managers are not uncommon, but it is not this type of family to which we refer. Cynicism, personal criticism, criticism that lacks a constructive framework, use of exclusive language, use of derogatory terms and gossip, repetitive use of expletives, manipulation and language that undermines others are all too commonplace in organisations. They are ultimately destructive and will inhibit wellbeing, learning, growth, engagement, performance and sustainability. They must be confronted immediately and firmly by leaders.

The enterprises embraced a variety of ways of fostering the family-like environment. The physical premises are infused with simple symbols of philosophy and purpose – Bees and wellness at Comvita, the environment and outdoor lifestyles at Patagonia, healthy living and yoghurt at Stonyfield Farm. The family history is portrayed in innovative ways using milestones and momentos; for example, the visitor's centre at Comvita traces the history of the company and what it stands for in quirky and innovative ways that demand attention. Family members and visitors are enabled to understand their history, people and relationships to connect past, present and future.

This provides a sense of personal pride and engagement. Achievements and performance, both personal and organisational, are symbolised through awards and trophies that hold pride of place. Achievements and milestones are celebrated in ways that are inclusive and related to purpose. Family activities often involve activism and philanthropy related to purpose that serve to provide personal fulfilment and engagement with the enterprise, its purpose and its people. For example, trips to the Patagonian wilderness region to help protect endangered rainforest are a much valued honour for the people

Fifteen.

of outdoor clothing and equipment manufacturer Patagonia. Closer to home, they engage in family outings to nourish natural places and wildlife in the vicinity of Ventura, California.

Sustainable enterprises hold purposeful family gatherings where the whole group is invited. Fun and food feature as part of these gatherings, and operations are often shut down for the event. Traditions define the spirit. For example, when surf is up, Patagonia family members go surfing. This tradition symbolises the company's spirit as well as its engagement with the natural world and its products, which make the experience of the natural world safer and more rewarding. At Dilmah, the tea ritual symbolises the purpose of producing the finest single-origin ethical tea. Founder Merrill J. Fernando treated us to an extensive array of tea with a multiplicity of flavours and aromas during our visit. The tea tasting arena holds pride of place in Dilmah. Teas and their origins and their modes of production, picking and packing are revered in the same way as fine wines. These rituals and places provide a platform for storytelling about what is important.

Conclusion

The practices of sharing the purpose, creating value and nourishing a family-like environment provide the context or necessary preconditions for the achievement of Sustainable Peak Performance. In particular we have emphasized sustainable enterprise practices as enbling opportunity creation, risk minimisation, cost reduction and revenue enhancement. This stands in contrast to traditional business perspectives on sustainability as a cost and impediment to profitability.

Practices create the context for Sustainable Peak Performance. It is the energising effect of positivity that makes it happen. We explore positivity in the next chapter.

Sixteen.

Positivity

In this chapter we explain the three concepts related to the principle of positivity and how this principle contributes to the Sustainable Peak Performance action model in Figure 15.

The three concepts that comprise the principle of positivity are:

Wellbeing

Flow

Making a difference

With people, potential, philosophy and practices all in place, positivity is the almost inevitable outcome. Positivity is about optimism, enthusiasm, passion and joy; the inherent energy, ability and capacity to live the purpose. The sustainable enterprise founders and their people exuded positivity in thought, word and deed. You could not help be

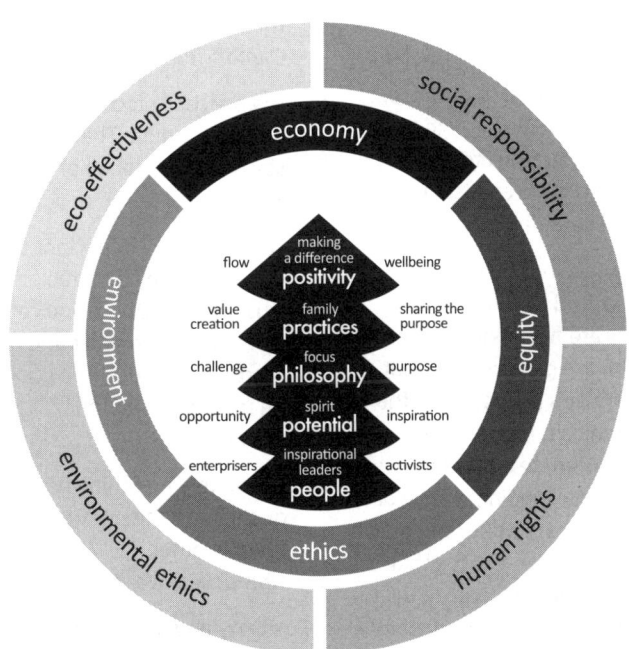

Figure 15 – Positivity

Sixteen.

infected by the enthusiasm, and people were.

Each of the case study enterprises had experienced defining crises which only the unswerving positivity and mental toughness of the enterprisers got them through; for example, the bankruptcy of a partner in the early days of Stonyfield Farm, the sleeves sewn on backwards in a vital export order at Snowy Peak, the financial crisis at Patagonia. Thoughts and emotions are energy. If you focus on positive outcomes by imagining a positive image of the future, positive energy will be created. In turn positive energy inspires positive ideas and solutions aligned to purpose. Positive outcomes will unfold to match the energy you create. This is why success inspires sustained success and confidence.

Positivity is inspired by passion for the purpose and products. The enterprises are filled with interesting people who are passionate about their enterprise's purpose and the causes to which it is dedicated. They are passionate about learning, growing and succeeding. Above all they are passionate about the quality of the products and services that are imagined and delivered. Quality was the single most used substantive word in our interviews. Quality is seen to be about a well-made,

durable product that delights the user and is aesthetically designed to last and be loved. Ingredients are carefully selected and authentically disclosed. Their story of origin is carefully researched and told. The experience of the product is seen to be as important as its physical features and functions. Quality, durability, reliability and aesthetic design are seen as the key ingredients to longevity and sustainability.

The success of the business is quality, freshness and integrity of the brand.
Dilmah Tea

We are really focused on the best quality product. That would be the starting point for all of our apparel.
Patagonia

Quality is very important to us. We don't have any bad tracks. People trust us, it's not like you can buy an album by an artist and maybe there are two or three good tracks on the whole album.
Putamayo

Absolutely first thing had to be the quality and the performance for the customer.
Untouched World

Positivity and passion are the primary recruitment and promotion criteria. People have the ability and are expected to make passionate choices about their work, and this passion becomes the wellspring for creativity and great new ideas.

Wellbeing

About the same time as *Peak Performance* was published, Martin Seligman and Mihaly Csikszentmihaly instigated the Positive Psychology project, building on Csikszentmihaly's earlier work on flow (see next section).[76] Whereas 20th century psychology was based on deficits, abnormalities and negative behaviour (and this has found its way into a lot of management thinking), Seligman and Csikszentmihaly's project is to explore what makes for positive behaviour, happiness and wellbeing. Seligman sees happiness and wellbeing as synonymous, and we treat the two concepts as such in this chapter.

One stand-out feature from our sustainable enterprise research was the evident positivity and happiness that shone through the enterprises we visited. By happiness we do not just mean the ephemeral happiness of 'pleasures of the moment' or hedonism, but rather a more enduring and deepseated sense of wellbeing that derives from pleasurable and meaningful activities and emotions. Happiness can be

envisioned across three levels:

1. Joy and ephemeral pleasures of the moment, such as good food, wine, sex, time with family and friends,

2. Satisfaction on achievement and success, such as meaningful work, successfully accomplishing a rewarding task, feeling healthy and financially secure,

3. Quality of life, fulfilling one's full potential in relation to skills and abilities and making a difference in the world.

Some variant of happiness or wellbeing lies at the heart of most philosophies.

"Happiness is the meaning and the purpose of life, the whole aim and end of human existence.[77]" The Greek philosopher Aristotle (BC 384-322) differentiated happiness from pleasure. He saw pleasure as ephemeral animal emotion and not therefore the true manifestation of what it is to be human. For Aristotle, happiness was a life well-lived, the good life based on good moral character, reason, values and virtues.

By contrast Epicurus[78] (BC 341-270) based his philosophy, which became known as Epicureanism, on pleasurable existence: the absence of pain and fear, a tranquil life, with

Sixteen.

sufficient wealth and good friends. He became regarded as a proponent of hedonism (the passionate pursuit of pleasure) although in fact he did argue for restraint.

The Scottish philosopher, economist and historian David Hume (1711-1776) is often regarded as the instigator of modern Western philosophy. He affirmed Aristotle's view – "The great end of all human industry is the attainment of happiness.[79]"

Like Epicurus, Jeremy Bentham (1748 – 1832) defined happiness as pleasure and the absence of pain. His proclamation "The greatest happiness of the greatest number is the foundation of morals and legislation[80]" has informed many generations of politicians, economists and philosophers.

Along with Bentham, John Stuart Mill[81] (1806 – 1873) was the instigator of utilitarianism which provides the foundation for much of modern economics. Mill predicated his analysis of happiness on actions which generated pleasure, although unlike Bentham, Mill did identify different types of pleasure, with 'higher pleasures' being more valuable.

Karl Marx[82] (1818-1883) also perceived the ultimate destiny for mankind as happiness. He saw this being achieved through widespread material wellbeing, which could only be achieved through collectivism. This necessitated the overthrow of the extant system of capitalism by the proletariat, by force if necessary, to put in place a more equitable economic system. He eschewed organised religion as a fraud on the proletariat, like capitalism.

Perhaps the most famous commitment to happiness as the primary goal of human existence rests with the American Declaration of Independence[83]:

We hold these truths to be self-evident, that all men are created equal and that they are endowed by their Creator with certain unalienable rights: that among these are life, liberty, and the pursuit of happiness.

Not all philosophers agree that happiness is humanity's ultimate purpose. For Einstein, "Wellbeing and happiness never appeared to me as an absolute aim. I am even inclined to compare such moral aims to the ambitions of a pig[84]." Nietzsche stated that happiness was something for British shopkeepers. For him the purpose of life was "the will to power" or self-determination; happiness was "the feeling that power is growing, that resistance is overcome"[85].

Happiness is also a central tenet of the world's great religions.

Happiness is central to Buddhism. Buddhist teaching comprises an eightfold path which leads towards nirvana, a state of ultimate happiness and everlasting peace. In Buddhist philosophy, transcendental happiness is achieved through overcoming all forms of desire and the development of compassion – the commitment to the wellbeing of others.

The 13th century philosopher-theologian Thomas Aquinas in his *Treatise on Happiness*[86], asserts "every man necessarily desires happiness". Aquinas was extremely influential in the development of Catholic theology with blessed happiness (felicity in Latin or eudaimonia in Greek) explained by Aquinas as a 'beatific vision' of God's essence in the next life.

Islamic rules and principles are designed though moral development to enable man to live in peace and happiness in this world and to achieve eternal happiness in the next life after death.

All of these perspectives – philosophical and religious – place humanity at the centre of all things and essentially disregard other life on earth. Deep green ecologists offer an entirely different perspective. For example, James Lovelock[87], a British scientist, environmentalist and futurist, theorises the earth as a natural living system which he describes as Gaia. Sustained happiness can only be achieved when humans learn to live in harmony with this system rather than seeking to dominate it. He believes that there are altogether too many of us for that to happen without a dramatic change in lifestyles and a reduction in global population.[88] Lovelock believes global societal collapse is possible before the end of the century. Yvon Chouinard of Patagonia agrees – "We are all toast!"

The nature and extent of the unsustainability issues summarised earlier in the chapter and at www.sustainableenterprise.org certainly give profound cause for alarm, with climate change being but one of a number of potential cataclysmic events that could cause the collapse of human life on earth as we know it within the foreseeable future. The fact that 20% of the earth's population is starving while more than 20% should be dieting[89] is not sustainable; the health costs (by 2050 the cost of obesity is estimated to be $45 billion a year in the UK alone) and unhappiness costs of both these

Sixteen.

extremes necessitate radical action. Conflict over resources will escalate, whether it is oil in the Middle East, productive land in Darfur[90], or water in Australia or Iowa.

So it is a tenable proposition to suggest that human happiness and wellbeing and sustainability are irrevocably interlinked. They are interlinked through the potential for societal collapse and the misery and suffering that will engender if we fail to act. They are also interlinked through increasing consciousness about the issues, and the fact that the will of people to do something about these issues may have reached a tipping point. Humans need meaningful activity to achieve enduring happiness, and we know that higher states of happiness are achieved when that activity is directed towards the greater good, beyond our own immediate desires. The ability to contribute therefore in some small way to making the world a better place, and to feel part of an organisation that is dedicated to doing so, may be the most profound way in which humans can achieve sustainable happiness.

"There is no business to be done on a dead planet." This famous mantra from David Brower, environmentalist, and founder of the Sierra Club and Friends of the Earth, is what confronts you as you enter the Patagonia headquarters in Ventura, California. Business performance will be increasingly linked to sustainability for all the reasons considered in Chapter 1, and because enterprise participants are happier when their own organisation is successful and sustainable. Sustainability, happiness and performance are intertwined.

If wellbeing is the ultimate purpose for humanity, then it follows that enterprises within which, in some form, most people pursue their daily lives must have a role to play in enabling wellbeing. In the next few pages we share what we have learned from the sustainable enterprise case studies about how enterprises can enable wellbeing amongst their people, users and investors.

Seligman and Csikszentmihaly[91] identified the positive emotions that comprise Positive Psychology related to past, present and future:

Past

Satisfaction, contentment, pride, serenity

Present

Pleasure

- Bodily pleasures of the moment – eg food, sex

- Higher order pleasures – eg music, stimulating

- Conversations, inspirational surroundings

Gratification

- Gratifications involve full engagement, flow, achievement and elimination of self-consciousness

- When gratifications finish then positive emotions remain

Future

Trust, hope, optimism.

You will observe elements of each of the great philosophers' perspectives embraced in these ideas. Happiness then is an attitude or an approach to life, based on optimism, virtue, courage, love and fulfilment. It is both emotion and action; or in the words of Sigmund Freud "lieben und arbeiten". Happiness is about positive:

- **emotions**: eg comfort, delight, joy, ecstasy

- **activities**: eg absorption, engagement, flow.

It will not be surprising to learn that happy workplaces create engagement and performance[92]. The best companies to work for

deliberately create happy work environments. Happy companies significantly outperform their peer group. But what is happiness and how do we achieve it? How can enterprises contribute to individual and collective happiness?

To this end we observed a number of characteristics within the case studies that are both consistent with and inform positive psychology and earlier philosophies of happiness. Moreover these characteristics appeared to apply both at the level of the individual enterpriser, and at the level of the enterprise.

Seligman explains the basic tenets of authentic happiness[93]:

- Gratifications can be achieved or enhanced by developing signature strengths and virtues. Signature strengths are your most significant skills and abilities.

- Authenticity is the achievement of gratification and positive emotions from using signature strengths.

- Happiness derives from using signature strengths to obtain high gratification, eg by enjoying work and creative activities.

- The greatest sense of happiness is experienced through the

Sixteen.

meaningful life, which is achieved by using unique signature strengths and virtues towards a higher purpose beyond one's own needs or desires.

We have developed the following two models – *Choice* and *Actions* – based on a synthesis of the happiness literature and on our sustainable enterprise case study experiences. These are offered as practical tools for reflecting on how to enhance individual and enterprise wellbeing.

Happiness – Choice

Happiness is achieved through choice, both in a Nietzschean sense of the will to power, or **self-determination**, and in the Aristotelian sense of virtues or **self-discipline**. These choices are depicted through the following Figure 16.

The extent of self-discipline over mind, body and spirit is depicted on the vertical axis. Self-discipline is defined as control of personal

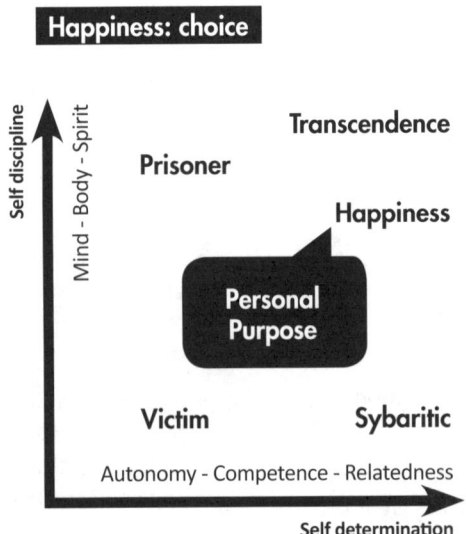

Figure 16 – Happiness: choice

emotions, desires and actions by one's own will. It is the ability to reject immediate pleasure, relaxation and satisfaction for a higher goal. Self-discipline provides the ability to take action for success, achieve your personal purpose, persevere and be resilient in the face of difficulty, failure and setbacks.

High levels of self-discipline can lead to transcendence, or going beyond ordinary levels of consciousness. It leads to self-control, self-confidence and self-esteem, and as a consequence to happiness. Self-discipline of the mind can be strengthened and developed through training in the same way as the body can be trained through physical exercise. Buddhist philosophy illustrates this path to happiness; transcendence beyond ordinary earthly desires.

"The first and best victory is to conquer self".
– Plato

"We are what we repeatedly do, excellence then is not an act, but a habit".
— Aristotle

"Mastering others is strength. Mastering yourself is true power".
— Lao Tzu

"It's not the mountain we conquer, but ourselves". – Sir Edmund Hillary

"The guy who is controlling his emotions is going to win".
— Tiger Woods

"Mental toughness is many things and rather difficult to explain. Its qualities are sacrifice and self-denial. Also, most importantly, it is combined with a perfectly disciplined will that refuses to give in. It's a state of mind – you could call it character in action".
— Vince Lombardi

Self-determination is the determination of one's own fate or course of action without compulsion across all walks of life: work, social and family. It is depicted on the horizontal axis of Figure 16. Key aspects of self-determination that appear to lead to happiness are: autonomy (feeling that your activities are self-chosen), competence (feeling that you are effective in your activities), relatedness (feeling a sense of closeness with others in the undertaking of meaningful activities) and self-esteem[94].

Self Determination theory was developed by Richard M. Ryan and Edward L. Deci to explain human motivation[95]:

- Physiological needs: food, water, shelter, sex, social

- Psychological needs:

Sixteen.

- Intrinsic motivation: an interesting, meaningful activity that is authentic to the individual's values, and provides for curiosity, affiliation and personal growth

- Extrinsic motivation: an activity undertaken because of external rewards such as wealth, recognition, acknowledgement, power, fame or image

• Self-determination of activities reflects one's own will, and leads to enhanced motivation, performance and happiness

• Authentic activities derive from one's core beliefs and spirit.

It is a characteristic of enterprisers that they need and seek high levels of self-determination. This spirit of self-determination is central to the enterprise drive. Dan Storper, founder of Putumayo World Music, noted:

> I've seen so many people that I know who have sold their businesses for millions and millions of dollars and have been required to stay on and have not been as happy afterwards as they were when they controlled their own destiny.

People who are self-determined are more deeply engaged, productive, happier and perform better than those who are not. This is especially the case in the context of ideas-based, creative, and complex activities. People feel more related to those who support their autonomy, and this inspires greater wellbeing. Intrinsic motivation, for the love of the activity, is most likely to provide feelings of autonomy and self-determination. When controlled, people tend to do only that which is directed. Extrinsic rewards (eg bonuses, recognition, surveillance, meeting expectations, evaluation, threat of punishment) can all diminish feelings of autonomy, and happiness. Information, a clear explanation for required actions, feedback and opportunity for choice all enhance feelings of autonomy. Feelings of self-determination can still be achieved under conditions of external rewards when the person fully identifies with the actions and their purpose. However, powerful incentives can cause people to forego autonomy, act against needs and neglect or destroy what they value most, from relationships to the environment.

Those with low self-determination, self-esteem and self-discipline are described as 'victims' in Figure 16. Unless they can break out of this psychic prison they will be doomed to a life of unhappiness. People in abusive relationships (domestic or work) fall into this category. Those with high levels of self-determination, but low levels of self-discipline are described as 'sybaritic', or devoted to pleasure and luxury. Children from third generation rich families can sometimes be seen to fall into this category; easy access to money enables them to buy self-determination, but this can be counter-productive to happiness unless matched with self-discipline.

High levels of self-discipline can enable people to survive and find meaning in seemingly hopeless situations of imprisonment. For example, Viktor Emil Frankl's experiences as a Holocaust survivor[96], or Nelson Mandela's experiences[97] on Robben Island illustrated how those with extraordinary levels of self-discipline can transcend the most terrible experiences and injustices to find a measure of meaning.

Self-discipline and self-determination go hand in hand for successful enterprisers. The drive to be in control of one's own destiny is matched by the drive to succeed. When times got really tough in the early days of Stonyfield Farm, Gary Hirshberg, and his family and friends just dug deeper (literally through the snow, and metaphorically); these 'bad old days' became part of the defining spirit of determination.

The most sustainable levels of happiness are experienced through high levels of self-discipline and of self-determination. Key to their achievement is the development of a personal purpose, akin to the organisational purpose described earlier in this chapter. Self-discipline and self-determination are both enhanced by the creation of a personal purpose because this clarifies authentic spirit and beliefs, thereby enabling choice about identification with intrinsically and extrinsically motivated goals and activities. Personal purpose clarifies what is important thereby providing a focus for self-discipline and mastery; it facilitates people's sense of choice and volition, and enhances their sense of self-esteem.

Happiness – Activities

Happiness is about choice and action. It involves activities that generate pleasure in the Epicurean sense, and activities that lead towards gratification through achievement. The extent to which the achievements relate to compassionate acts which benefit others also influences levels of perceived happiness. Positive emotions and happiness are achieved through activities that provide gratification **and** activities that provide pleasure. Progress

Sixteen.

towards meaningful goals engenders gratification. Happy people take time to do multiple activities that give them pleasure. The integration of gratification and pleasurable activities maximises happiness.

In Figure 17 below, the vertical axis depicts the extent of gratification through the achievement of authentic (to one's personal purpose) meaningful goals. The single-minded pursuit of work related accomplishments or 'workaholism' can lead to breakdown in family or social relationships, and, potentially

to reduced happiness.

The horizontal axis in Figure 17 records the nature and extent of pleasurable activities. Happy people create time to do things that give them pleasure. Multiple studies[98] have shown that pursuit of a variety of activities that you enjoy appears to promote increased happiness. However, the single-minded pursuit of pleasure can engender 'hedonism'; the more we get, the more we need. Wellbeing appears to be enhanced more by

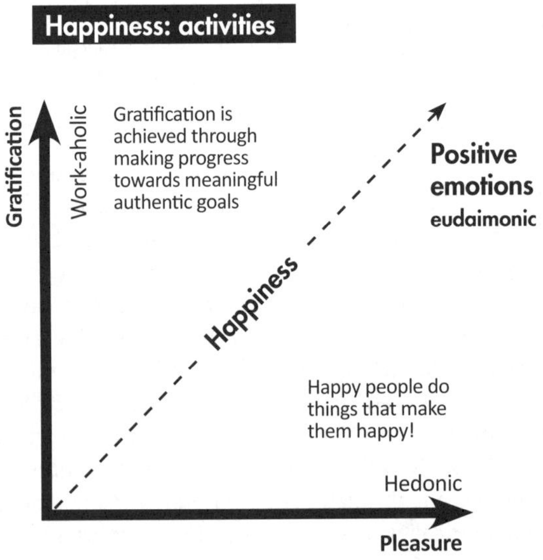

Happiness: activities

Gratification

Work-aholic

Gratification is achieved through making progress towards meaningful authentic goals

Positive emotions
eudaimonic

Happiness

Happy people do things that make them happy!

Hedonic

Pleasure

Figure 17 – Happiness: activities

activities which are directed towards outcomes that benefit others.

In summary, happy people appear to choose meaningful personal and work-related goals, undertake activities that enable them to exercise their 'signature strengths' and virtues, make meaningful progress towards the achievement of their goals, and embrace altruistic goals and activities. Research over the last decade within the positive psychology movement has demonstrated that it is possible for almost everyone to choose to take active steps to become happier. For example, deliberately creating regular time for moments of happiness (a cup of coffee with a friend, listening to music you love) has a disproportionate effect on wellbeing and productivity. By practising being happy (deliberately reframing negative emotions) you become happy, and help to make those around you happy too in a virtuous cycle. Spontaneity seems to enhance happiness, as does active engagement with life rather than passive entertainment[99]. Quality time with friends and family seems to have the greatest potential to maximise happiness. Expressing gratitude to others enhances the happiness of all involved.

We have used Positive Psychology, together with its intellectual antecedents amongst the great philosophers, as a means to develop the two models of happiness enhancement described above. They can apply to individuals and enterprises. The models are an attempt to theorise the evident and extensive happiness that we experienced in the enterprises that we visited, with a view to developing a practical approach to enhance happiness, wellbeing and performance for people and enterprises.

Creating enterprise wellbeing

Defining features of enterprise wellbeing appear to be:

1. There is a higher order purpose for the enterprise which has as its outcomes the generation of wellbeing for people and the planet. This provides a sense of meaning for enterprise participants, and sets the stage for their own personal purpose and achievements (**self-determination**).

2. People can co-create meaningful work-related goals aligned to purpose (**autonomy**) and are provided with the resources, training and experiences necessary to achieve them (**competence**).

Sixteen.

3. A positive work environment is engendered that inspires mutual support, recognition, confidence, self-esteem and friendship (**relatedness**).

4. **Self-discipline** is encouraged and role-modelled; the enterprise itself is disciplined with simple, effective policies, procedures and processes that are consistent with purpose, well communicated and well executed.

5. Policies and actions are in place to nurture **mind**, **body** and **spirit**: for example, access to knowledge sources and training is appropriately available; healthy living is encouraged through availability of gym or other exercise facilities and healthy food is available in cafeterias; the organisation's spirit and legacy are cherished as primary assets.

6. People are assisted to identify and nurture their 'signature' strengths and 'virtues' and to exercise them through **'just right' challenges**; that is, challenges that are sufficiently stretchy to provide growth, learning and development but not so demanding as to create unreasonable stress and anxiety.

7. Mentoring, coaching, resources and training are available to support people towards the achievement of demanding challenges, the achievement of which yields enduring **gratification**; achievements are recognised, rewarded and celebrated.

8. Sufficient space is available in people's working lives to ensure quality personal time for a variety of **pleasurable activities**, both within and outside the workplace.

9. **Philanthropic activities** in which staff can be involved are actively supported and promoted.

10. Trust, hope, optimism and **successful achievement** for the enterprise and its people are nurtured. **Gratitude** is freely and appropriately expressed.

The net result of our brief review of happiness theory as seen through the lens of Positive Psychology and sustainable enterprise is that Aristotle and Epicurus and Nietzsche are all right; happiness is a function of self-determination and self-discipline and achievement and pleasure. Enterprises that are able to create the context for their people to achieve happiness and wellbeing will be rewarded by the ability to attract and retain great people and their deep emotional commitment to purpose. From this engagement derive flow and productivity and performance in all its dimensions. For example, Patagonia is widely recognised as a great place to work. For every job available it will receive upwards of 1,000 applications enabling the company to select the very best people, both in attitude and capability.

The combination of these two models of Choice and Action, when based on a commitment to sustainability, constitute our concept of sustainable wellbeing.

In the earlier chapter on philosophy we introduced the work of Saatchi & Saatchi S. Their primary service is workforce engagement through their Personal Sustainability Practices™ [PSP]. Their foundation client is Wal-Mart. Founder and CEO Adam Werbach was the recipient of strident criticism from environmentalists and green movement colleagues for working with the 'Bully of Bentonville'.[100] Wal-Mart's alleged treatment of staff and the effect on local communities as well as accusations of exacerbating consumerism with low quality imported goods were all cited as reasons whereby working with Wal-Mart should be incompatible with sustainability credentials. Yet Adam correctly identified that

the world's largest company has incomparable potential to tip the world towards sustainability through its own actions, and its influence on consumers and on supply chain partners. In a startling speech entitled 'Twenty-First Century Leadership'[101] in October 2005, Lee Scott, CEO of Wal-Mart, declared his company's commitment to sustainability, and put in place an impressive agenda of action to make it real. At the end of February 2009, Scott handed over the reins to Mike Duke, Vice Chairman of the international division. In his incoming speech, Duke declared that "sustainability is not optional" and stated that in the current economic climate eliminating waste and making effective use of resources is fundamental to their business model and 'always lower prices' commitment. He went one step further by telling staff that their ability to move up in the company would be tied to their commitment to sustainability.

There has been much speculation as to what instigated this dramatic strategic change at Wal-Mart. One theory was that Wal-Mart's success in being the first into storm ravaged New Orleans after Hurricane Katrina with a fleet of vehicles carrying relief supplies prompted the epiphany. Another was the need to improve

Sixteen.

its public image. Insiders say that the real story is much simpler; and entirely consistent with sustainable enterprise. Sustainability creates value and enables Wal-Mart to enhance its focus of 'always lower prices'. Sam Walton's original dream for Wal-Mart was to bring good quality affordable products to Americans everywhere. Lee Scott and the Wal-Mart leadership realised that environmental sustainability was a way of further developing this dream. The unwanted and unwarranted packaging that cluttered Wal-Mart bins outside their stores cost money to remove, increased the cost of products, took up unnecessary space on the shelf, and irritated consumers. The pressure went on suppliers to minimise packaging except that necessary for health and safety. Next was the size of product packages and how much went in them. If a product, for example detergent, could be compressed then the size of packages would be smaller. This in turn meant less space on shelves and less room taken up in transport vehicles, all of which meant reduced costs. The shape of packages too was considered. Round packaging takes up more space than square for a given content because of the air gaps. Excess materials are waste and consume excess transport, energy and storage space. A systematic review of environmental sustainability in products and operating costs of stores revealed dramatic opportunities for cost saving. Economic and environmental sustainability work together.

Wal-Mart was attracted by the Saatchi & Saatch S (formerly Act Now) PSP™ programme because they could see that by engaging the entire workforce in a practical understanding of sustainability issues in their own lives, some of this may flow into insights for the business as well as enhancing the wellbeing of individuals and their commitment towards the company. More than one million associates at Wal-Mart have experienced PSP™ training with sometimes dramatically positive effects on their wellbeing. In the PSP™ programme people learn key elements of wellbeing and how the adoption of personal sustainability practices can enhance their wellbeing and that of their family, friends and workmates. They are encouraged to adopt one practice until it becomes habitual, rather than a laundry list of commitments all of which quickly become forgotten.

Lee Scott had this to say about the purpose of the programme[102]:

> We are living in a time that presents many uncertainties and a rapidly changing global landscape.

Such times demand forward-looking leadership. The Wal-Mart organisation is committed to becoming a world leader in sustainability, bringing positive change both inside and outside of our company. Imagine what we will be able to achieve when the 1.3 million men and women of Wal-Mart and Sam's Club step up and take the lead for sustainability!

We believe that this simple yet powerful idea should form part of every sustainable enterprise implementation as both a means of enhancing staff wellbeing and as a means of enhancing understanding of the value of sustainability for the benefit of the business.

Flow

We have seen that higher order wellbeing is achieved through meaningful activity and successful progress towards satisfying goals. And this is the domain of flow and performance.

Flow is defined as the complete engagement of mind, body and spirit in the pursuit of challenging and meaningful activities. We observed the idea of Flow during the case study research for *Peak Performance*. Flow was identified as a key concept in peak performance theory, but how to achieve it eluded

us until we worked with the ideas of Mihaly Csikszentmihalyi[103] to implement flow as a step towards peak performance in a range of large and small corporations throughout the world.

Csikszentmihalyi instigated the concept of flow. He explains flow as a state of complete concentration, attention or absorption in the current moment in a challenging and meaningful activity. Flow is equivalent to the sporting analogy of 'being in the zone'. It is experienced when the activities themselves are intrinsically[104] rewarding to the participants, and when the activities are sufficiently challenging to provide growth through learning and achievement and ultimately mastery, but not so overwhelming as to engender high levels of stress, anxiety or hopelessness. We call this 'the just right challenge'.

Csikszentmihalyi describes the experience of flow thus:

- Clarity of focus and concentration is achieved,

- Irrelevant clutter disappears from the mind, and worries and concerns are suspended,

- Time passes quickly,

- A sense of control over actions,

Sixteen.

extraordinary awareness, confidence and power takes place,

• Identity with surroundings and colleagues is felt,

• Joy, happiness and fun is experienced by everyone,

• Loss of self-consciousness and a sense of becoming part of some greater entity is experienced.

Dan Storper of Putumayo told the story of 'store-busting', the process of landing in a strange town and hunting down the most likely stores to stock their music. It was fun and challenging, and the store-busters developed a sixth sense of where to go and which stores would be the winners; intuitively they could glance at a store, at each other, and 'know'.

Although the power of flow is proven for engendering fun, creativity and performance, Csikszentmihalyi demonstrates that the majority of people in the majority of organisations spend the majority of time not in flow; that is, not actively engaged in useful and meaningful activity. The enterprise upside to this is the huge potential for productivity and performance gains and personal wellbeing through the enhancement of potential for flow experiences. In summary, this is achieved by:

1. Enabling people to engage in challenging, meaningful and achievable tasks that stretch skills,

2. Involving people in their choice of activities,

3. Providing real time feedback on performance,

4. Giving feedback based on actions and outcomes,

5. Creating opportunities for learning and skills development,

6. Imagining new activities as skills develop.

Some people have a greater natural propensity for flow than others. Csikszentmihalyi describes this as 'flow personality'. Such people strive to find meaningful activity even in apparently mundane circumstances. They will strive to undertake an activity to the best possible extent, and improve on the way that it is done. They find ways of making even the most boring or undesirable work challenging, interesting and rewarding for its own sake. It's who they are. They are positive and optimistic and joyful in a constructive, not Shangri-La[105] way. Flow personality is an essential attribute for sustainable enterprisers, and one overwhelmingly evidenced by all the founders who we interviewed.

Csikszentmihalyi sees flow as naturally energising creativity; indeed, creativity is an intense form of flow experience[106]:

Creativity is a central source of meaning in our lives...most of the things that are interesting, important, and human are the results of creativity... [and] when we are involved in it, we feel that we are living more fully than during the rest of life.

... for better or worse, our future will be determined in large part by our dreams and by the struggle to make them real.

We also need a positive goal, otherwise why keep going? Creativity is one answer to that question: It provides one of the most exciting models for living.

The sustainable enterprises are awash with innovation in products and processes. New inventions emerge that can shape and re-shape the business model, and sometimes whole industries. For example, Comvita's honey-based wound dressings, promise to transform conventional wound care and healing for certain types of injury. These innovations and inventions will be informed by the sustainability issues, opportunities and risks outlined earlier in this chapter. Insights will emerge from the practices set out in the value creation section.

As well as energising creativity and providing motivation towards sustained engagement, flow experiences also lead towards great execution and getting things done. Because people are fully engaged with the project and each other and totally focused on the activities at hand, projects are effectively completed on time with all details resolved. Flow is about mastery. By practising together over a long period of time, people develop an intuitive understanding of individual and group responses to challenging situations and can respond instinctively, covering for each other as necessary to ensure flawless execution. Execution can't be managed; it's a process of achieving clarity of purpose, inspirational leadership, people with appropriate capacity and capability, putting in place effective practices and creating the context for flow. Great ideas and great execution are the natural results.

Making a difference

Sustainable enterprises make a difference through:

- the sustainable products and services that they deliver,

Sixteen.

• role modelling a more sustainable way of doing business,

• their advocacy for social and environmental causes,

• their philanthropy.

The primary platform for making a difference is the set of products or services that the enterprises provide. Defining characteristics of these products or services are:

• authentic with the enterprise purpose and philosophy,

• premium quality and value for money,

• differentiated and innovative,

• eco-effective,

• socially responsible,

• respectful of human rights,

• environmentally ethical,

• transparently described and explained through an authentic story.

The founders of sustainable enterprises develop their organisations to be role models to show how business can do well by doing good. They share their stories of a better way of doing business through books, presentations, influence on other businesses with whom they trade, and openness to those who seek to learn from them.

Many of the enterprisers from our case study companies have written books[107] about their experiences; most give regular presentations to academic and business audiences. Not only are they activists for the causes to which their enterprises are dedicated, they are also activists for a new paradigm of doing business. Not for them Milton Friedman's self-referential mantra of 'the business of business is business'; for them the role of business is to make a difference – to make the world a better place. In this sense the sustainable enterprises become theatres of dreams that can inspire and provide role models for others.

Here is how Carmelle Druchniak of Stonyfield Farm explains their philosophy:

The purpose of business to Gary Hirshberg is to change the world for the better. He really thinks that the role of business can be to advocate for positive change and he's using Stonyfield as an example to do that. Our healthy vending initiative is a perfect example. Just as the child obesity debate was about to enter the mainstream consciousness, Gary picked his kid up at school and found out he had pizza and skittles and chocolate milk for lunch and said, hey there has got to be a way to get healthier food to the schools here. Because I know if it tastes good kids will eat it, it doesn't matter if it's healthy. And we ended up giving away machines filled with Stonyfield products and kids ate it. We were at the forefront of healthier foods in schools debate because we came up with a solution. And where did the solution come from? Business.

Dilhan Fernando explains the thinking behind Dilmah's philosophy:

The MJF Charitable Foundation exists because of Dilmah, and it grows as Dilmah grows. Whilst a significant part of the revenue of the Foundation comes from my father's personal income, much of it is derived from our now formalised commitment to donate 10% of the profits from Dilmah to the Foundation. This adds meaning to our commercial activity because we know that commercial success brings with it greater ability to do good. In the past two years the work of Dilmah Conservation and our partnership with IUCN[108] has meant that we have similar emphasis on the environment, again structured in the same manner, although the percentage in that case is much less than 10%, our core objective being humanitarian.

Beyond the specific activism inherent in the enterprise models, there is an intent to demonstrate that there is a better way of doing business; or in Anita Roddick's words "business as unusual"[109]. From their enterprise success and advocacy an emergent philosophy of business can be deduced, one that sees the primary outcome of the activities of the enterprises in terms of the goods and services delivered and profit generated, and in terms of the extent to which the wellbeing of people and the planet is advanced. Ray Anderson is an early pioneer of sustainability through his company Interface. Interface[110] is the world's largest supplier of industrial carpet tiles, and has as its purpose "To show the entire industrial world what sustainability is in all its dimensions: People, process, product, place and profits[111]."

This new philosophy of business does not eschew money; far from it. As Yvon Chouinard explained, "Every time we make a decision to do good, it makes us more money[112]." The enterprises strive to be financially successful because this is what enables them to advance their activist agendas in a virtuous cycle.

We introduced construction company Gazeley Ltd in the chapter on potential. Our work with Gazeley commenced with a fascinating

Sixteen.

philosophical conversation with Frank Dixon, their sustainability advisor. Frank prompted us to think deeply about the need for whole system change. Gazeley is passionate and thoughtful about the need for system change. Frank explained:

> System change is like sustainability was ten years ago. In the same way that I knew sustainability would become mainstream, I am certain that system change will soon dominate the sustainability movement.
>
> Sustainability is not possible without system change. I've developed the names mid-level and high-level system change to differentiate the area. Mid-level system change is focused on sectors, stakeholders and specific environmental and social issues. Through its Sustainable Value Networks, Wal-Mart is pioneering mid-level system change. Gazeley's Expert Networks also are an example of mid-level system change.
>
> The most important sustainability issue by far is high-level system change – practically and collaboratively improving overarching economic, political and social systems. Systemic issues essentially make it impossible for any firm to act in a fully responsible manner (ie mitigate all negative impacts) and remain in business.
>
> System change typically has not been the responsibility of business. However, since systemic issues essentially compel business to negatively impact society, growing pushback from society is inevitable as the human economy continues to expand in the finite Earth system. Business is the most powerful force in society. If business does not drive system change, in collaboration with others, business problems inevitably will increase and sustainability will not be achieved voluntarily.
>
> High-level system change is a hugely complex issue. There are no easy and almost certainly no short-term answers. However, by simply putting the issue on the table (ie adding it to the sustainability equation), we take the sustainability movement to a new level.
>
> We put these issues on the table in a non-threatening, pragmatic way. We are simply acknowledging their presence and committing to move forward on them in a practical way, which means in a way that enhances Gazeley's business.

Gazeley confronts directly the question we posed in Chapter 1. Can sustainable enterprise be achieved in the context of an unsustainable global economic system? They seek to play a role in changing that system itself, and modeling the way for other enterprises to do likewise, thereby exemplifying par excellence the making a difference concept in Sustainable Peak Performance theory.

All the enterprisers embrace philanthropy as a natural expression of their enterprise philosophy and means of sharing the dream. Each of the enterprises featured in this book makes philanthropic contributions to organisations or causes relevant to its purpose.

- 1% For the Planet was launched in 2001 by Yvon Chouinard of Patagonia, Inc, and Craig Mathews, owner of Blue Ribbon Flies. Their intent was to inspire other companies to help solve the environmental crisis and to build the success of their businesses through environmental activism. There are over 930 company members now.

- Putumayo World Music donates to enterprises in the communities from which its music derives.

- The Body Shop Foundation donates funds to causes related to its beliefs.

- Stonyfield Farm donates annually 10% of its profit for the planet.

- Dilmah embraces humanitarian service on the principle that business is a matter of human service, and this is discharged through the MJF Charitable Foundation[113]. The activities of the foundation extend to most areas of humanitarian service in the area of economic empowerment, education, improved healthcare and vocational training. The programmes are all aligned with the objective of dignified empowerment to avoid dependency and promote self-reliance and sustainable development through individual and community talents and abilities.

- Patagonia people are actively involved in environmental projects to clean up the natural environment. This personal involvement builds spirit and connectivity amongst the people of the sustainable enterprises, their communities and their customers. It makes the sustainability commitment real.

- Snowy Peak's Untouched World Foundation is committed to developing the next generation of leaders for sustainability through its work with school students.

Sixteen.

Sustainable enterprise philanthropy goes beyond the donation of funds to worthy causes related to the purpose of the enterprise. There is often the active involvement of sustainable enterprise people in the causes themselves, in a way which enhances the participants' wellbeing for reasons explained in the wellbeing section above, and enhances a sense of camaraderie within the enterprise and deep engagement with its purpose and spirit.

For example, Children on the Edge is a charity instigated by Anita Roddick and The Body Shop Foundation. Assistant Director and close friend of Anita, Simon Dowe tells the story:

> Children on the Edge strives to find the most marginalised and the most vulnerable children and make a difference to their life... wherever we work, whatever country we work in, we always manage to find the most godforsaken place and work there and often it is the place that other people won't work. Often it is the place that other people can't work because they can't get funded.

The actual beginnings of the organisation, the founding of the organisation dates back to 1990. Obviously in 1990 when much of the Eastern Bloc was falling and Nicolae Ceauşescu was deposed and executed in Christmas 1989, in the UK and I think probably all around the world, there was a lot of media coverage when they discovered these orphanages and much of the media coverage was based around pictures of neglected children, children being stuck in cots and covered in faeces and never being picked up. And all these kinds of very disturbing things – particularly for our societies – were all over the television screens and I think it was probably the first time something like that broke.

In response to that, Anita decided that she had to do something about it. What she did was she visited Romania and was shown round a variety of different institutions and she ended up in this little village called Halaucesti which had three institutions and the institutions were graded like high schools. They would have like your baby orphanage or middle school orphanage and then your older kids' orphanage. And all these orphanages, these three orphanages, were in this village in the middle of nowhere, bleak Romania, and she decided that was where she wanted to focus her attention, or the company's attention. So she then went back to the company and she organised a collection of goods such as clothing, plumbing stuff, building materials, electrical stuff and initially they took a coach load of employees out to Romania along with some skilled tradesmen and a truck full of all this stuff that had been donated.

From these beginnings in physical infrastructure the Romania project developed initially with four people involved [including Anita's daughter Sam] to work with at risk children directly, a model which continues to this day now in seven countries. Children on the Edge operated as a project within The Body Shop Foundation for the early years of its life until five years ago when it moved to become an independent charity. Although no longer funded by the Foundation, it still has close ties to The Body Shop.

We have an amazing relationship with The Body Shop at home which is the direct sales arm, they fundraise at their parties for Children on the Edge, we have the very close relationship with Body Shop New Zealand who registered as Children on the Edge New Zealand and support most of our work on the Thai-Burma Border. These are all things that just are in the very kind of veins of the company...

As well as fundraising from The Body Shop, volunteering was the power behind Children on the Edge as well as an energiser of spirit within the company. We ran the play schemes where I first came in to contact with Children on the Edge, we ran those in Romania for I think 15 years and every year it was a six week play scheme over the summer and we'd take three teams of about 25 people and they were all company employees and they were from across the globe. There were people from Japan, America, UK, all over Europe, Australia, New Zealand, and they'd all come together in this godforsaken village in the middle of Romania and they'd all sleep on the floor in the school house and they'd all wash under a bucket in the field, and all these people had in common the fact that they worked for this company... The experience of being there with your fellow colleagues from around the globe -- and it was literally people who were working on the shop floor to the head of Communications or the head of HR. It was across the board and everybody was equal there, and I think that is one of the ways that we are so well known in the company because every single one of those people went back to

Sixteen.

that shop floor and told everybody else about it.

Sustainable enterprises make a difference by what they do and what they stand for. And they enable their people to make a difference, thereby enhancing their ability to feel good about themselves and the company through action and achievement.

Conclusion

Through clarity of purpose, nourishing a family-like environment, and following the concepts set out in the section on wellbeing, enterprises can create the context for performance. The concept of flow provides the mental models and tools to enable enterprise participants to experience satisfaction and gratification through achievement of meaningful stretch goals. As these are aligned to enterprise purpose, individual and enterprise performance are maximised. The highest sense of wellbeing is experienced through the feeling of achieving one's full potential and making a difference to something larger than oneself or organisation. The enterprise cause provides this opportunity. Sustainability, wellbeing and performance are thereby inseparably interlinked.

Seventeen.

Performance

We discussed the concept of sustainable development in Chapter 1 and adopted for the purposes of this book the Forum for the Future definition:

"a dynamic process which enables all people to realise their potential and to improve their quality of life in ways which simultaneously protect and enhance the Earth's life support systems".

Or more simply – 'making the world a better place'.

In the preceding pages we have explained how enterprises can infuse the principles of sustainability into their organisational development towards achieving Sustainable Peak Performance.

In this concluding chapter we contemplate the nature of performance in a sustainable

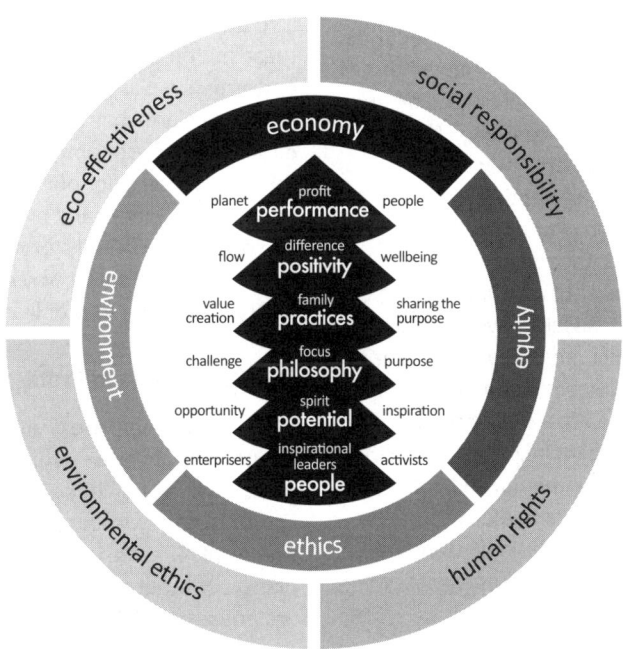

Figure 18 – Performance

Seventeen.

enterprise, and suggest an expanded set of concepts from the usual narrowly defined focus on profitability or economic value added – people, planet and profit. We explain how the principle of performance contributes to the Sustainable Peak Performance action model in Figure 18.

The three concepts that comprise the principle of performance are:

- People
- Planet
- Profit.

Performance is the primary focus of business, so we have retained this as our ultimate principle in Sustainable Peak Performance theory. One definition of performance is the results of the activities of an organisation over a specified time period; another is the working effectiveness of a business, team or individual. Results have traditionally been measured in economic terms, but more recently there has been a move towards 'triple bottom line[114]' performance monitoring of social, environmental and economic outcomes. Sustainable enterprises hold themselves to high standards across all of these dimensions.

A third definition of performance relates to a theatrical or artistic show, presentation or acts that inform, entertain and/or inspire. In this sense sustainable enterprises are 'performances' that inspire a different philosophy of business and of living.

The primary definition of performance in Webster's Dictionary is the simple 'something accomplished'[115], and this is the basis for our formulation of the performance principle in Sustainable Peak Performance theory. What is to be accomplished?

In this chapter we explore what is to be accomplished through these multiple perspectives on performance. Sustainable enterprises pursue performance across the three dimensions of economy, society and the environment (for our purposes here people, planet and profit). They do so with drama and storytelling which inspires a better way of doing business, a better way of living.

People, Planet and Profit

Sustainable enterprise is ultimately about achievement – people, the planet and profit. They go hand in hand. Profit without people is irrelevant. There's no profit on a dead planet. Without profit, enterprises are not sustainable.

The term 'triple bottom line' was

first minted by John Elkington[116], founder and Chief Entrepreneur of SustainAbility, one of the world's pre-eminent consultancies and thinktanks on matters of sustainability. Triple bottom line (TBL) reporting relates to social, environmental and economic outcomes of enterprise activity, normally reported in a single document. Purists argue that the TBL concept perpetuates the problem of divisiveness across these three dimensions which are seen as being irrevocably interlinked. But no-one has been able so far to develop a model quantifying such inter-linkage. Sustainable enterprises do report their outcomes across these three dimensions, but to date no common set of reporting standards has emerged (unlike financial reporting where international accounting standards do provide a framework for comparison).

One area where theory and practice is emerging is in carbon accounting[117], which in the wake of the publicity around climate change has enjoyed considerable attention. It is axiomatic that sustainable enterprises will seek to make rapid progress towards becoming carbon neutral, then positive. We have some anxiety though that the publicity attached to climate change is tending to overshadow other dimensions of sustainability which also have profound potential for creating cataclysm – the global population explosion and shortages of food and fresh water are obvious examples.

We therefore advocate action and reporting across all dimensions of sustainability set out in sustainable development earlier in this chapter, emphasising those aspects that are core to an enterprise's beliefs:

- healthy food for Stonyfield Farm,

- the environment for Patagonia,

- wellness for Comvita,

- human and animal rights for The Body Shop,

- ethical trade for Dilmah

- leadership for sustainability at Snowy Peak

- cultural understanding through music at Putumayo

- people and plants at Eden

- education about sustainability at Forum for the Future.

Although some aspects of sustainability are susceptible to measurement (eg carbon emissions, energy use, philanthropy), many are not. Storytelling is an engaging way of communicating sustainability actions. The Body Shop provides an excellent example[118] of how to

Seventeen.

weave facts into compelling stories of action related to all their beliefs. These stories are complemented by stakeholder commentary and critique related to each belief; for example, actions in regard to 'Against Animal Testing' are commented on by Michelle Thew, Chief Executive, of the British Union for the Abolition of Vivisection. Stakeholder commentary authenticates the stories.

Growth, Financing and Succession

Growth and the challenge of succession beyond the entrepreneurial founders test the new philosophy of sustainable enterprise, and various responses have emerged. The founders of The Body Shop, Ben & Jerry's, Stonyfield Farm, and Tom's of Maine have sold all or a majority of their shares to larger and more traditional companies.

On the other hand some of the enterprisers, such as Yvon Chouinard and Merrill J. Fernando, have vowed never to sell because of concern that their activist agendas would be overwhelmed by the whims of short-term capital markets. They believe that sustainability is simply incompatible with the ethics and values that drive stock markets and multinational corporations. Merrill sees sustainability as embedded in

the family values that he espouses. The company he founded is fortunate in the sustainable leadership of his sons Dilhan and Malik in creating the future. Yvon has concluded that further significant growth in size is not essential for Patagonia's activist agenda, and indeed could be antithetical too it. Growth in environmental activism is the focus.

Others such as The Eden Project and Forum for the Future were established, after careful consideration, as charitable organisations so that their sustainability commitment and activist intent could overtly be framed within their constitutions.

Ben & Jerry's icecream was an early leader in the sustainable enterprise movement, and acted as a role model for many of the organisations cited herein. The founders sold to Unilever in 2000 in an early deal that brought dismay to advocates of sustainable business, who feared that the global corporation would dilute their sustainability beliefs and suck them into the treadmill of quarterly economic results. Ben Cohen and Jerry Greenfield were reputed to be unhappy with the outcome although it appears that Unilever has enabled Ben & Jerry's to remain true to its core beliefs. Jonathon Porritt of Forum for the Future explains it thus:

Unilever has always been a very progressive company and has always had strong commitment to bringing forward more sustainable ways of doing things, with a very strong emphasis on supply chain issues, sustainable agriculture and so on. The statement of business principles in Unilever is one of the most progressive statements you'll find anywhere.

In the years immediately after the acquisition by Unilever, Ben & Jerry's appeared to become a little more conservative and Ben and Jerry themselves were inconspicuous, but under their new CEO Walt Freese the old social activism appears to be back and Ben & Jerry's are actively campaigning for action against global warming and switching expenditure from nuclear bombs towards child health. And Ben and Jerry are back in the fold actively helping. Executives at Ben & Jerry's were told to keep Unilever at the outer edge of their comfort zone, although at times they felt they were pushing them over the edge! For example, the company was overt in its opposition to a genetically modified ingredient for icecream that Unilever is pushing for approval in Europe; Ben & Jerry's have vowed they would never dream of using it.

Anita Roddick explained to us her perspective on the acquisition of

The Body Shop by L'Oreal in 2007 as a "Trojan horse moving into L'Oreal". She hoped that The Body Shop business philosophy would rub off on L'Oreal thereby enabling a transformation in business that the scale of The Body Shop could never achieve alone – to move sustainability into the main stream of global corporations. But Porritt is less sanguine:

That's a tougher one. That's much tougher than Ben & Jerry's into Unilever because L'Oreal doesn't have Unilever's sustainability commitment. The Body Shop's rather harder values frankly clash at L'Oreal, and people are much more sceptical about whether it's going to work compared to Ben & Jerry's.

Simon Dowe of Children on the Edge had a different point of view:

I think that Anita had a very clear vision as to what she was going to do to change L'Oreal, and I honestly believe she would have achieved it, because I think she was so determined and she so believed that she could do it that I think she would. And she wasn't scared of anybody from as far as senior as you can possibly be to as lowly as you can possibly be, she was scared of nobody. And that was why she probably would have

Seventeen.

made huge differences. I think because of her loss, that impact will be lessened. However, they've already launched their Foundation. They've never had a Foundation before. They've launched their Foundation and I know she was key in that happening. Over the next three years I think they are giving 30 million euros away. That is a direct result of her I believe.

Gary Hirshberg of Stonyfield Farm had similar aspirations for the sale of 80% of Stonyfield Farm to Danone in 2004. But he took counsel from Ben and Jerry and developed what's become known as the Hirshberg contract in sustainable enterprise circles – the sale came with a contractual agreement that entrenched the Stonyfield beliefs, kept Hirshberg as CEO and gave him majority control of the subsidiary board. It seems that Danone genuinely wants to learn from the Stonyfield ways, and in the process Stonyfield gets access to Danone capital, technology and channels to new markets. The business is enriched and the theatre of sustainable enterprise is expanded.

Tom Chappell followed the Hirshberg contract model when he and Kate sold a majority shareholding in Tom's of Maine to Colgate-Palmolive. They retained a minority ownership in the company as well as continuing as CEO and Vice President.

The agreement we have worked out succeeds in preserving the character, spirit and values of our company as we grow. You will continue to be able to rely on our tried and true Natural Care products based on our model of stewardship and sustainability. We will continue to make products without artificial preservatives, sweeteners, or dyes and without animal testing or animal ingredients. It will probably become easier for you to find more of our products in a variety of stores. You will still write or call us here in Kennebunk, Maine and we will still be called Tom's of Maine. We will continue our Common Good Partnerships, and to give 10% of what we earn to community efforts, and to support 5% of employee time for volunteering.[119]

Comvita went public quite early in its multinational development with a view to dramatically energising the global growth of its pioneering honey wound dressings. Its initial public offering statement made very clear the sustainability philosophy, purpose and beliefs of the company. So investors knew what they were buying into as an ethical investment within a portfolio.

Is there a right way for sustainable enterprises to finance their growth and expansion? We believe this depends on the philosophy and purpose established for the enterprise. In the case of Forum for the Future, establishment as a charitable organisation gives them the independence to talk tough to their clients about sustainable development. In the case of Patagonia, sustained family ownership enables them to prioritise profits towards environmental activism, and Dilmah towards social activism. For Stonyfield Farm, merging with Danone gave them scale to bring their eco-effectiveness messages to the world.

The Wise Group – a brief case study of Sustainable Peak Performance Implementation

The Wise Group is a large (850 people) social enterprise dedicated to the enhancement of mental wellness, which operates throughout New Zealand. Wise operates a diverse group of companies covering research, information and workforce development for the mental health industry, mental wellness services for women, community-based mental health services, training and education, work placement, software and systems development, and enterprises that create work opportunities for people who are experiencing mental illness.

The business of Wise is social outcomes. They are also economically extremely successful having grown from very small beginnings in just 20 years to NZ$100 million turnover on an investment base of retained earnings. The business generates surpluses that enable them to make further investment in their social purpose.

The enterprise has been a peak performance partner for a decade. So it was interesting for us to work with the senior leadership team including board members to identify those further actions necessary to embrace Sustainable Peak Performance. We commenced by co-creating a sustainability philosophy:

WISE sustainability philosophy

We're a charitable organisation committed to doing our part to create a sustainable future. Sustainability naturally fits with our business philosophy. Our dream is creating fresh possibilities and services for the wellbeing of people, organisations and communities. We see wellbeing as a positive, sustainable state in which people can flourish.

Seventeen.

It's about social equity and contributing towards making the world a better place.

For us sustainability is the holistic integration of social responsibility, economic growth and environmental ethics. This means contributing to a future that is socially just and environmentally sustainable.

We are activists for change towards a more inclusive society. We work to inspire the future and create solutions with government, non-government organisations and communities. As a major non-government organisation we influence others towards sustainability.

Economic independence and profitability are essential for us to fulfill our dream of creating fresh possibilities. We believe everyone in the organisation has a part to play. Through lean thinking and the power of ideas we will create enduring value for people and the planet.

Environmental responsibility means being authentic. We've built Kakariki House, the Waikato region's first certified green building, as a catalyst for our environmental sustainability aspirations. We know it's just the start. We're committed to re-imagining and continually refining our business practices to help us live sustainably.

Sustainability doesn't just happen. It's a belief, an attitude, a journey of social responsibility, and we know that together everything is possible. Everyone can do something.

The Wise purpose is about social sustainability. Peak performance has helped them towards economic sustainability. In 2008 the enterprise made an important overt step to embrace environmental sustainability through the retrofit construction of their national office in Hamilton, New Zealand's fourth-largest city. The building achieved Green star[120] certification and is a source of pride amongst Wise people as well as an inspiring place in which to work and live. It provides a perfect example of the nexus between sustainability and wellbeing and creativity. A gym is included. The offices are light and airy, with natural ventilation and lighting. Central foyer areas use greenery to create calm and positivity. Conference rooms are set up with creativity in mind. The main conference room is 'The Flow Zone'. Across one entire large wall are beautifully designed and illustrated inspirational quotes that were contributed by people from throughout the enterprise. All conference rooms are connected by teleconferencing to the Wise network of companies and offices throughout the country, to minimise travel costs and carbon footprint. The building did cost more than would have been the case had it been built conventionally. But this is offset by reduction in running costs, and by the intangible yet visceral benefit of the building's contribution to wellbeing and productivity as well as symbolising the enterprise's purpose.

A small but symbolic example of how social systems conspire against sustainability was illustrated through the car park story. As part of the building consent for the new headquarters, the local Council insisted on additional car parking space being provided. Another building at the back of the property would have needed to be removed to achieve the additional space. But Wise did not want more people bringing cars to work, or to remove the building which could be used as part of its operations, because this would increase their carbon footprint. They intended to build secure cycle racks for staff bicycles and to encourage people to walk for health, or car pool if too far away. But the Council building requirements provided for one car park per 40 m² of gross floor area regardless of sustainability commitments, so 83 were required, compared with 74 proposed by Wise. CEO Julie Nelson has a gift in inspiring people towards new points of view and after much negotiation, and a proposal to the Council that focused on sustainable transport options, the reduced car parking was accepted by the Council meaning that the building didn't have to be removed.

Because of Wise's role as a health services provider, quality systems are embedded throughout the organisation. The enterprise is certified to ISO 9001 and some parts of the group are also subject to external government quality audit. One of the key insights from our Sustainable Peak Performance workshop was the nexus between the enterprise's sophisticated systems of quality, health and safety, and human resources, and the integrative potential of embracing all of these within an overall system of wellbeing and sustainability. This latter approach would be more in keeping with the purpose and philosophy of the enterprise, and would enable them to continue the process of systems innovation. The process towards this exciting development is currently under way.

CEO Julie Nelson summed up their commitment:

Seventeen.

As a charitable organisation, sustainable enterprise is inherent. It's who we are. We're determined to contribute to a future that is socially just and environmentally sustainable, and we know ours is a continual journey.

Conclusion

Performance relates to what is to be accomplished. This in turn derives from the philosophy and purpose of the enterprise, and embraces positive outcomes for profit, people and the planet. The products and services of the enterprise are designed to achieve strong economic performance, and improve people's lives and nurture or do no harm to the natural environment. The performance principle also includes the meaning of public presentation or exhibition, with the enterprise as a role model, and enterprisers as advocates for a better way of doing business. Performance is the last of the six principles which in combination constitute Sustainable Peak Performance theory.

The pioneering sustainable enterprises in this book have shown the way to a new philosophy of business that can make the world a happier and more sustainable place. The extent to which this new philosophy is embraced by more traditional businesses will be dependent on inspirational leaders in those businesses showing the way (eg Lee Scott and Mike Duke at Wal-Mart and Ray Anderson at Interface), pressure from consumers and from the growing shift towards ethical investment.

The complete Sustainable Peak Performance theory is depicted in Figure 18, and is summarised as follows:

- The macro-context is set by the four sustainability dynamics – ethics, economics, equity and the environment. These inform all aspects of sustainable enterprise.

- People are at the heart of Sustainable Peak Performance. Activists, enterprisers and inspirers define the spirit which becomes the driving force for the enterprise.

- The potential for new business opportunities is enriched by deep understanding of sustainability issues.

- The philosophy and purpose are co-created in a way which provides clarity of purpose, and direction and intent for the organisation based on sustainable value creation.

- Practices are reviewed across all the sustainability drivers to create the context for performance and to ensure that eco-effectiveness and social responsibility are consistently achieved.

- Positivity derives from passionate commitment to creating sustainable products and services that both delight and educate users and enhance people's lives.

- Performance, or what is to be achieved, plays across profit, people and the planet. Sustainable enterprises dramatise a new philosophy of business.

In the following and final chapter we re-assert that sustainable enterprise is simply good business, explain how to get started and emphasise the urgency.

Eighteen.

Just do something!

Sustaining the Future – The Solomon Islands revisited

Everyone we spoke to for this book had a sense that they were preserving something for the future, whether it be resources, the environment, cultural heritage or a community. Charlie Panakera from the Solomon Islands, who we introduced in Chapter 1, puts it succinctly: "I see myself now as being a custodian of resources," he told us. "I'm also responsible for passing on the wealth of knowledge I've accumulated to the new generation, and then they will do the same."

Twenty years ago, Charlie was a trailblazer for sustainability in the tourism industry in the Solomon Islands. With his Western education and position as paramount chief of Rannong island, he was uniquely placed to realise that what he and his people took for granted was something Western tourists would pay good money to experience – money that used wisely could help secure the future of the local people.

Unusually for the 1980s, he also realised that unless tourism was managed sustainably, it had the power to destroy exactly what it sought: an unspoiled corner of paradise with unique cultural traditions.

Charlie's ability to marry traditional island hospitality with entrepreneurial flair made him a magnet for journalists the world over, who flocked to his hotel on Gizo island, the scuba diving capital of the Solomons. "My face was all over the covers of Pacific magazines as I was the only black man running hotels," he remembers.

The experience Charlie offered his guests was a far cry from that of the glossy international resort chains, well insulated from the surrounding local community. At Charlie's places, tourists got to experience island life at grassroots level, in modest accommodation with opportunities to mix in with the locals. It was in fact what we now know as ecotourism.

From hotels, Charlie moved on to tour operations, dive shops, game fishing businesses, and even a logging microenterprise supplying sustainably harvested logs to New Zealand and Australia. He was also active in public life, serving as a Member of Parliament for 12 years, and as Deputy Managing Director of the Solomon Islands Development Bank.

Charlie is still digging into his wealth of accumulated experience to give back to his community. Now an academic based in New Zealand, he's developed the curriculum for the Solomon Islands' first School of Tourism and Hospitality, which opened in the capital Honiara in 2009, with funding from the United Nations Development Programme (UNDP) and Taiwan. Charlie hopes that from among its graduates will emerge the next generation of ecotourism entrepreneurs.

"All the courses have indigenous, cultural and environmental sustainability concepts built in," Charlie told us. "Tour operators need to be able to tell our stories when they take visitors through the bush. And we are dealing with unique marine resources that need to be managed sustainably."

Charlie remains optimistic on the outlook for sustainable tourism in the Solomons. "We're seeing the globalisation of sustainability and ecotourism," he says. "It's quite amazing that today someone can sit in front of a computer in Europe and call up a website showing sustainable hotels in a remote corner of the Solomon Islands, and book a holiday online."

That particular initiative grew out of a chance contact Charlie had with the International Finance Corporation, part of the World Bank Group, which helps private sector development initiatives in poor countries with finance and advice. The Solomons is now part of the WorldHotel-link.com project, an online hotel booking system. The IFC provides training and support to small local tourism operators to help them access the global e-marketplace through this site.

With the current Solomon Island government committed to easing red tape for international investment and two new Pacific airlines, Charlie says tourism could bring huge benefit to the Solomons. But he's also mindful in his role as custodian of resources that ensuring any development remains true to the principles of sustainability is no easy task. Better education should help, and he believes the new School of Tourism and Hospitality is a step on the way to a brighter future for the next generation.

We admired our friend's enthusiasm and were amazed by his ability to make things happen despite lack of infrastructure, impoverished civil society and corruption. We were excited by the sustainable enterprise ventures we experienced

Eighteen.

from seaweed to eco-tourism, sustainable logging and natural sponge harvesting. It will take all this positivity to enable sustainable enterprise value creation to endure in a global economic context where the short term is privileged, environmental costs are externalised and social costs are deferred to the next generation.

Sustainability, value and quality

We completed our research adventure at the end of 2007, with Anita Roddick's closing words to us echoing in our ears – "just do something!" By the conclusion of our research we were very confident that it is possible to create enterprises based on sustainability principles and for them to be as or more enduringly financially successful than their econo-centric counterparts. We are confident that sustainability lies at the heart of enduring value creation.

Sustainability can be seen in a similar light to the quality movement of the closing decades of the 21st century. The story of W. Edwards Deming, the quality pioneer is well-known in the annals of business. Unable to make himself heard in his home country the USA, Deming[121] became the leading light of the transformation of the Japanese economy in the years following World War II with his pioneering quality principles. His ideas were rejected in his home country with claims that there was nothing wrong with American products; and even if there was, quality costs more; that people did not want quality and even if they did they would not be prepared to pay for it. Far from costing more, Deming demonstrated that by building in quality, costs of both manufacture and re-work reduced, often dramatically. His work contributed to the dominance of Japanese manufacturing methods to this day. It is no coincidence that Toyota, who were at the forefront of the quality movement, were early adopters of environmental sustainability as a core strategy nearly ten years ago. The Prius Hybrid has given Toyota an image of green leadership as well as a brand that commands premiums.

We can expect sustainable development to follow a similar pattern as quality. Those who claim it can't or shouldn't be done will be forced out of the market by those who are already doing it. Like quality, sustainable development is a state of mind as much as it is a set of management practices. It is this state of mind that will reveal opportunities where others only see cost and risks.

By using the analogy of quality we can make a number of predictions:

1. People will come to expect sustainability; they will not be willing to pay a premium for it in the long run; instead they will reject companies that fail to deliver sustainable products and services.

2. The transition towards sustainability will take several years; it will move more quickly than the quality transition because of the speed with which unsustainable practices can be revealed through the web and citizen media.

3. It will be difficult for companies that are late adopters of sustainability to catch up with the leaders because of the self generating cycle of efficiency gains, brand enhancement, technological development and staff engagement that comes with the adoption of a sustainability paradigm.

4. Those who embrace sustainability at the heart of their business models will discover that it saves rather than costs money and enhances rather than reduces profitability.

The global economic crisis which unfolded during 2008/9 was a crisis of capitalism as we have known it. We have witnessed the worldwide spectacle of developed world banks and private enterprise going cap in hand to their own nation states and sovereign wealth funds of developing or oil-rich nations to bail out their bankrupt businesses.

Yet we believe it is not the principles of capitalism that created the crisis, but rather the short-termist orientation of their execution. We hope that a new understanding of capitalism can emerge from this wreckage, based on a regained understanding of the need to create enduring value to enhance wellbeing for people and society. Such was the foundation principle of classical economics.

Research by global management consultants A.T. Kearney, gives cause for encouragement. They demonstrate that businesses with a genuine commitment to sustainability are coping significantly better in the new economic reality than their peers. Their February 2009 report, *Green Winners: The Performance of Sustainability-Focused Companies in the Financial Crisis*[122], looked at 99 companies on the Dow Jones Sustainability Index and/or the Goldman Sachs Sustain focus list. Their conclusion was that companies committed to sustainability were outperforming their industry peers by 10% over

Eighteen.

three months of the economic crisis, and by 15% over six months.

Is Sustainable Peak Performance for everyone?

Can any enterprise aspire towards Sustainable Peak Performance? Or are the principles limited to the small and medium-sized organisations from whence they derive?

We believe the principles are generalisable to all enterprises, except for those that are based on fundamentally unethical business propositions (tobacco companies would be an obvious exclusion[123]).

Our work through Inspiros Worldwide has demonstrated over the last decade that peak performance principles can lead to enhanced performance in multinational corporations and small and medium-sized enterprises alike.

"Peak Performance is unleashing and inspiring P&G leaders around the world."
— AG Lafley, worldwide CEO, Procter & Gamble

"I think Peak Performance will inspire you to rethink your business from the inside out."
— H. Okuda, Chairman, Toyota Motor Corporation

"Peak Performance has added two billion dollars worth of value to the Saatchi & Saatchi global network."
— Kevin Roberts, Worldwide CEO, Saatchi & Saatchi[124]

Sustainable Peak Performance Principles are consistent with the earlier peak performance work in so far as the need for clarity of purpose, inspirational leadership, energising practices and flow are concerned.

Additional theoretical elements from this sustainable enterprise project relate to the need for:

1. An underlying philosophy that explains what the enterprise believes about sustainability and what it is going to do about it.

2. Leadership for sustainability.

3. Sustainability opportunity and risk recognition as potential for value creation.

4. A set of sustainability practices that create the context for sustainable enterprise.

5. The development of positivity through, in addition to flow, enterprise development that enhances wellbeing and making a difference for people, organisations and society.

6. The expansion of performance to embrace people and the planet as well as profit, and role

modelling a better way of doing business.

Each of these elements can enhance and sustain performance in every sense, and as a consequence are entirely consistent with the traditional business imperative of profitability. It is perhaps the extension of the notion of performance itself to embrace people and the planet that causes economic purists to baulk at the sustainability agenda. But here is a summary of why embracing sustainability in its totality is good for the bottom line as well as people and the planet:

Human relations

- Ability to attract and retain top talent

- Improved employee productivity

Eco-effectiveness

- Reduced or avoided costs

- More effective use of available resources

Quality and risk management

- Minimised reputation risk

- Minimised legal and regulatory risks

- Enhanced quality of products or services

Right to operate

- Reduced compliance, licensing and insurance costs

- Enhanced reputation with key stakeholders including regulators

Marketing

- Stronger brands and consumer loyalty, and avoidance of consumer backlash

- New products, technologies, processes or services

- New market opportunities.

In combination these benefits can result in reduced costs of capital, increased resilience, enhanced market share, profits and shareholder value.

The Potential for Sustainable Peak Performance

We completed ten sustainable enterprise consultancy engagements during 2008 to share the ideas and learn from the experiences.

Collectively and individually these experiences confirmed our conviction in the principles of Sustainable Peak Performance –

People who are inspirational leaders, enterprisers and activists passionate about making a difference are essential for

Eighteen.

sustainable enterprise success,

Unsustainability risks and sustainability opportunities can inspire insight about **potential** for business ideas,

At the heart of Sustainable Peak Performance theory is clarity of **philosophy and purpose,**

Practices are the everyday activities that create sustainable enterprise value and the context in which Sustainable Peak Performance can be achieved,

Positivity of attitude is the energy for Sustainable Peak Performance,

Performance is explained in terms of creating value for profit, people and the planet.

We concluded our year of pilot projects on the one hand enormously encouraged that almost any type of company can embrace Sustainable Peak Performance with positive effect. On the other hand we were even more puzzled why such a small proportion of companies are actually doing so, when the benefits to performance, wellbeing and brand are so evident.

We are not sure why this is so, but the following explanations may form part of the answer:

The global economic system tends to privilege the short term through stock market quarterly investment earnings reports, and senior executive incentives. Sustainability is a long term agenda, and although it can be demonstrated that financial performance over the long term will be maximised through adopting sustainability practices, business leaders fixated and incentivised to the short term may not see the benefit.

There is a widespread view that sustainability is just about the environment. As such it has been easy for sustainable business advocates to be dismissed as 'greenies', not serious about business.

Many business people and business academics who create business theory tend to be inherently conservative. We tend to borrow our theories metaphorically from other domains – for example, strategy derived from the military, organisation behaviour from behavioural psychology, culture from anthropology. Often the ideas that we import are dated or discredited in their source domains only to be used with impunity in business. New ideas, as J. Edwards Deming found in the 1960s with quality, can often be treated with scepticism and sometimes ridicule.

To date there hasn't been sufficient thought put into the development of simple, practical ways of transitioning towards sustainable enterprise; to enable enterprises to "just do something!"

During the three years it has taken to research this book and write the stories, a series of unrelated global events has tipped the world towards a greater awareness of the compelling need for sustainable development. The fourth assessment report of the Intergovernmental Panel on Climate Change was published in 2007[125]. It was unequivocal in its convictions about anthropomorphic induced global warming and the consequences for humanity if we fail to act to contain it. Al Gore's documentary *An Inconvenient Truth* popularised these ideas and made people around the planet aware of the serious consequences of delay in acting to mitigate greenhouse gas emissions. Business leaders of mainstream global businesses have placed their commitment to sustainability on record and dedicated their companies to its achievement, Lee Scott and Mike Duke of Wal-Mart for example. But the most compelling transformation is likely to be from the global economic transformation

that is currently unfolding.

Consumer reaction has been swift[126]. Consumers have reduced their purchases especially of long term assets such as vehicles, and luxury items. They are looking for value, reframing what constitutes value and conducting due diligence to find it. Quality is paramount. There is a rediscovery that wellbeing is not defined by what you buy, but by what you experience; that joy can be found in simple pleasures and rituals. Frugality has become the new cool, together with a sense of not wanting to appear too well off. Consumers are feeling good about making do. It is too early to say whether these changes will be enduring. But we can assert that the conditions that led to the dramatic global growth in consumer spending of the last decade are unlikely to be repeated.[127]

How to get started

The best way to get started is 'just do something'!

We have presented Sustainable Peak Performance theory in the logical sequence of how the sustainable enterprises featured in the book came into being and developed – people, potential, philosophy and purpose, practices, positivity and performance. And this can be a practical series of steps to take to

Eighteen.

develop an overall action plan for engaging with sustainable enterprise and sustainable peak performance.

1. People

- Develop an education and training programme for everyone in the enterprise to learn about the potential from sustainable enterprise.

- Consider ways in which the senior leadership team will embrace and become ambassadors for sustainability.

2. Potential

- Conduct a comprehensive review of sustainability issues that may affect the enterprise and consider their implications for value creation and strategy.

- Complement the enterprise's quality, lean and innovation systems and attitude with a sustainability frame of reference to ensure that opportunities from sustainable enterprise become a natural aspect of the way the enterprise does business.

3. Philosophy

- Develop a sustainability philosophy that explains what the enterprise means by sustainability and what it intends to do about it.

- Review the company's Purpose and business model to ensure that a commitment to sustainability is explicitly incorporated.

4. Practices

- Review the enterprise's practices across all aspects of the business, using the checklist in Chapter 15

- Start on a programme to measure, reduce and offset carbon emissions. Tracking carbon can lead to a wide range of cost savings and efficiency gains as well making a demonstrable commitment to a key sustainability issue.

5. Positivity

- Introduce a wellbeing programme directly connected with your health and safety programme, people and performance.

- Review the product/service portfolio as the primary means whereby you make a difference, to ensure consistency with sustainability principles.

6. Performance

- Develop sustainability reporting, storytelling and stakeholder dialogue as means of learning as you go, and demonstrating transparent commitment to sustainability.

- Network with other organisations as a means of learning and sharing.

- Celebrate.

Sustainable enterprise, like lean, quality and innovation, is a journey rather than a destination. Our experience is that the steps above work well as a means of getting started. Each journey will be unique, but the principles above have proved in our experience to be robust across multiple businesses and industries. The need for a comprehensive and holistic approach, fully integrated across all business activities is paramount.

Conclusion

Sustainability is a state in which current generations can meet their needs without compromising the ability of future generations to meet their own needs. Sustainable development is a process of development that moves towards sustainability.

Sustainable enterprises are committed to sustainable development. They view the burgeoning global social and environmental needs and issues described in chapter 1 as

opportunities for private enterprise to provide entrepreneurial and innovative solutions. Sustainable enterprise is simply good business.

We have presented a model of sustainable enterprise as describing enterprises founded on principles of sustainable development, which we define as embracing economy, equity, environment and ethics. We consider that the addition of ethics to the usual sustainability elements of economic, social (equity), and environment brings robustness to the model, and extends business sustainability thinking to encompass its near cousin, corporate social responsibility.

We have emphasised the inter-connected nature of these elements of sustainability. In particular we have noted the commonly held misapprehension that sustainability is just about the environment. We reject the notion that any one of the elements can exist without the others, and as a consequence advocate against the separable description or use of ideas of environmental sustainability, or economic sustainability or social sustainability.

The alternative of unsustainable enterprise is clearly not attractive. As the 21st century unfolds there will be no enduring ethical enterprise

Eighteen.

success without embracing sustainability principles.

We have shared a series of stories about enterprises that have based their global success on adherence to sustainable enterprise principles. The stories cross cultures, countries and industries. In so doing we found that these enterprises exemplified many of the principles and concepts of the earlier peak performance theory, but with additional elements.

Sustainable enterprise provides the context and philosophy within which peak performance can unfold. Sustainable Peak Performance theory provides six principles and 18 concepts which together explain how Sustainable Peak Performance can be achieved. Sustainable Peak Performance is defined as "continuously exceeding the enterprise's best performance in pursuit of a sustainable purpose". A sustainable enterprise purpose is one that aspires to meet a social cause and customer needs, whilst nurturing or doing no harm to the natural environment and generating adequate economic returns to stakeholders.

Sustainable Peak Performance theory is a comprehensive and holistic approach towards sustainable development and enduring enterprise success. It enables and

encourages the adoption and integration of sustainability principles across all dimensions of the enterprise.

Because we advocate integration of sustainability throughout the enterprise, we advise against the establishment of separate sustainability departments and separate sustainability strategies. Sustainability is everyone's job and should form a fundamental and integrated aspect of enterprise development – leadership, business philosophy and purpose, opportunity recognition and strategy development, business models, value creation, product design, marketing, people policies, processes and practices, spirit and culture, and performance measurement and development.

Initial attempts by businesses to develop a 'sustainability strategy' often focus on brand, image or marketing with scant regard to substance. These will inevitably fail, and will probably be damaging. Customers, consumers and the business's own people will quickly see through such ploys with consequent undermining of credibility. NGOs, blogs and citizen media-based web retribution can be swift and devastating.

There are no short cuts. It has

been our experience through the project that the most progressive and best managed companies are the ones most likely to embrace sustainable development, as a natural progression of performance development. Toyota plays General Motors is a case in point. In fact we have reached the conclusion that it's probably not possible (as well as not likely) that sustainable development can be successfully achieved by companies that are not well led or managed and whose purpose lacks clarity. Inspirational leadership and clarity of purpose are departure points for Sustainable Peak Performance.

The rewards of Sustainable Peak Performance, both in traditional economic terms and in terms of making the world a better place, are substantial. The risks of failure to embrace sustainability individually and collectively are that enterprises, and ultimately humanity, may not endure.

We wish you well on your own continuing story of sustainable enterprise, and would love to hear from you at Stories@SustainableEnterprise.org.

Endnotes.

Preface

1   SMEs represent over 95% of enterprises in most of the 30 OECD countries and generate over half of private sector employment.

CHAPTER 1
Why Sustainable Enterprise?

2   Stiglitz, J.; & Charlton, A. (2007). *Fair trade for all: How trade can promote development.* Oxford: Oxford University Press.

3   Prahalad, C. K., & Hammond, A. (2002). Serving the world's poor, profitably. *Harvard Business Review, 80*(9), 48-57. Prahalad, C.K. (2006). *The Fortune at the Bottom of the Pyramid.* New Jersey: Wharton School Publishing, pp. 235-245.

4   Power, prestige or influence in inidigenous languages of the South Pacific

5   Gossip network

6   Diamond, J. (2005). *Collapse: How societies choose to fail or succeed.* New York: Viking Press.

7   United Nations. (1987, December 11). *Report of the World Commission on Environment and Development.* General Assembly Resolution 42/187. Retrieved June 19, 2008, from http://www.un.org/documents/ga/res/42/ares42-187.htm

8   Forum for the Future. (2008). *Formal definitions.* Retrieved June 19, 2008, from http://www.forumforthefuture.org.uk/node/327

9   Gilson, C., Pratt, M. J., Roberts, K. & Weymes, E. (2000). *Peak performance: Business lessons from the world's best sports organisations.* London: Harper Collins.

10   See for example Eisenhardt, K. M. (1989). Building theories from case study research. *Academy of Management Review,* 14(4), 532-550.

11   Cooperrider, D., Sorenson, P. Jr., Whitney, D., and Yager, T. (2000). *Appreciative inquiry: Rethinking human organization toward a positive theory of change.* Champaign, Ill: Stripes Publishing.

12   Burke, W. (1987). *Organization Development: A Normative View.* Reading, MA: Addison-Wesley.

13   Anderson, R. (1998). *Mid-course correction: Toward a sustainable enterprise: The interface model.* Atlanta: The Peregrinzilla Press.

14   We understand that Ben Cohen has now re-established connections with the company he co-founded following a change of leadership.

15   Chappell, T. (1999). *Managing upside down: The seven intentions of values-centered leadership.* New York: William Morrow and Company.

16   Peters, T., & Waterman, R. (1982). *In search of excellence.* New York: Harper & Row.

17   Collins, J. (2001). *Good to great.* New York: Harper Collins.

CHAPTER 3 Stonyfield Farm

18   Gerber, M. E. (1995). *The E-myth revisited: Why small businesses don't work and what to do about it.* New York: Harper Business.

19   Bovine somatotropin is a protein hormone produced in the pituitary glands of cattle. Monsanto first synthesised this hormone using recombinant DNA technology [genetic engineering] – hence recombinant bovine somatotropin or rBST – and marketed it in the USA as POSILAC from 1994. It was said to increase milk yields by 25% or more. The non technical name is bovine growth hormone. Canada, Australia, New Zealand, Japan and the European Union all refused to approve it. In 2007 Starbucks announced it would cease using milk derived from rBST treated cows. By 2009 consumer resistance because of health concerns about use of the growth hormone and concerns about the welfare of treated cows had

dramatically reduced the use of rBST.

20   Jensen, R. (1999), *The Dream Society – How the Coming Shift from Information to Imagination Will Transform Your Business*, McGraw-Hill, New York, NY .

CHAPTER 4 The Body Shop

21   The *Letters of Delegates to Congress, 1774-1789* provide an in depth account of the operations of the Continental Congress during the critical years of the founding of the United States.

22   A personaility questionnaire, designed to discover a person's inner feelings

CHAPTER 5 The Eden Project

23   Smit, T. (2001). *Eden*. London: Bantam Press.

24   Smit, T. (2001). *Eden*. London: Bantam Press. (pp14-15)

25   Diana Mullis, D. (2005). *West Country Faerie*, Launceston: Bossiney Books

CHAPTER 6 Forum for the Future

26   Plan A is Marks & Spencer's 100 point eco-pan that will see them working with customers and suppliers to combat climate change, reduce waste, safeguard natural resources, trade ethically and build a healthier nation – see http://plana.marksandspencer.com

27   For example, ICI's Ecosure, paint, Sustento, a new property fund for sustainable properties, forest-backed bonds, Landrover's CO2 offset, BP's Target Neutral.

28   Porritt, J. (2007). *Capitalism as if the world matters.* London: Earthscan.

CHAPTER 8 Comvita

29   Good manufacturing practices for natural health products.

30   MRSA stands for *methicillin-resistant Staphylococcus aureus*

31   These children are born with skin as fragile as a butterfly's wing which can blister at the slightest touch. Normal day-to-day life can cause constant

pain and scarring, which, in the worse forms, leads to eventual disfigurement, disability and often early death. EB cannot be cured, however Comvita's Medihoney™ is proving beneficial for healing lesions with minimal scar tissue.

CHAPTER 9 Patagonia

32   Chouinard, Y. (2006). *Let My People Go Surfing: The Education of a Reluctant Businessman*, New York: Penguin Books

CHAPTER 10 Dilmah

33   From BBC news report http://news.bbc.co.uk/2/hi/south_asia/8062922.stm

34   Gin & and tonic, the classic drink of the British in the colonies of Ceylon and India.

35   Mike has a lifetime interest in manufacturing and recently chaired for New Zealand Trade and Enterprise the development of a national vision for manufacturing.

CHAPTER 11 Sustainable Enterprise

36   Genetically Modified Organisms

37   David, L., Bender, L. & Burns, S. (Producers), & Guggenheim, D. (Director). (2006). *An inconvenient truth* [Motion picture]. United States: Paramount Classics

38   McDonough, W., & Braungart, M. (2002). *Cradle to cradle: Remaking the way we make things.* New York: North Point Press.

39   You can learn more about the story of peak performance in Gilson, C., Pratt, M.J., Roberts, K. and Weymes, E. (2000), *Peak Performance*. London: Harper Collins, and Pratt M.J., A Story of Peak Performance. *Management Communication Quarterly*, 14(3), February 2001, 476-483, or at www.inspiros.org.

CHAPTER 12 People

40   Albrecht, K. (1994). The northbound train: Finding the purpose, *setting the direction, shaping the destiny of your organization*. New York: AMACON.

41   Capparell, S., & Morrell, M. (2001). *Shackleton's way: Leadership lessons from the great antarctic explorer.* New York: Viking Press.

42   The model is informed by – Maslow, A. A Theory of Human Motivation. *Psychological Review, 50(4),* 370-396; Beck, D.E., & Cowan, C.C. (1996). *Spiral Dynamic: Mastering Values, Leadership and Change.* Cambridge: Blackwell; Barrett, R. (1998). *Liberating the Corporate Soul.* Boston: Butterworth; Seligman, M. & Csikszentmihalyi, M. (2000, January) Positive Psychology. *American Psychologist.*

43   Bill Gates, *Fortune,* January 26, 2004, p. 124

44   Inspiros Worldwide provided inspirational leadership training for A.G. Lafley and the senior leadership of Procter & Gamble from 2001-2008.

45   Ben-Shahar, T. (2007) Happier: Learn the secrets to daily joy and lasting fulfilment. (p.127) New York: McGraw-Hill.

46   Chouinard, Y., Lecture at Stanford Business School, October 2006, see http://www.gsb.stanford.edu/NEWS/headlines/2006-07vongugelberg.shtml, accessed 27 September 2009

CHAPTER 13 Potential

47   For example the Murray-Darling basin in Australia

48   Lovelock, J. (2000). *Gaia: A new look at life on earth* (3rd ed.). Oxford: Oxford University Press.

49   Developed from Zadek, S. (2004, December). The path to corporate responsibility. *Harvard Business Review,* 82(12), 125-132.

50   A Google search on Nike and sweatshops will reveal scores of entries and whole web-sites dedicated to essays on the topic.

51   Greenpeace. (2006). *Green my apple.* Retrieved July 3, 2008, from http://www.greenmyapple.org

52   Anderson, R. (1999). *Mid-course correction: Toward a sustainable enterprise – the Interface model.* White River Junction, VT: Chelsea Green.

53   Chouinard, Y. (2005). *Let my people go surfing: The education of a reluctant businessman.* New York: Penguin Press.

54   Hirshberg, G. (2008). *Stirring it up: HowUp; how to make money and save the world.world,* New York: Hyperion. Hyperion

CHAPTER 14 Philosophy

55   See http://www.forumforthefuture.org.uk/about-us downloaded 20 August 2009

56   See http://comvita.com/ourworldatcomvita.html downloaded 20 August 2009

57   Greenleaf, R.K. (1977). Servant leadership : A journey into the nature of legitimate power and greatness (p. 16). New York: Paulist Press.

58   Lovemarks is an approach to branding adopted by Saatchi & Saatchi. See http://www.lovemarks.com/

59   Collins, J. & Porras, J. (1996). Building your company's vision, *Harvard Business Review,* 74(5), 65-77.

60   Capodagli, B. & Jackson, L. (2000). The Disney way fieldbook : How to implement Walt Disney's vision of "dream, believe, dare, do" in your *own company.* New York; London : McGraw-Hill.

61   See http://www.interfaceglobal.com/Sustainability/Our-Journey/Vision.aspx, downloaded 27 September, 2009

CHAPTER 15 Practices

62   The traditional business language to describe people who use a company's products is 'consumer'. We eschew this term in favour of 'user' on the basis that consumption implies 'using up; burning up', whereas 'user' can be more benign. We advocate renewable use rather than consumption.

63   See http://www.stopgreenwash.org and Aitken, L. (2007, November 19).

Wiping out 'greenwash' companies. *The Guardian*, p. 9

64 The initial version of this model was first developed as part of a research project entitled Manufacturing+, A Vision for World Leading New Zealand Manufacturers, commissioned by New Zealand's Minister for Economic Development – see http://www.nzte. govt.nz/section/14454/16182.aspx.

65 There are many books available to assist you to embed sustainable development into your enterprise practices. We invite you to review http://www. sustainableenterprise.org/bibliography. htm for a selection of our favourites.

66 Opinions on the use of GMOs are polarised, with passionate advocates on both sides of the divide. Sustainable enterprises should have a thought-through position on where they stand on this issue. Our point of view is that the risk of consumer rejection of brands revealed as tainted by GMOs is likely to be too high to be sustainable [eg rBST].

67 See http://www.ipcc.ch/

68 Benyus, J. (1997), *Biomimicry: Innovation Inspired by Nature*. London: HarperCollins Publishers Inc,

69 http://www.oecd.org/department/.

70 "Human beings are powered by emotion not by reason. Study after study has proven that if the emotion centers of our brain are damaged in some way, we don't lose the ability to laugh or cry, we lose the ability to make decisions." Roberts, K. (2005). *Lovemarks*. (p. 42). New York: Powerhouse Books.

71 as stated on their website www.wbcsd. ch

72 Womack, J., Jones, D. and Roos, D. (1990) *The Machine That Changed the World: The Story of Lean Production* New York: Maxwell Macmillian.

73 Womack, J.P., & Jones, D.T. (1996). *Lean Thinking: banish waste and create wealth in your corporation*, New York: Simon and Schuster

74 Differing definitions of family business are used by different researchers; the usual parameters include significant (>10%) family ownership, a family member is CEO or chairman and family control of the board

75 Poutziouris, P. (2006). *The UK family business PLC economy: A report on the performance of UK family controlled quoted companies*. London: Institute for Family Business (UK).

CHAPTER 16 Positivity

76 Seligman, M. E. P. & Csikszentmihalyi, M. (2000, January). Positive Psychology. [Special issue]. *American Psychologist, 55*, 5-14.

77 Aristotle, *Nichomachean Ethics*, book 1, section 7

78 See http://www.epicurus.net/

79 Hume, D. (1826). *The Stoic, Essays, Moral, Political and Literary*, part 1, essay 16, in *The Philosophical Works of David Hume*, vol. 3, p. 167

80 Bentham, J. (1789). *An Introduction to the Principles of Morals and Legislation*, Oxford: Clarendon Press

81 Mill, J. S. and Benthem, J. edited by Ryan, A. (2004). *Utilitarianism and other essays*. London: Penguin Books

82 Marx, K. and Engels, F. (1975). *Collected Works*. New York and London: International Publishers.

83 See http://www.ushistory.org/ declaration/

84 Quoted in C P Snow, *Variety of Men*, (Harmondsworth 1969) 77

85 Nietzsche, F. (1968). *The will to power: In science, nature, society and art*. New York: Random House.

86 St. Thomas Aquinas (1983). *Treatise on Happiness*, University of Notre Dame Press

87 Lovelock, J. (2006). *The revenge of Gaia: Why the earth is fighting back – and how we can still save humanity*. London: Allen Lane.

88 Lovelock postulates that one billion people would be comfortable; WWF believe about 4.5 billion may

be sustainable; the current global population is 6.7 billion and moving rapidly to 9 billion by mid century.

89   For example, the Foresight Report on Obesity published in the UK in October 2007 forecast that more than 60% of men and 50% of women would be obese by 2050 unless dramatic change occurred.

90   The desertification, and scarcity of water and fertile land in Darfur in the Western Sudan is at the root cause of the widespread violence reputed to have led to the deaths of an estimated 500,000 people.

91   Seligman, M. E. P. & Csikszentmihalyi, M. (2000, January). Positive Psychology. [Special issue]. *American Psychologist, 55,* 5-14.

92   Smithey Fulmer, I., Gerhart, B., & Scott, K.S. (2003). Are the 100 best better? An empirical Investigation of the relationship between being a "great place to work" and firm performance. *Personnel Psychology, 56,* 965-989.

93   Seligman, M. (2002). *Authentic happiness. Using the new positive psychology to realize your potential for lasting fulfillment.* Sydney, Australia: Random House.

94   Sheldon K., Elliot A., Kim Y. & Kasser T. (2001). What is satisfying about satisfying events? Testing 10 candidate psychological needs. *Journal of Personality and Social Psychology, 80(2),* 325-339.

95   Ryan, R. M., & Deci, E. L. (2000). "Self-determination theory and the facilitation of intrinsic motivation, social development, and well-being." *American Psychologist,* 55, 68-78.

96   Frankl, V. (2004). *Man's search for meaning. An introduction to logotherapy.* London: Rider

97   Mandela, N. (1994). *Long walk to freedom.* New York: Little Brown and Company.

98   Sheldon, K.M. & Lyubomirsky, S. (2006). Achieving sustainable gains in happiness: change your actions not your

circumstances. *Journal of Happiness Studies,* 7, 55-86.

99   Maestri , (2009). M.,*Wal-Mart's incoming CEO to expand environmental push,* New York: Reuters, Jan. 26

100   Bianco, A. (2006). *The bully of bentonville.* New York: Broadway Business.

101   Scott, L. (2005). *Twenty first century leadership.* Retrieved March 16, 2009 from Walmart Web site: http://walmartstores.com/ViewResource.aspx?id=1965

102   From Saatchi & Saatchi S marketing material

103   Csikszentmihalyi, M. (1990). *Flow: The Psychology of Optimal Experience.* New York: Harper and Row.

104   Seen as having meaning in their own right beyond the extrinsic monetary or other tangible rewards to which they may give rise.

105   Hilton, J. (1933). *Lost horizon.* New York: William Morrow & Co.

106   Csíkszentmihályi, M. (1996). *Creativity: Flow and the psychology of discovery and invention.* New York: Harper Perennial.

107   See http://www.sustainableenterprise.org/bibliography

108   The International Union for Conservation of Nature and Natural Resources (IUCN) is dedicated to natural resources conservation. It was founded in 1948 and is based in Switzerland.

109   Roddick, A. (2005). *Business as Unusual,* Chichester: Anita Roddick Books

110   Anderson, R. C. (1998). *Mid-course correction: Toward a sustainable enterprise: The Interface model.* White River Junction, VT: Chelsea Green Publishing Company.

111   See http://www.interfaceglobal.com/Company/Mission-Vision.aspx

112   Chouinard, Y., Lecture at Stanford Business School, October 2006, see http://www.gsb.stanford.edu/NEWS/headlines/2006-07vongugelberg.shtml, accessed 27 September 2009

113   http://www.mjffoundation.org

CHAPTER 17 Performance

114 Elkington, J. (1994). Towards the sustainable corporation: Win-win-win business strategies for sustainable development. *California Management Review, 36*(2), 90-100
115 See http://www.merriam-webster.com/dictionary/performance
116 See http://www.johnelkington.com
117 See http://www.ghgprotocol.org/standards/corporate-standard
118 See http://www.thebodyshop.com
119 Retrieved July 10, 2008, from http://www.tomsofmaine.com/about/Colgate.asp
120 Kakariki House has now become the Waikato region's first certified green building after receiving a 4-Star Green Star rating under the Green Star NZ Office Design programme from the New Zealand Green Building Council. See http://www.nzgbc.org.nz/main/greenstar/elaboration/certifiedprojects.

CHAPTER 18 Just do something!

121 The W. Edwards Deming Institute. See http://www.deming.org
122 See http://www.atkearney.com
123 We acknowledge the libertarian argument that people should be allowed to choose to risk their health and morbidity if they wish, in return for the addictive pleasure of smoking. This argument would have greater validity if presented simultaneously with a commitment by tobacco companies to cover the health costs of their products that are currently externalised to the taxpayer.
124 Retrieved July 10, 2008 from http://www.inspiros.org/our_clients
125 See http://www.ipcc.ch
126 Based on January 2009 research by Saatchi & Saatchi
127 The developed world led by the United States fuelled its growth in consumerism through ever increasing balance of payments deficits funded by debt from the sovereign wealth funds of developing and oil-rich nations. Enhancement of first world lifestyles was based on rapidly escalating consumer debt supported by escalating house values. The situation was not sustainable. First world borrower nations will need to pull back their debt to more manageable levels, whilst developing nations will need to spend more of their sovereign wealth on developing the wellbeing of their own citizens to avoid civil unrest. This rebalancing of the global economy has unknowable potential implications, but potential positive impacts could include an increased awareness amongst individuals of priorities for wellbeing in their own lives, and a greater propensity towards sustainable development in the global economy.

Index.

activism 32, 161, 166, 176, 179, 192, 219–20, 240, 241, 254; The Body Shop 61, 70, 71, 76, 77, 173; Comvita 173; Dilmah Tea 148, 173; The Eden Project 173; Forum for the Future 100, 173; Patagonia 127, 128–30, 133, 164, 173, 250; Putumayo World Music 40, 173; Snowy Peak 106–7, 173; Stonyfield Farm 52–3, 173
activities 231–3, 235, 237
Anderson, Ray 31, 104, 173, 241
animal welfare 64, 69–70, 74, 77, 120, 173, 192, 200, 215

Ben & Jerry's icecream 31, 39, 51, 58, 62, 67, 250–1
The Body Shop 28, 30, 39, 60–77, 156, 161, 168, 176, 184, 191, 215, 218, 243, 244–6, 249–50, 251–2
Bougen, Alan 30, 111, 112, 114, 116–17, 118–19, 153, 162
Boyden, Peter 78, 79–80, 85–6, 88
brand development and positioning 33, 137, 141, 142, 148, 156, 168, 172, 173, 190

capacity building 99, 207
Chapman, Carol 54–5, 163
Chappell, Tom and Kate 31, 252
choice 228–31, 235
Chouinard, Yvon 30, 122, 124, 125, 126, 128, 130, 132, 153, 163, 166, 169, 176, 241, 243, 250
Cohen, Ben 31, 39, 62, 69, 250–1
commitment 17, 30, 33, 34, 91, 94, 101, 108, 109, 131, 142, 143, 146, 160, 166, 180, 213, 235
communication 61, 65, 73, 74, 81, 164, 210, 213, 240; see also marketing; storytelling
community 60, 66, 67, 68, 69, 206–8
Comvita 30, 111–21, 181–2, 185, 239, 252–3
consumer/customer education 33, 48–9, 51, 52, 54, 55–6, 75–6, 79, 81, 97–8 , 147, 192, 208–9
consumer/customer relationships 32, 41–3, 48, 49, 51–3, 55–6, 57, 115, 116, 118–19, 140–1, 145, 146, 147, 169, 170, 190
core business 33, 50, 173

creativity 73, 239, 254
cultural issues 13, 32, 36–7, 38, 40, 41, 44, 47, 51, 56, 106–7, 173, 180

Dilmah Tea 30, 31, 134–48, 179, 184, 186, 207, 215, 220, 243
Dowe, Simon 30, 60, 244–5, 251–2
Druchniak, Carmelle 50, 53, 54, 161, 240–1
Drysdale, Peri 30, 101–7, 153, 176, 186

eco-effectiveness 156, 201–6, 240, 263
economic issues 27, 34–5, 51, 93–4, 119, 154, 155, 156, 254, 265; see also profits
The Eden Project 30, 78–89, 168, 178, 184, 187, 190, 250
employees, see staff …
equity 27, 153, 154–5, 156
enterprisers 161–3, 166, 193; see also philosophy and beliefs, founders; and specific enterprisers
environmental issues 26, 27, 32, 33, 34, 154, 155, 156, 171, 225–6, 240, 248–50; The Body Shop 65, 67, 70, 73, 191; Comvita 117–19, 120, 181–2; Dilmah Tea 143, 146, 147; The Eden Project 78–9, 80, 87, 173; Forum for the Future 90–1, 92, 93–5, 97–8, 99, 100, 173, 180–1; Patagonia 122, 123–4, 125–33, 156, 164, 173, 191; Putumayo World Music 40; Snowy Peak 102–3, 104, 106, 107–8, 109, 110; Stonyfield Farm 48–9, 50–1, 52–3, 54, 55, 56, 57, 58; sustainable enterprise practices 196–201; Wal-Mart 235–7; Wise Group 254–6; see also eco-efficiency
ethical issues 27, 28, 63, 64, 66, 69–70, 73, 74, 76, 114, 120, 141, 147, 148, 155, 156, 171, 191, 213, 215

fair trade 69, 72, 74–5, 76, 140–1, 212–13
family-based suppliers 50, 54, 55, 66, 74–5, 218
family-like working environment 33, 44, 65–6, 108–9, 116–18, 123, 125, 133, 142, 217–20
Fernando, Dilhan C. 134, 135, 136, 140,

142–3, 144, 145–7, 153, 250
Fernando, Merrill J 30, 31, 135, 136–41, 142, 143, 144, 147–8, 153, 163, 179, 207, 220, 250
flow 237–9
For the Planet 129, 131, 243
Forum for the Future 27, 30, 90–100, 161, 180–1, 201, 247, 250, 253
founders, see enterprisers; philosophy, founders; succession
franchises 63, 64, 65, 66–7

Gazeley Ltd 173–4, 241–3
genetically modified organisms (GMOs) 26, 120, 155, 199–200
globalisation 45–6, 67–8, 79, 98, 115–16
Greenpeace 61, 62, 172, 191, 194
Greenfield, Jerry 31, 62, 250–1
greenwashing 73, 76, 120, 193–4, 214
Groupe Danone 57, 58, 59, 170, 252
growth, business 33, 34, 250–3; The Body Shop 61, 68–9, 73, 74; Comvita 113–14, 115–16, 119–20; Dilmah Tea 146, 147, 148; Forum for the Future 95–7; Patagonia 125; Putumayo World Music 46; Snowy Peak 110; Stonyfield Farm 57, 58; see also globalisation

happiness 154, 166, 223–33, 238; see also positivity
Hirshberg, Gary 30, 48, 49, 50–9, 153, 161, 162, 176, 252
human rights 65, 70, 73, 76, 154, 156, 171, 173, 191, 210–16, 240

Interface 31, 104, 173, 241
investments, ethical 87, 114, 121

Kaymen, Samuel 30, 49, 50–1, 54, 59, 162
Kraus, Michael 30, 36, 39, 41–2, 45

Last Man Standing theory 82, 168
leadership, inspirational 74, 91, 110, 163–6, 176, 193
L'Oreal 74, 75, 76, 176, 192, 251–2

Lost Gardens of Heligan 80–1, 82, 84, 168

Madden, Peter 90, 91, 97, 98–9
marketing 32, 33, 169, 190, 192, 209–10, 263; The Body Shop 61, 68–9, 75; Comvita 112, 113, 115; Dilmah Tea 141, 142; Patagonia 130; Putumayo World Music 41–5, 46, 47, 191; Snowy Peak 103–4, 108; Stonyfield Farm 48–9, 52–3, 54, 55–6; see also brand development and positioning; communication; greenwashing; storytelling
media relationships 68, 69, 76
mission statements 65, 126, 127
model, enterprise 164, 165, 169–70
motivation 65–6, 69, 72, 156
MJF Charitable Foundation 143, 144, 146, 241, 243

not-for-profit (NGO) alliances 40–1, 61, 62, 63, 70, 72, 73–4, 90, 94–5, 192, 213–14

optimism 33, 54, 58–9, 61, 75, 76, 123, 179, 238; see also positivity

packaging 40, 52, 53, 181, 198, 236
Panakera, Charlie 258–60
Parkin, Sara 30, 94–5, 96
partner relationships 42, 55, 57, 90, 91–2, 93, 94–5, 98–9, 106, 119, 129, 130–1, 133, 148, 166, 170, 181, 191, 200–1, 212, 241
Patagonia 28, 30, 58, 122–33, 156, 161, 163–4, 169, 176, 180, 187, 191, 219–20, 243, 250
Patagonia National Park, Chile and Argentina 127–8
peak performance 28, 156–7, 165, 175; see also sustainable peak performance
people 159, 160–6, 193, 248–50, 256, 263–4, 266
performance 159, 247–57, 264, 266–7; see also peak performance; sustainable peak performance
philanthropy 34, 40, 53, 57, 58, 76, 87, 114–15, 117–18, 127–30, 141, 143–4,

145–8, 206–8, 219–20, 234, 243–6; see also community; social enterprise; social issues/responsibility

philosophy and beliefs, enterprise 32–4, 159, 170, 172–3, 175, 178–88, 184–5, 215–16, 256, 264, 266; The Body Shop 62–3, 64, 65, 68, 69–70, 73, 74–5, 77, 176, 191; Comvita 115, 116–20, 121, 181–2, 185; Dilmah Tea 142–3, 147, 241; The Eden Project 81–2, 87, 178; Forum for the Future 90, 93, 94–5, 180–1; Patagonia 125–33, 180, 191, 241–2; Putumayo World Music 44, 47, 180; Saatchi & Saatchi S 182, 183, 185; Snowy Peak 103, 108–10, 176; Stonyfield Farm 51, 54, 56, 176, 240–1

philosophy and beliefs, founders 32–4, 160, 162–3; The Body Shop 61–2, 176; Comvita 112; Dilmah Tea 135, 142; The Eden Project 78–9, 84–5; Forum for the Future 93–4; Patagonia 122, 124, 176; Putumayo World Music 44; Snowy Peak 101, 104, 110; Stonyfield Farm 51, 54, 56

Porritt, Jonathon 30, 91, 92, 93–4, 95, 96, 98, 99, 100, 153, 161, 250–1

positivity 59, 65–6, 133, 136, 159, 168, 221–46, 257, 264, 266; see also happiness; optimism

potential 159, 167–77, 256, 264, 266

practices 159, 189–220, 256–7, 264, 266

products 192, 198–200, 203–5

profits 46, 47, 51, 64, 65, 68, 92, 115, 121, 132, 138, 147, 148, 154, 179, 180, 248–9

purpose 182–5, 208, 256, 264; sharing 190–4

Putumayo World Music 30, 31, 36–47, 156, 169, 180, 187, 243

quality 33–4, 46, 47, 49, 50–1, 53, 59, 101–2, 106, 139, 148, 164, 222, 240, 263, 265

recycling 109, 123–4, 130, 131, 198, 203

Roddick, Dame Anita 30, 39, 60–77, 153, 161, 168, 170, 176, 177, 186, 218, 244–5, 251–2

role models 34, 58, 148, 240

Saatchi & Saatchi S 182, 183, 184, 185, 187, 235, 236

Setnicka, Lu 127–8, 128, 129

Sheahan, Casey 122, 123, 125, 127, 128, 130–1, 132–3, 161, 180

Smit, Tim 30, 78–9, 80–5, 88, 89, 153, 168, 177, 178, 190

Snowy Peak 30, 101–10, 176, 186, 243

social enterprise 78–9, 81–2, 85–7

social issues/responsibility 26, 27, 32, 33, 35, 75–6, 154, 156, 171, 206–10, 240; The Body Shop 65, 73; Comvita 114–15, 117, 119, 181; Dilmah Tea 143–6, 147, 148; The Eden Project 78–9, 81–2, 85–6; Forum for the Future 92, 94, 95, 180–1; Putumayo World Music 40, 44, 47, 156; Snowy Peak 106, 207; Stonyfield Farm 51, 52, 55–6; Wise Group 254–6; see also equity; philanthropy

Solomon Islands 22–5, 258–60

spirit 175–6, 193

staff education and training 69, 70, 71–2, 117, 208–9, 234

staff engagement 164–6, 193, 233–7, 239, 263; The Body Shop 65–6, 67, 68, 70–2, 73, 74, 245–6; Comvita 115–18; The Eden Project 83–4, 85–6, 87; Forum for the Future 92–3; Patagonia 123, 127, 128–9, 133, 235; Snowy Peak 108–9; Stonyfield Farm 43–4; Wise Group 254–5; see also family-like work environment

Stonyfield Farm 30, 48–59, 156, 161, 162, 163, 170, 176, 184, 187, 191, 192, 215, 218, 240–1, 252

Storper, Dan 30, 31, 36–43, 44–5, 46–7, 153, 162, 169, 170, 180, 238

storytelling 48, 60, 61, 70, 71–2, 77, 80–1, 88–9, 115, 163, 190–1, 192–3, 249–50

Stratford, Claude 3, 111–12, 153, 162

success 25, 27, 28, 29, 32, 33, 41, 46, 64, 74, 96, 108, 116, 123, 146, 147, 164, 165

succession 34, 57, 59, 96–7, 110, 250–3

supplier relationships 32, 55, 87, 119, 125–6, 130–1, 132–3, 142, 190, 191, 200–1; see also family-based suppliers

sustainable enterprise 152–8, 258–69; cost 35, 152, 155; definition 27, 247;

dynamics 154–6; making a difference
239–46; and "market for convictions"
56–7; patterns 32–4, 152; reporting
249–50; see also social enterprise; and
names of specific enterprises
sustainable peak performance 157–9, 262–9

technology 57, 58, 101, 119, 131–2, 170,
194, 203–4
The Natural Step (TNS) framework 118, 205
Tinkerbell Theory 82, 83, 168
Tompkins, Doug 125, 126–7, 127, 128
Tompkins, Kris McDivitt 124–5, 127, 128
Tom's of Maine 31, 57, 252
trust-based relationships 91, 94, 164

Untouched World Charitable Trust 101,
105, 107–8, 110, 243
Untouched World brand 101–2, 104,
105–6, 176
Uren, Sally 92–3, 95–8

value creation 35, 158, 194–6, 196–217
values, see philosophy and beliefs
volunteering 66, 67, 69, 72, 128, 245–6

Wal-Mart 75, 132, 182, 235–7, 242
wellbeing 33, 77, 100, 112, 115, 119–20,
121, 154, 156, 158, 174, 180, 182, 195,
223–37, 253–4, 255, 265
World Business Council for Sustainable
Development 214–15